Advance Praise for
Girl, Stop Passing Out in Your Makeup

"Zara has the rare talent of marching into the deepest, darkest moments of life—the mascara-teared and alcohol-soaked—scooping them up, and thrusting them into the light with amazing clarity, forgiveness, and compassion. As her editor at *Elite Daily*, I had the honor of watching Zara blossom into the emotionally raw and poetic writer she is now. Her gripping first-person narratives help every woman (including me) come to terms with her own demons or insecurities in a refreshingly comfortable way. There's a reason she's built up an army of 'babes' who are empowered by the words of their dear big sister, Z: Her candid honesty and no bullshit advice are simply addicting."

—FAYE BRENNAN, Sex & Relationships Director, *Cosmopolitan*

"Reading Zara is like reading your own thoughts—only sexier and much more brilliantly written."

—KAITLYN CAWLEY, former Editor-At-Large,
Bustle Media Group and former Editor-in-Chief, *Elite Daily*

"Reading Zara's writing will make you feel like you're at your cool-as-hell big sister's sleepover party. You will be transfixed by her unflinching honesty and words of wisdom, and she'll successfully convince you to not only ditch the shame you feel about the raw and messy parts of yourself, but to dare to see them as beautiful."

—ALEXIA LAFATA, Editor, *New York Magazine*

"If Cat Marnell and F. Scott Fitzgerald had a literary baby it would be Zara Barrie. She's got Marnell's casual, dark, downright hilarious tone of an irreverent party girl. But then she also has Fitzgerald's talent for making words literally feel like they sparkle on the page. You instantly feel more glamorous after reading a page of Zara's writing, even when the page is talking about getting into a screaming match with her girlfriend outside of a bar on a Sarasota street corner while high on benzos. I've always been a fan of Zara's writing but *Girl, Stop Passing Out in Your Makeup* takes it to the next level. With shimmery words that make her dark stories sparkle, she seamlessly manages to inspire even the most coked-out girl at the party to get her shit together."

—CANDICE JALILI, Senior Sex & Dating Writer, *Elite Daily*

"Self-help meets memoir. Party girl meets wise sage. Beauty meets reality. Zara Barrie is the cool older sister you wish you had. The one that lets you borrow her designer dresses and ripped up fishnets, buys you champagne (she loves you too much to let you drink beer), and colors your lips with bright pink lipstick. She'll take you to the coolest parties, and will stick by your side and she guides you through the glitter, pain, danger, laughter, and what it means to be a f*cked up girl in this f*cked up world (both of which are beautiful despite the darkness). *Girl, Stop Passing Out in Your Makeup* is for the girls that are too much of a beautiful contradiction to be contained. Zara is a gifted writer—one second she'll have you laughing over rich girls agonizing over which Birkin bag to buy, the next second she'll shatter your heart in one sentence about losing one's innocence. Zara is the nuanced girl she writes for—light, irreverent, snarky, bitchy, funny; and aching, perceptive, deep, flawed, wise, poised, honest—all at once. Perhaps the only thing that can match Zara's unparalleled wit and big sister advice is her candid humor and undeniable talent for the written word. Zara is one of the most prolific and entertaining honest voices on the internet—and her talent is only multiplied in book form. *Girl, Stop Passing Out in Your Makeup* is for the bad girls, honey."

—DAYNA TROISI, Executive Editor, *GO Magazine*

"Love this book! Zara Barrie has a wicked skill for spinning vulnerable, piercingly honest tales of sex, drugs, and transgression while poignantly leading her reader and herself towards hope and enlightenment. A book about GIRL Power in the age of anxiety that will resonate with today's women looking for something much more than just happy ever after—at least in the traditional sense. Read it to understand what dangerous girls with glittering eyes are thinking and feeling as they learn to conquer their demons and triumph."

—KT CURRAN, Writer/Director of the internationally acclaimed, award-winning *SOURCE PRODUCTIONS*

*Girl, Stop Passing Out
in Your Makeup*

Girl, Stop Passing Out in Your Makeup

THE BAD GIRL'S GUIDE
TO GETTING YOUR SH*T TOGETHER

Zara Barrie

Post Hill PRESS

A POST HILL PRESS BOOK

Girl, Stop Passing Out in Your Makeup:
The Bad Girl's Guide to Getting Your Sh*t Together
© 2020 by Zara Barrie
All Rights Reserved

ISBN: 978-1-64293-463-2
ISBN (eBook): 978-1-64293-464-9

Cover art by Cody Corcoran
Interior design and composition by Greg Johnson, Textbook Perfect

Post Hill Press
New York • Nashville
posthillpress.com

Published in the United States of America

For girls who live on Long Island
and listen to Lana Del Rey.
I get it.

Medical Disclaimer: I'm not a doctor, don't sue me.

"Being young was her thing, and she was the best at it. But every year, more and more girls came out of nowhere and tried to steal her thing. *One of these days I'm gong to have to get a new thing,* she thought to herself—but as quietly as she could, because she knew that if anyone caught her thinking this thought, her thing would be right over right then."

—B.J. NOVAK, *One More Thing: Stories and Other Stories*

CONTENTS

FOREWORD

I Slept in My Makeup Last Night

Song: "Grigio Girls" by Lady Gaga

I have a confession to make: I couldn't care less if you fall asleep in your makeup from time to time. Just last night I passed out with a full face of foundation, blush, highlighter, bronzer, mascara, eyeshadow, and liquid eyeliner. What can I say? I went to a karaoke bar in midtown and sang my heart out to all of my favorite '90s girls: Alanis Morissette, Janet Jackson, Liz Phair, Lisa Loeb, Sheryl Crow, Whitney Houston, and TLC. After an impossibly long, arduous week involving extreme family drama and a vicious fight with my best friend, mixed in with the typical day-to-day New York City traumas, it felt *good* to blow off some steam. It felt *good* to slug back a hefty pour of whiskey. It felt *good* to slap pizza into my mouth at two o'clock in the morning. It felt *good* to puff on my CBD pen in bed, with my dog snuggled up on the pillow over my head and my new weighted blanket thrown over my body, soothing my exhausted limbs and easing my underlying anxiety.

Girl, wash your face. I coached myself. *You'll regret it in the morning.* But I was so warm and cozy and content in the safe confines of my bed. The last thing in the world I felt like doing was disrupting the first moment of peace I'd experienced in *weeks* by subjecting myself to the nuisance of harsh tap water and soap splashing across my face. Also, if you're a girl like me, a girl who *really* piles on the mascara, then you most definitely understand that removing your makeup is a process—to say the very least. It takes far more than the delicate dab of a Neutrogena makeup wipe when your lashes are two thousand layers deep in inky-black goo. It takes oils, and cold-creams, and triple-cleansing sessions, and the soiling of pristine white towels (that will forever be mascara-stained no matter how many times you soak them in bleach).

So I decided that, against my better judgment, I would sleep in a full face of makeup. And guess what? I didn't feel bad about it.

Look, life is *hard*. Certain days *test* you. And certain nights you just need to put yourself to bed before you do something unnecessarily destructive like write an unhinged tweet or send a hateful text to that colossal asshole you slept with last month. And sometimes you're just too damn tired and too damn sad and too damn *lazy* to exfoliate the day away. And that's *OK*. Even beauty gurus sometimes get too wasted, too wracked with depression, too emotionally depleted to partake in their seventeen-step nighttime skincare routine.

About a year ago, I read Rachel Hollis's book *Girl, Wash Your Face*, the unlikely inspiration behind this book. It was gifted to me by a friend, and I suspected perhaps it would be a book about skincare (I enjoy skincare but not nearly enough to read a book about it). I was sitting on a plane, gnawing at my fingernails and bored to tears when I found the book buried at the bottom of my messy purse, nearly lost in the sea of crumpled bills and lip glosses and shameful taxi-cab receipts. I decided, what the hell? Might as well give it a gander. As I tore through the pages, I was delighted to discover that the book had nothing to do with skincare. In fact, it was just what I needed to read at the time. It was a no-holds-barred, woman-to-woman, real-life advice book that explored everything from staying true to your word to diving head first into risks, to knowing your worth. In fact, the book was really about taking *control* of your life. I loved that title: *Girl, Wash Your Face*. I could see why the phrase resonated with so many women all over the world. It wasn't so much about the importance of a clean face as it was about getting off your ass and making *your life* happen.

While I loved Hollis's book, I felt her audience was vastly different from the girls I knew. A lot of the themes in her book centered on the nuances of motherhood and marriage. I longed for a version of her book that spoke to girls like me and *my* friends. Single, millennial girls reared in the age of social media and Kate Moss and leaked sex tapes. Girls who have done drugs and slept around. Girls who are wracked with guilt over what they did last night. Girls who burn so intensely, they often end up unleashing their fire unto themselves, leaving them scorched and scarred.

So I decided to follow the advice of the late Toni Morrison who famously said: "If there's a book that you want to read, but it hasn't been written yet, then you must write it."

So here it is. A book I've always wanted to read. A book made specifically for girls who not only need to traipse over to the bathroom and scrub their faces, but who also need to confront the lifetime of mascara residue resting beneath their eyes, the stained-into-the-skin leftover bits of eyeliner that give them a forever raccoon-like appearance. And I don't mean that *literally*. Because this book has nothing to do with beauty or skincare hacks, and it's certainly not about products. When I say "girl, stop passing out in your makeup," what I really mean is: Let's look at the naked reality of our lives. Let's allow our skin to *breathe* so it can actually heal for once. Let's examine all the beautiful grit that lives beneath the shiny exterior we are forever presenting to the outer world. Because if we get down and dirty with what this book is really about, it's about digging deep and pulling out the truth. And the truth—unlike the shimmery blush and the creamy lipstick we slather across our skin like armor every morning—doesn't have to be *pretty*. All it has to be is true. Isn't that a relief?!

And here's the beautiful thing about confronting the truth: Once we gaze into our unfiltered reflections and get comfortable in the discomfort of how we look barefaced, we'll relearn how to fall asleep. There is a stark difference between falling asleep and passing out. Falling asleep is a choice. Passing out is not. Passing out is the body shutting down without your permission. Us girls who pass out on the regular, makeup caked on or makeup cleansed off, we're too tightly wound to let go and allow our bodies to relax into the vulnerability of a true night's rest. So we find ourselves going to extreme measures in order to escape the prison of our ever-vibrating brains and exit our bodies for a while. Maybe we pop Ambien or Xanax into our mouths or smoke loads of weed or down a bottle of red wine or workout for three hours a day or type until our eyes feel like they're bleeding from the artificial light of the computer screen, until—BAM—our bodies have shut down and we're out. Cold. There is no falling.

I didn't sleep, I just passed out throughout the entire decade of my twenties. I didn't take off my makeup for the entire decade of my twenties, either. I bought into the bullshit notion that I somehow owed the world this sparkly, polished version of myself. If I wasn't a size zero, I felt invisible. If I didn't show up to the party glittery and smiling, then I was convinced I didn't deserve to be at the party. That if I wasn't witty and pretty and charming, I was letting everyone down. Who? I don't know, babe. All I know is that I never wanted to remove my makeup and gaze into the unfiltered truth of my life. I never let myself break down. I never let myself cry in public. If something bad happened to me (and a lot of bad things happened to me), I would isolate myself in my apartment for three days and have endless panic attacks, and then on the fourth day, I would shower and shave and flatten the kinks of my untamable mop of curls with a blazing hot iron and paint my face and cartwheel into the world like none of it had ever happened.

But here's the real tea: If you keep sleeping in your makeup, you're going to eventually wake up to that beautiful reflection riddled with acne. If you keep swallowing secrets, you'll eventually combust.

Before you know it, all the shit you've been running from will catch up to you—and it will knock you right the fuck down. Trust me. By the time I reached twenty-six, I nosedived so hard into the pavement, I'm amazed I didn't die from the impact.

But I didn't die. I made it out alive. And so can *you*.

So if you're feeling lost, lonely, sexually confused, afraid, a bit queer, too sick-humored for your friend group, born into the wrong family, kind of like you're always teetering between hating yourself and feeling like a queen, or like you're blindly falling through outer space not knowing when (or if) you're going to land on solid ground, come inside. You're under my wing now. And guess what? You're safe here. I *promise*.

And together we'll work through our druggie issues, our love addictions, our teenage traumas, our partying mishaps, our STD scares. We'll fucking laugh and we'll fucking cry, but we will learn to forgive ourselves for our mistakes and will eventually become empowered by the lessons of our magnificent failures.

After all, tasting the pavement on the ground only means you fell from a really high place! And really high places are dangerous, it's true, but they have the most beautiful views, don't they? And I don't know about you, but I think a pretty view is always worth the pain of a fall.

But if your scar is too fresh and too grotesque for you to look at right now, I'll find you the prettiest pink Band-Aid and we'll cover up the bloody mess for now, and I'll sit with you and wait for it to heal. Then, when it's time, we'll rip it off and gaze into that gorgeous fucked-up scar together. And we'll admire it, because it's weird and different and what's weird and different is high fashion. And while we might not be perfectly manicured little angels, we're *most definitely* high fashion.

So get as cozy as possible, grab the blanket of your choice, curl up on the couch in that oh-so-comforting Juicy Couture velour sweatsuit that you haven't rocked since the seventh grade, and dive recklessly into this book. Because I'm here to serve as your big-sister guide and will help you, little sister, navigate the dark and stormy waters of adulthood. I'm going to provide you with the razor-sharp, real AF kind of advice only a *real* big sister can provide. Because it's my life's mission to help all of you messy girls get your shit together. And let me assure you: There is no one in the world more qualified to help you figure this complicated grown-up mayhem out like yours truly.

'Cause I'm the messiest bitch you'll ever meet.

Even so, after years and years of falling on my face, my bruises have turned into stunningly beautiful scars. After years and years of teetering between hating myself and feeling like a queen, I'm no longer seasick. After years and years of self-destruction, I've finally learned how to channel my fiery, crazy-girl energy into wild creativity, passionate yet healthy relationships, a career that feeds my soul *and* pays my bills, and ultimately, an adventurous, fulfilling, nuanced life.

The most precious gem I've unearthed in my journey? I haven't lost myself in the process of bettering myself. I'm still the klutzy girl with the big opinions and the loud mouth. Only my extraness no longer comes with a side of pain. It comes with a giant, family-sized portion of self-love and self-worth that I never knew could taste so sweet.

Big sisters never lie and I'm no exception. I'll admit that the depression and the anxiety and the panic attacks and the desire to chug white wine in order to silence the demons definitely still attempt to hold my spirit hostage from time to time. But unlike before, I now have the tools to keep those pesky monsters at bay. And instead of trying to ignore the bad feels that occasionally pound down my door at 3:00 AM, I let them in. Because I am no longer afraid of them. See, I now understand that feelings—no matter how painful or big or unfamiliar they are—can't ever physically kill me. Running away from them can.

This book is going to be a wild ride. Together we're going to stop running away from our fears and learn how to deal with all the shit us unhinged girls are afraid to deal with. Like the terrifying realities of money (shudder), or the toxic person you're fucking who takes up so much space in your life there isn't any room for anything else. We're going to talk about the prescription speed you think you need in order to function, but is actually holding you back from living your truth. We're going to help you find your purpose and build a career you love. We're going to improve the relationship you have with yourself, so when love and opportunity *do* come waltzing into your world, you won't screw it up because you're afraid of good things or addicted to chaos or crazy-clingy because you have no self-worth without the validation of another person. In fact, we're going to SQUASH your need for validation entirely! We're going to learn that validation is like a bump of shitty coke. Just like that heartless bitch blow, validation gets you high for fifteen minutes, then crashes your spirit into the ground and leaves you crawling on the carpet, desperately searching between the floorboards for *MORE MORE MORE*. Enough of that bullshit, sister.

In *Girl, Stop Passing Out in Your Makeup,* we're going to fuel your confidence so it sustains you in the long term—no more quick fixes, you hear? That means no more chill pills or reckless shopping sprees or dark bouts of binge eating. We'll replace the fleeting feel-goods with something far more powerful than a temporary high. We'll replace it with something real. We'll replace it with *love.*

And together, we'll stop giving a shit about what everyone else thinks and start embracing the essence of who we actually are! Because if there is one thing I've learned in this haphazard whirlwind of a life, it's this: If you don't honor who you are, if you don't worship at the altar of your natural rhythms and fierce eccentricities and extraordinary talents, you'll never love the girl that gazes back at you in the mirror. And when you don't love that girl, you'll end up destroying that girl. And that girl is all you really have.

She's far too beautiful to destroy.

Speaking of beauty and mirrors and all that jazz, we're going to deep-dive into all of your body-image issues, too, which I know is triggering and uncomfortable, but also super important. Take it from me. I wasted far too many precious years of my life waging a war against my body. Secretly vomiting into nasty toilet bowls. Sucking my stomach in during sex. I know firsthand that you can't manifest shit when you treat your body like shit. You live in your body, and if you detest your home, you'll always feel unstable no matter how many downward dogs you do or how many self-help books you devour.

By the end of this book, we'll channel our collective fire into one giant, beautiful flame that will light up the goddamn world. Because I swear to my higher power, Lana Del Rey, there is nothing more powerful than a wild-child who has finally decided to channel her messy girl prowess into a fabulous, fulfilling, productive life.

Good girls, watch out. We "bad girls" aren't taking a backseat anymore. In fact, we're driving the goddamn car. And the road we take might've gotten off to a rocky start, but it's leading us to a magical place.

CHAPTER 1

Feelings Can't Kill You

Song: "I Am Not A Robot"
by Marina and the Diamonds

I am sitting pretty in a tiny, trendy, wannabe Bushwick speakeasy-style bar in Sarasota, Florida. I am with my girlfriend Lila, and our three best friends Josh, Matty, and Eduardo. We are hungrily slugging back booze as if it's the last time our lips will ever grace a wine glass.

Even though I have slurped back *at least* six cocktails in the span of four drunken hours, this particular night I feel very...*on edge*. On the verge of inexplicable tears. I'm too fuzzy-brained from the mix of booze and my daily cocktail of antidepressants to know *why* I'm suddenly overcome with such acute feelings of restlessness. Big, dramatic fire alarms begin to sound off in my brain. Suddenly I hear a loud, screeching voice boom through a megaphone. "ATTENTION, ZARA," the voice screams. "YOU'RE IN A STATE OF EMERGENCY. YOU'RE STARTING TO FEEL THINGS." I take a prim sip of my cocktail and dab the corners of my mouth with a pale pink silk napkin. The screams carry on despite the calm, debutante energy I am attempting to radiate into the universe.

"EMERGENCY! CODE RED! YOU'RE EXPERIENCING EMO-
TIONS. THIS IS VERY, VERY DANGEROUS. EMERGENCY!" I
reach into my makeup bag. I pull the wand out of my brand new
"Two Faced Better Than Sex" mascara and apply a fresh coat of inky-
black goo onto my lashes. I grab my lip-gloss and smother it across
my mouth. I can feel my lips gleaming in the candlelight that softly
flickers at the center of our table. I take another (very prim) sip of my
cocktail. The screams are so loud now, I swear I can see the wall-
paper of the bar starting to curl.

Screw it.

I dig my fingertips, the nails bitten down, into my messy purse.
My heart races as I furiously search for a prescription bottle. I touch
a comb. A pack of gum. My cellphone. Where the hell is my Clonazepam? I can feel my blood pressure rise. Finally, my fingers brush
against that oh-so-familiar plastic bottle with its oh-so-comfortingly
sweet child-proof cap. I keep my eyes fixated on my friends' giggling
faces and let my fingers do the work. POP. The cap pops off. Never
underestimate the muscle memory of a pillhead's fingers.

I laugh along with my friends as my hands fish out a sapphire
blue pill from the bottle and discreetly shove it into my mouth. Just
as my tongue basks in the bitter-chemical taste of a waterless pill, I
feel daggers in my face.

"Why are you taking pills?! We are *drinking*!" Lila screams, her
larger than life Mickey Mouse eyes stretched open so wide I can see
the whites all the way around them, like Joan Crawford's character in
Mommie Dearest.

"Shh, Lila! Everyone is *staring* at us!" I whisper. The cold-sweat of
embarrassment tiptoes down my spine. I need rumors flying around
about my pill-popping habits like I need a hole in the head. It's a
small town.

Lila takes a fat swig of her whiskey. Steam pours out of her ears,
like a chimney in a Christmas cartoon. I pray to my higher power
(Lana Del Rey) that the pretty blue chill pill will please, please, *please*
kick in. Fast.

"I DON'T CARE WHO THE HELL HEARS US!" Lila roars, her shiny mane of stick-straight, perfect hair eerily juxtaposed against her demonic looking face.

Matty's soft blue eyes stare into the untouched plate of truffle fries that dangerously teeter toward the edge of the table. Josh smiles wickedly, as if he is about to witness a table-flipping, *Real Housewives Of New Jersey* moment. *Prostitution Whore!* I think to myself, fighting back the strange urge to giggle.

Eduardo firmly touches Lila's arm. "Lila, calm down," he says, his Mexican accent rich with an exotic authority one would be damned to question.

Lila freezes like a statue. "You're a drug addict," she says slowly, as if she is explaining quantum theory to the village idiot. "A. Drug. Addict."

I kick her under the table. "I am not. I have *anxiety!*" I can feel the eyes of a couple I know, a couple my parents frequently cocktail-party with, watching us like we are polar bears behind glass in the Central Park Zoo.

"My girlfriend is a drug addict," Lila says, this time casually, as if it's yesterday's rag mag gossip.

The voice booms once again through the megaphone: "You're FEELING FEELINGS! RUN! RUN!" I imagine the voice attached to a scary, impossibly pale, inbred-looking woman—the kind of woman you see protesting at gay pride parades.

I slither out of my seat and grab my handbag in one elegant swoop. I gallop out of the bar with the grace of a gazelle even though I am just an inebriated twenty-five-year-old girl teetering in six-inch heels, hopped up on a cocktail of pharmaceuticals.

The moment I step outside and breathe in the balmy summer air, I feel a lump in my throat. I fight the lump. I try to swallow the lump. Crush it with my teeth. Spit it out onto the pavement. It's always *Zara Vs. The Throat Lump* and tonight we are duking it out in a courtroom.

"Zara! What the *hell!*" Lila shouts. The bitch has chased me outside. I look around for my gentle army of homosexual boys but they are tucked inside the safe four walls of the bar, politely avoiding the primal lesbian drama taking place in the wild.

I lean my body up against an ATM machine. I hold my breath. I know that breathing means feeling, and feeling means, well, *dying*— perhaps. I kick the ATM machine and clench my fist so hard I feel calluses form on the inside of my hands.

I take in the vision of Lila. She is *beautiful*. Even in the throes of a tantrum. She is curvy and swaggy and ethereal all at once. Her waist-length hair looks like two silk champagne-colored curtains that frame her bone-white face. I *love* her. She is good. I am good. But together, we are *bad*.

Maybe it's all the booze in my bloodstream, or maybe it's the great divine. Truthfully I don't know what the hell it is, but I feel a very sudden shift inside of me. A shift that is so powerful it feels almost… spiritual. I know right then and there that I can't live like this anymore. See, I've always known since I was a little kid that I am supposed to do big things with my life. Big, extraordinary things! Things that don't involve discreetly tossing numbing chemical mechanisms into my body, things that don't involve a toxic relationship that drains me of my energy, things that don't involve kicking poor ATM machines on beautiful summer evenings.

The truth is this: This behavior, this pill-popping, booze-swigging, girlfriend-fighting, ATM-attacking behavior, none of it is *me*. I know that. My core nature has always been honest, raw, funny, wild, expressive. Gentle. The foundation of who I once was has been stepped on one too many times and my real self has slipped through the floorboards. I *miss* her. My old self. The opinionated teenager who made art in her bedroom till 2:00 AM on a school night. The eighth-grader who furiously scrawled poetry all over her binders during Algebra. The ambitious eighteen-year-old who blasted angry nineties girl music in her car and screamed along to every single lyric as she happily tore through the suburbs in her bright yellow beetle.

"I can't do this anymore," I hear myself say.

Lila's eyes bulge. She looks like a pretty female toad. That's what happens to her face when she fights back tears. It breaks my heart.

I frantically wave down a taxi—a rare find in a small town. The second the rough leather texture of the backseat rubs up against my shivering bare legs, the pill kicks in.

The next morning I wake up in the same bed I slept in as a teen. In a wise move for a girl deep in a benzo-haze, I had requested the taxi drive me to my parent's house rather than to the apartment I share with Lila. I pull the comforter over my head. It still reeks of adolescent hormonal fervor. I stare at the Bright Eyes poster still duct-taped to the wall by my bed. My heart feels hollow.

Pills. My girlfriend is a drug addict. You're a drug addict. Cocktails. Fire alarms in my head. Pills. Can't live like this anymore. Zara vs. Lump In Throat. Taxi. Freedom. (Pill Freedom).

Holy shit. When did my life become such a hot mess?

But oh, on the outside? On the outside my life looks perfect. I am a natural-born party girl and no one can fake it like a natural-born party girl.

For example, I have *a million* friends. I have a fabulous wardrobe. I have the ~dream~ job. As a side hustle, I star in a popular fashion video series for a local publication. I live with my hot girlfriend in a retro-looking apartment complex that has a gym and an *Olympic-size* pool. Lila and I get invited to all the parties, from the grunge to the glam to the gay to the high society. Young girls look up to me, they invite me for coffee and ask me for career advice. My family is the coolest. My hair extensions are extra-virgin and I didn't even have to pay full price for them, the salon gave them to me at *cost*—that's how fucking good my life is. Or at least, how good I make it look.

But the inside is an entirely different story. No one knows that I experience vivid, horrifying nightmares every single night. Nightmares so dark I have grown to fear sleep. I haven't fallen asleep in years without the help of Ambien or Clonazepam. And girl, I'm not stupid. I know that this little habit is quickly metamorphosing into a dangerous addiction. I am throwing up my food at least three times a week thanks to my escalating eating disorder, a secret not even my live-in girlfriend is privy to. I suspect I will never, ever know life without antidepressants. When I go to all those glittery parties I am not having fun, I can tell you that much. Yes, I show up to the parties dressed to the nines, all red lipstick and heels, but not because I want to have *fun*. I show up because I want to cop a hit of the shittiest, most fleeting, most defective quick-fix drug on the market: validation.

And deep down in the underbelly of my gut, lives a top-secret trauma. I stay still in bed, frozen. The images and words from the night continue to play on and on in my head on a loop.

Pills. My girlfriend is a drug addict. You're a drug addict. Cocktails. Fire alarms in my head. Pills. Can't live like this anymore. Zara vs. Lump In Throat. Taxi. Freedom. (Pill Freedom).

Just as I'm about to fall back asleep, I hear a voice.

"It's time," I hear a woman's voice gently purr. It's the voice of the wise woman who lives inside of me. She lights up a cigarette and looks at me with warm eyes.

"Time for *what*?" I ask. Some might call the wise woman who lives inside of me "my instincts" or my "higher self" or my gut or whatnot. I call her Sharon. Sharon is safe and reliable, and I am always grateful when she unexpectedly shows up and provides me with some of her maternal guidance. Come to think of it, Sharon hadn't been around in a while.

"Therapy," she replies, carefully examining her manicure. It is French and square-shaped, very early 2000s. I side-eye her and cross my arms.

"Therapy, Zara!" she practically sings, twirling her Virginia Slim in the air. She runs her fingers through her blonde bob haircut. A sensible Coach bag dutifully hangs from her broad, sturdy shoulder. I conclude then and there that Sharon is *definitely* from the Midwest.

"You know what you need to do," she says, lowering her voice a good three octaves. She winks. And off she goes, leaving me choking in a cloud of cigarette smoke and musky fragrance.

Sharon is right. Sharon is always right.

I spend the rest of the afternoon googling therapists. I finally stumble across the website of a woman named Catherine. Catherine has short, cool-blonde hair and a smile so kind you can feel it heat up your skin through the screen. She reminds me of someone. She reminds me of *Sharon.* I book an appointment with her for the following day.

That night I crawl into bed completely sober for the first time in at least a year. By sober I mean no sleeping pills. No downers. No wine. No weed.

And I sleep like an angel who has finally landed upon Heaven's first cloud! Ha. More like I sleep like a junkie withdrawing from heroin. I writhe around in bed that night like a python suffering through its first night of captivity.

I'm not sure I slept a wink that night. All the pills I could ever dream of sit pretty in their plastic-bottle homes a few drawers south of my bed—for whatever reason I don't feel tempted to take them. I let myself simmer in the sleepless hell. Because I know the pills are only going to send me into a different kind of hell, a hell that stops me from being able to tell which flames are real and which flames are fake. If I am going to *burn*, I want to at least know what is burning me, you know?

* * *

Catherine's office smells like Nag Champa incense and is far more bohemian than I expected. I had envisioned white leather upholstery, smooth white marble coffee tables, the smell of Chanel No. 5 softly lingering in flower-fragrant air. Instead, I am met with a heavy antique wooden table, Tibetan peace flags, and pale pink crystals. I spot a dreamcatcher hanging in the window.

Oh dear.

Something about the earnestness of Catherine's faux-hippy office soothes me, even though I resist feeling that way. The snob in me never wins in the end. I'm too soft to be a snob.

"How are you?" Catherine asks me, looking at me intently.

That's when it happens. I break down. After five minutes of uncontrollable sobbing, I am finally able to muster up a simple few words. "I am" *sob* "so" *sob* "sorry" *sob. Sob. Wail.*

"Why are you *sorry?* It's OK to feel. I suspect you haven't been allowing yourself to feel much of anything at all, huh?"

I want so badly to ask Catherine why she feels that way. What is it about my behavior, my energy, that has made her so quick to conclude that I haven't experienced a real feeling in years? But I can't ask her. The fact that this total stranger, the fact that a blonde woman with a Kate Gosselin–style haircut—a woman who has a *dreamcatcher* in her window—has somehow seen through my glittery armor of fashion and makeup and jewelry—the same armor that fools everyone around me (even my blood family) into thinking I AM JUST GREAT—makes me cry even harder. I feel exposed but I don't feel embarrassed. I feel relieved? I feel like a cozy blanket has suddenly wrapped itself around my body. I feel *seen.*

"It's OK," Catherine says, gazing into my subconscious in a way that doesn't feel violating, just hyper-attentive and loving. "You know feelings can't *kill* you."

"They can't?" I whimper. I feel like a little girl who is just finding out that the monsters she is convinced lived beneath her bed aren't real, just figments of her wild imagination, and that she is safe and everything is going to be OK.

"No. Feelings can't kill you." Catherine pauses. "Running from them *can.*"

I blow my nose. A lifetime of green snot splatters into the Kleenex. When was the last time I blew my nose? How much toxic bullshit have I been storing inside of myself?

"What does that *mean?*" I am starting to feel desperate. Like I am sitting in a coffee shop with God and have only five minutes to be explained the true meaning of life. I want answers now! Before it's too late!

"Running from them by doing destructive things. Drinking yourself to death. Blacking out. Abusing drugs. Or suicide." She says all of this without an ounce of emotion in her voice. This isn't a performance. This is the real shit.

I am *shook*. This is exactly what I've been doing. I have been running away from my feelings, and my tactics are all deadly. Pill-popping. Binge drinking on antidepressants. Climbing into cars with inebriated friends.

"But the bad feelings, they're so, so painful." I shiver. "What if they never go away?"

"The beautiful thing about feelings is that they're temporary, Zara. Feelings…they fade. And when you stop fearing your feelings, you just might find they aren't as bad as you think they are."

A timer goes off. The session is over. Catherine hugs me. I exhale into her arms. It is the first time in years I have really let myself be hugged.

That night I don't take any Clonazepam for the *second night* in a row. I don't drink wine, either. I don't puff on a joint. I lay in bed and stare at the ceiling, sober as a nun. I repeat Catherine's words in my head like they are one of those new pop songs you can't get enough of, so you just replay 'em over and over again to scratch the itch. *Feelings can't kill you. Running from them can. Feelings are temporary. They fade. When you stop fearing them you'll realize they aren't so bad. Feelings can't kill you. Running from them can.*

Over the course of the next several months, I see Catherine twice a week. I trade in my monthly session with my psychiatrist (more like a very expensive drug dealer) for bi-weekly sessions with a therapist I actually speak to. I cut my antidepressant dose in half. I am committed to finding Zara again. Which really means: I am committed to learning how to feel again. Because I am no one without my feelings.

Going to therapy twice a week is not easy. I have to face some *serious* shit in therapy. Nestled in Catherine's couch I cry more than I've ever cried before. My face is swollen for two months. Yet at the same time, it is the most exciting and uniquely empowering journey I have ever been on.

Each week I dig into the folds of my mind and pull back a new layer. I stare at the raw naked truth. Every time I pull back a fresh layer, I am met with a different, forgotten memory to unearth. I dig so deep inside of myself, I eventually find diamonds buried in there! But before I get to the pretty things, I have to deal with the ugly things.

* * *

I am a twelve-year-old girl telling a grown-up man that I'm eighteen. My face is round like a child's but my tits are round like a woman's. The man invites me to a party in his hotel room and I say yes because he's looking at me like I'm a fabulous piece of art, and I love the attention. His lips brush up against mine and his large, man hands make their way down my pants. I let him touch me. I am frozen, paralyzed, asleep like Snow White. He lets me go, probably sensing I am younger than I had claimed. I run into the night. An IV drip of shame hooks into my vein and doses me with embarrassment and humiliation and guilt every hour on the hour after that night. The following Monday in social studies class I decide I'm going to start counting calories. Counting calories is its own form of self-medication. It's such an obsessive habit, one that it allows my mind to focus on that singular task while everything else fades away. I begin to fixate on numbers and math, calories in and calories out, which is so much easier than fixating on this strange sexual experience I can't make sense of or talk to any of my friends about. I fear my parents will be ashamed of me if I tell them what happened that night. And my friends? They already call me a slut behind my back because I'm a young girl with boobs, and that's what happens to young girls with boobs.

I am sixteen and my parents are out of town, so I let this senior boy come over to my house. He is armed with a bottle of 151. We listen to Elliot Smith on my back porch and chain-smoke cigarettes and take swigs right out of the bottle. I quickly realize he is way more drunk than I am, even though he weighs twice as much. We begin kissing which is like, fine, I guess. But then he pushes my skinny limbs onto my bed, my teenage bed with the tacky leopard-print sheets I had begged my mother to buy me. His clammy, drunk hands rip my Victoria's Secret underwear right in half. He throws them like a baseball across the room and tries to push himself inside of me. This time I don't go limp. I fight him. I scratch him with my baby pink acrylic nails. He is so drunk he can't fight back and he ends up passing out in my bed, snoring and drooling on my beloved leopard-print pillowcase. I relocate to my brother's room (he is away at college) down the hall. I hear his footsteps creep down the stairs at 5:00 AM. That old familiar asshole shame wraps his long, spindly fingers around my neck. I am angry. I am angry at myself. This is my fault. I am suddenly overcome with the very real Fear of Being a Girl. A Girl doesn't invite a Boy over to her house if she doesn't want to have her underwear torn in half.

This is when I discover white wine. Oh, white wine. I could write poetry about white wine! That soothing, velvety pale-yellow liquid derived from grapes. Chic grapes from places like New Zealand and France and Napa Valley. The substance that Lady Gaga promises will put an end to all of your blues in her song "Grigio Girls." I began stealing wine out of my parent's stash regularly after that night. I really, really like wine. The razor-sharp edges of reality are nice and ROUNDED OUT when I drink wine.

The hardest memory to plunge from my subconscious is strangely the most recent. It is only a few years old, but I had stuffed that one down so deep, I had to remove it with pliers.

I am living in Notting Hill in London. In a speck of a studio, all alone. I am twenty-three. I don't have that many real friends in the UK, but I do boast a roster of drinking buddies. I trudge over to my local pub a lot because I am starting to experience panic attacks for the first time, and my beloved white wine seems to be the only thing that halts that scary rush of adrenalin. Plus, did you know that in British pubs you can order small, medium, or large glasses of wine? I *always order large wines (duh) and suck down at least three a night (two equals a full bottle). This particular night at my local pub I have sucked down at least four large wines. I realize it's 11:00 PM and I work the early shift at the makeup counter the following morning, so I stumble home, trying to ignore the shadow of a boy creature stumbling behind me. The boy follows me into my tiny, bright pink, girl-sanctuary of a flat and pushes me onto the couch and manically begins grabbing me by my braids. It hurts. I am wearing a spandex, bright-yellow Betsey Johnson dress and he's pulled it over my head. He's kissing me with rough lips and he smells like poison. The rest fades to black. The next morning the boy is gone but I can smell his venom on my skin. I wash him off me with water so hot the smoke alarm goes off in my apartment. I call out sick from work. My Scottish boss is very sweet and nice and tells me to feel better and to drink a hot toddy. I trudge into a pharmacy and request the morning after pill—just in case, you know? (I knew.) In England they make you go into a little booth and make sure you weren't assaulted before giving you the pill. "No way!" I say, smiling like a psychopath. The counselor is visibly freaked out by my superficial grin. I bat my lashes at him, and I see he has decided it's OK. I'm just one of those overly friendly American girls with overly bleached teeth. I go back home, splash my face with arctic cold water, and stare at myself in the mirror. I look thin, which pleases me. "Zara, you can let this destroy you or you can pretend it never happened." I choose the latter and go on my first antidepressant, Lexapro. I start dabbling with quick-fix pharmaceuticals like Valium and Xanax and Clonazepam and Ambien, and continue to count calories and drink wine, too.*

* * *

In order to feel feelings—whether they're happy or sad, blissful or devastating—one thing is required: vulnerability. That steel wall that you've spent so many years hiding behind? It needs to be knocked the fuck down if you want to feel.

I don't think there is anything on the planet more vulnerable than sex. I like to think of myself as a modern, sex-positive feminist, but I would never, ever, ever downplay the vulnerability of sex. Especially when penetration is involved. Someone is inside of you. It's intense. It's more intimate than anything else in the world. I never even realized the weight of sex until I spoke about it with Catherine in therapy.

When your first few experiences with the most vulnerable act in the world are frightening, it's understandable that you never want to put yourself in a vulnerable position ever again. Anytime you feel vulnerable—even if it's not sexual, even if it's merely opening up to a friend or mentor—automatically reminds you of the trauma you endured.

So you shut down shop. Lower the blinds. Lock the door. Tape a "DO NOT ENTER" sign to the shattered glass storefront. At least that's what I did.

Because I put this protective armor over myself every single day, I cut myself off from all feelings. After all, you can't just experience just the "good feelings." It doesn't work like that. If you numb yourself to the bad feelings, you're numbing yourself to the good feelings too. And since not feeling anything is against the very nature of the human experience, my feelings fought back. Feelings long to be felt. I didn't care. I fought *them* back. I found ways to knock 'em into the ground no matter what was what going on in my life. The death of a friend. Heartbreak. Career rejection.

I kicked the shit out of my feelings with the help of the two toughest brutes on the planet: booze and drugs.

I watched my friends fight their own battles against feelings too. Violet jogged so much she broke every single one of her toes. Beatrix online shopped her way into thirty thousand dollars of debt. We were all looking for a way to distract ourselves from the heaviness of real life. We were all looking for a way to nod out from reality.

There a million ways to numb. Two million. Probably more. I don't even know what half of them are, but here's what I *do* know:

Running away from your feelings can most definitely kill you if you dive head-first into the world of drugs and drinking and mindless risk. But those of you who excessively shop or have empty sex or simply binge watch TV as your drug of choice—yeah. You might not physically die.

But something *else* will die. Something deeper and more profound than your body will wither into nothingness. Your soul, the very essence of *you,* will be slaughtered if you continue to put roadblocks between yourself, your feelings, and the past you're so fucking terrified to confront.

Your spirit leaves your body when you stop being present. And you are not present when you're going through the motions in life. You're living in a fog. You're not experiencing the beautiful, nuanced, emotionally rich life humankind is supposed to live.

And what I find to be the most gut-wrenchingly sad part of it all is this: You lose your ability to evolve when you lose your ability to feel. Because your feelings exist for a reason, other than to simply torture you and keep you up all night stewing in your sweat.

For example, pain is a wise indicator that something is simply **not right**. Same with anxiety. Anxiety—which I find to be one of the most harrowing feelings of all—is also one I've learned to value the most. I'm anxious when I'm not in alignment with my purpose. I wake up with anxiety when I'm going to a job I detest. I feel anxiety in the presence of people who are inherently bad for me. Feeling anxious is wildly, wildly uncomfortable—but holy shit it's also quite beautiful. It's my higher-self saying, "Get the hell out of here! Make a change, bitch! Stay away from that damn friend...she'll screw you over!" If I numb my anxiety completely, I end up numbing the most important thing a woman has: her intuition. You can't have intuition without emotion. In fact, what if intuition and emotions are actually the same thing?

When you honor your feelings, you'll find that they're here to guide you back into the right place. Think of feelings as badass guardian angels who are whispering in your ear: "This job is bad for you. Apply for a new one." "This boy is a scum-bag, that's why you feel uncomfortable around him. Get the hell out of his house." "What happened to you was terrible, that's why this darkness is following you around. Let's get you help."

When I started embracing feelings, I realized I wasn't happy in Florida. I realized the underlying anxiety I was constantly numbing was my body telling me to go move back to New York. That I belonged in the frenetic energy of New York, and that if I could move there I might actually attain a sense of fulfillment—the kind that exists without a full glass of champagne and a purse full of pills. The fear I had about moving to New York, the incessant anxiety that I wouldn't "make it" was also important. It catapulted me into working my ass off and scoring my dream job. I was terrified about being jobless in New York, that's for sure. But rather than popping a pill to numb the fear, I let it be my driving force. I poured my fear into the deepest, most intense job search I've ever done in my life.

I came to realize that this incessant, restless fire that exists inside of me—the one that had been snuffed out by all those happy pills and drinks and tiny bumps of coke—wasn't actually dangerous. There wasn't something "wrong" with me like the doctors and teachers had told me when I was a kid. (Anyone else diagnosed with ADHD for daydreaming too much?)

It was actually my creativity. What if I channeled that burning sensation into a creative outlet? I started to think back to what I did as a teen with all these fiery feelings. What I did before I even knew *how* to self-medicate. Before the walls came tumbling up. What did I do with that fire?

I wrote. I journaled. In fact, I had a wildly popular LiveJournal in the early 2000s that described the day-to-drama of my angst-ridden teen life. I had loved my LiveJournal. It gave me so much...release. I processed the thoughts swirling through my head through writing and sharing.

So at twenty-five, I began to write again. I wrote furiously. I wrote feverishly. I wrote like my life depended on it, because it did.

Fuck it, I'll start a blog, I decided one day. I was scared as hell to put my work out there, but I did it anyway. And guess what? People actually *connected* to my silly little blog. Little by little I built a loyal, engaged audience.

Within six months after starting my blog, I got offered a full-time writing job in New York City at the popular millennial publication *Elite Daily*. Someone who knew someone at *Elite Daily* followed my blog and loved it and thought I would be a good fit. I wound up moving to New York with a decent salary, a dream job, and a passion for writing that no one could ever, ever take away from me. That's the beauty of passion. No person can snatch it from you. A job that doesn't work out can't snatch it from you, either. Only drugs can.

After so much therapy, I moved to New York with a newfound resilience about me. A strength that lived deep in my bones, a strength that was far more powerful than any of the social or drug-induced armor I'd ever tossed over my limbs. Because when I had finally cried, sobbed, and stared into the pain of my past, I wasn't so scared of it. I wasn't so scared of myself and the dark places my brain would venture off into if left unattended.

Obviously, the pain of sexual trauma will never leave me—but finally confronting the darkness of those times cracked open some *light* in my heart. I developed a deeper sense of empathy and connection to womankind, and in my willingness to be vulnerable I forged close relationships with my readers. My readers began to open up to me in a way they wouldn't have if I wasn't in touch with my past. Art only makes a real impact when it's authentic. I was finally authentically *me* because I was no longer disregarding my past.

I felt light. I didn't have to drag that heavy baggage around with me anymore. Feeling my feelings had been the ultimate cleanse.

So, to all of my babes who are reading this right now—actively numb or stuck in a shitty relationship or wracked with the kind of depression where you don't feel anything at all, scared of feelings for reasons unbeknownst to you—I want to encourage you to stop fighting the feelings. Don't just embrace them. Fuck them. Fuck them

like that rock star you've been dreaming of fucking since you were a
tween. Make love to them as intensely as you made love to that toxic
lover your body couldn't get enough of. Especially, the scary feelings.
The "demons." You'll realize that those demons that you so vehe-
mently fear are cowards (like that toxic lover). When you confront
the demon, when you gaze unblinkingly into his ice-cold eyes and
say, "I'm not afraid of you, in fact, I'm going to let you into my apartment and we're going to hash it out," he softens. He doesn't look so
much like a demon anymore. In fact, he looks kind of like *you*. Beautiful. Afraid. Scarred. Nuanced. And once you connect to him, you
will become one. You'll understand that the demon under your bed
isn't actually a demon, so there's nothing to be afraid of anymore. In
fact, the demon under the bed was actually a guardian angel who
was never there to hurt you. She was a feeling. A feeling that exists
to help you find your way in this world. And isn't that fucking beautiful? The demon was an angel all along!

CHAPTER 2

An Ode to The Girls
Who Grew Up Too Fast

Song: "This Is What Makes Us Girls" by Lana Del Rey

Let's talk about the girl who grew tits before she was ready for tits. The girl who got her period while she was still playing hopscotch. The girl who never had a curfew. This is my love letter to you. To me. To *us*.

I first began to bleed between my thighs during the spring of fifth grade, when I was still a ten-year-old kid with a mouth full of hot pink braces and a backpack full of Lisa Frank binders. I was mortified the morning I woke up with blood in my underwear.

I hung my head in shame as I tiptoed into the kitchen. "Don't tell anyone," was the first thing I said to my mother.

"Don't tell anyone what?" my mother chirped, happily clutching her morning cup of English Breakfast tea. She suddenly put her teacup down and stared at me for a good ten seconds, without blinking.

"Wait. I know."

Of course my British mother would instinctively know that her only daughter had gotten her period. I rolled my eyes, but secretly I was relieved that I didn't have to twist my tongue around that vile word "period."

"Swear you won't tell anyone? Swear to *god?*" I begged, my wide eyes filling up with pools of hormonal tears.

"I swear."

I crossed my arms. "Not even Aunt Marie?"

My mother paused. Like me, she takes promises extremely seriously. She took a deep breath and gazed at me with the loyal eyes of a noble lioness. "Not even Aunt Marie." She went back to her tea and kept her promise.

As I stuffed a wickedly thick cotton pad into my polka-dotted Gap Kids underwear, I felt betrayed by my body. My insides were all skinned knees and pigtails, but my body was ready to do what grown-ass women do: house a fucking *child.* I shuddered. *How dare my body make such a horrible mistake?*

The only silver lining was that at least getting my period could be "my little secret." I came tumbling out of the womb a very convincing liar, so it was easy to convince my blood-less peers I Was Just Like Them.

Boobs, on the other hand, are impossible to hide. The summer between fifth and sixth grade, during my annual eight-week stint at Camp Merriwood for Girls, I grew tits. I was dropped off in the White Mountains of New Hampshire and returned home to Westport, Connecticut with white mountains of my very own. I glared at them, and they glared back at me. They *taunted* me. *You might feel like a kid, but you're not a kid anymore, baby,* they teased.

"You need a bra, sis!" my older sister, Audra, blurted the moment I skipped off the camp bus. Audra was my half-sister from my dad's side, who was in her early twenties and currently living with us as she re-evaluated her current life choices. She took me to a swanky lingerie shop in downtown Westport and pointed me in the direction of the training bras, all cream-colored and cute, adorned with pink little cotton rosebuds.

"Oh, darling, you need a *proper* bra!" shouted the French sales-woman, whom I had not requested advice from. She pulled a scary looking contraption with sophisticated lace and vicious underwire off the rack and thrust it into my face. My cheeks suddenly felt very warm.

"You don't want to distract the boys with those things," she purred, hungrily eyeing my chest like a creepy uncle. My face went from warm to scalding fucking hot. My sister popped a piece of Bazooka bubble gum into her mouth, paid for my first bra (the scary one with the WIRE), and off we went, recklessly into womanhood, just like that.

Tanner Hastings, the most popular boy in school—a foot-ball-playing rich boy who had never even looked in my skater-punk direction—suddenly took to snapping my bra in the middle of math class. I would be blissfully doodling my usual drawings of hearts and stars and long-lashed girls into my notebook when I would feel the sting of a thick elastic band SNAPPING hard against the untouched skin of my back. His posse of frat-boys-in-training would high-five each other. The pretty, popular girls rolled their jealous eyes. The nerdy girls twisted their faces in horror as they slumped further into their chairs. And I would do the only thing I knew how to do: *giggle*.

It amazes me when people mock young girls for giggling so much. They chalk it up to silly vapidness, as if our tiny little brains are consumed with butterflies and pink puffy clouds, when really we're giggling because no one warned us that one day we would get sexually harassed while doodling in math class. We giggle because a part of us wants to scream bloody murder and rip our tits off our chests and hide for the rest our existence on earth. A part of us wants to deck all the boys who touch us smack in the center of their greasy faces. A part of us wants to kiss their smarmy little mouths.

But we don't do any of that because we're in the throes of a total mind-fuck. And when a human is being mind-fucked, they giggle. We're giggling because we're traumatized, but also because we're secretly thrilled. For we're being given the one thing we've wished for our entire lives: attention. And attention in middle school means one thing: *power*.

"You want to sit with us at lunch?" Beth Steinberg—the hottest, most badass girl in school—asked me out of nowhere. We had known each other since elementary school and had never exchanged more than a word, but now I was suddenly being granted a coveted seat at her *table*.

"Sure!" my tween heart fluttered like a moth intoxicated by the warm glow of a lamp. I paid for my turkey sandwich and followed her to the cool girl table, my chunky platform Steve Madden shoes loudly clanking against the cafeteria floor.

"Cool shoes," Beth's main minion, Tiffany, purred with the deflated, raspy voice of a thirty-two-year-old chain smoker.

"Thanks," I replied in my well-rehearsed vocal fry. This was the beginning of the rise of Paris Hilton, when apathy was at the height of fashion. Right before lunch ended I clanked over to the vending machine to buy a cherry Pop-Tart.

"She's a slut," I heard Tiffany say to Beth.

"I know," Beth answered, sweetly.

I took an indulgent bite of my pop-tart and smiled. I was *in*. Of course I felt degraded and insulted. But I would gladly accept those feelings, if it meant I could be popular.

I sort of loved my new tits, but I sort of hated them, too. Because while they garnered me all the attention I had ever dreamed of, they had a sneaky way of putting me in situations I wasn't quite ready for.

Like The Great Hotel Room Incident of 1998.

I was in the seventh grade now, and on vacation with my best friend Lauren Levine (who also bore a grand set of adult-sized tits—young girls with boobs stick together) and her father in Miami, Florida. We stayed at a gorgeous resort in South Beach. Her father was sick and slept most of the time, which was *totally fine* by us because that meant there was no one around to ensure we wait that infuriating "thirty minutes" after chowing down that monstrously large lunchtime burger before cannonballing into the pool. But most importantly, that meant no one was there to tell us to stay off the beach after 9:00 PM.

It was me, of course, who had the brilliant idea to go to the beach around that time. Lauren was nervous, but I assured her there was nothing to worry about.

"It's not like we have to go swimming! Let's just run around and explore!" I passionately begged her. I got down on my knees and seduced her with my hazel eyes. "Please," I whispered.

Her blue eyes glittered for a moment. "Fine!" she said, throwing her hands in the air.

Drunk on our newfound rebellion, we ran onto the sand, laughing like we had just smoked sixteen joints. Lauren wore the new tankini she had ordered from dELiA*s and I wore a striped halter-top and ripped denim short-shorts my mother had begrudgingly bought me at Wet Seal.

We were rendered breathless and wordless as our young eyes took in the sight of the beach. Nothing was more dangerously beautiful than that roaring ocean that night. The black waves looked so regal as they violently washed up against the sand, dissolving into nothing but a puke-green sea foam. The smell was dense and salty and intoxicating and I felt both massive and small, excited and afraid, adventurous and uneasy, old and young, wise and naive as hell—all at once.

"Hey," I heard a southern voice croon behind me. I turned my head and saw two older boys traipsing toward us. They looked older than my brother, who was a senior in high school. They didn't look like the hacky-sack playing rich boys posing as Phish Phans that I was used to seeing in Westport. Their shirts were tucked in. They were southern preps.

"Hi," I answered with the lazy confidence of a girl who is *constantly* bothered by men. My older sister, Audra, had taught me the mystical powers in being aloof. Lauren giggled.

"Where do you go to school?" the cuter of the two boys asked. Even though I was pretty sure I was gay and in love with Angelina

Jolie, I felt honored to be noticed by these strange, older boy creatures. Gay or straight, I was just like any other seventh grade girl. I was ravenous for attention.

"NYU," I answered without skipping a beat. It was the first of many times I would lie about my age.

"NYU! Wow, city girls!" The less cute one roared, smiling at our bodies like we were freshly sliced butcher meat. He reached into his cooler. "Want a beer?"

"Sure," Lauren answered. It was my turn to giggle.

I had never been offered booze before, but I'd watched my parents drink my entire life, so I decided to give it a go. I took a confident swig out of the ice-cold aluminum can and enjoyed the warm, fuzzy feeling that washed over my brain as the liquid made its way down my virgin throat. It helped to tone down the girl alarms loudly sounding off deep in my gut. I had never heard an alarm go off inside of me before, but it seemed to be sending me a dark signal: *Danger is looming ahead, danger is looming ahead, danger is looming ahead.*

The boys thought we were really "cool" and "sophisticated" because we were from *New York* and pretty soon they were oh-so-graciously inviting us upstairs to their hotel room, which was only a short walk away. As long as I kept my lips on the can of beer, I felt at peace. Beer seemed to beautifully silence those stupid alarms.

I don't remember much about the boys' hotel room except that it smelled like socks. There was a box of condoms clumsily thrown across the dresser. I went in for a sip of beer, only to realize it was empty. Suddenly I was suffocated with a crazy, intense anxiety, a visceral fight or flight rush of adrenalin I had never, ever experienced. What the hell was happening to me? These boys were southern. They were nice! I was acting like a freak.

"Can I have another beer?" I asked, fighting the shake in my voice.

"Babe, you can have as many beers as you want," the less-cute of the two boys answered, grabbing a can of Pabst Blue Ribbon from the mini-fridge. He cracked it open and handed it to me. He looked at me expectantly as I grabbed it out of his thick fingers.

"Thanks."

He smiled. "That's more like it."

I downed half the beer in one gulp.

And the next thing I know, I've knocked back three beers in thirty minutes and I'm stumbling around the hotel room giggling like I'm on *shrooms* and Lauren is sitting on one of the boy's laps (the less cute one) which seems SO WEIRD, so I down another beer and, like magic, the scene doesn't feel so weird anymore. It looks *fun*. So much fun that I hop on the other boy's lap (the cuter one!), and before I can even begin to process anything, I suddenly realize that I am beneath the sheets of the hotel bed with this dude and he is ramming his thick, furry tongue into my mouth. I am overcome with nausea. Like I'm going to throw up, NOW. My chest begins to pound so loudly I'm afraid he'll hear it and find out I'm lying, that I'm not even thirteen and I'm so not ready for beer and boys and bodies pressed up against bodies. I can't think of what to do so I weakly push his hand away. "I'm not feeling well," I mutter. But he grabs my skinny hand and purses his finger against his pouty chapped lips and goes, "Shh. You're gorgeous. Just. Enjoy. It." It's the first time I feel entirely out of control.

I was raised like most girls, to view "gorgeous" as the highest of compliments, and also to value compliments above anything else, so I stopped resisting and did as I was told. As he stuck his man-sized fingers inside of me, I felt my body ascend into the air. I was disconnected entirely. I hung out on the hotel room ceiling and stared down at the scene.

I remember his hands inside of me. I remember suddenly feeling very, very drunk. I remember pretending to fall asleep hoping it would all stop. Then, there's only a very dramatic blackness. Not a cinematic slow fade into blackness, just a harsh cut to black. No flashes. No feelings. No nothing.

Until I woke up at 6:00 AM, my twelve-year-old head POUNDING like a panicked heartbeat, my sore eyes scanning the room for Lauren. I found her curled up into a tiny ball in the corner of the room, sleeping like an angel, a beatific expression of purity and peace dancing across her little porcelain face. That's when I noticed a bruise-like hickey stamped on her neck.

"Lauren, wake up! Your dad is going to kill us!" I frantically whispered, not wanting to wake up the sleeping boys, as I grabbed her warm, sleepy arm and pulled her to her feet. I noticed the blisters on her feet. She was an amazing ballerina who had just given it up because her body was too "voluptuous" for the craft. My heart broke a little bit looking at those hard-earned scars on her feet.

Without speaking, the two of us quietly crept out of the grown boys' hotel room, disoriented, dehydrated, and dripping with shame. We didn't speak as we rode the elevator into the lobby. We didn't speak as we slowly walked down the boardwalk back to our resort. We didn't speak as we embarked into the pool area, holding our breath with all our might, because breathing meant feeling and feeling wasn't an option right then.

Lauren's dad refused to speak with us for the rest of the day. So the two of us continued our silence as we baked in the sun, parentless. We mourned for what we had lost.

Things would be different from now on. We both understood that childhood as we knew it was officially dead. We both had learned that booze can quell the pesky feelings of fear and panic, and can make intolerable, uncomfortable situations—situations that feel like they're poisoning your soul—feel far less toxic than they actually are. We both now understood that when your girl alarms sound off, they can be silenced with a single beer. We both now knew that when male creatures ask you if you want to "see their hotel rooms" it's not because the hotel room is pretty or cool or has a pool table. It's not because they want to talk and laugh with you, either. It's because they want to touch your body, which I was beginning to understand wasn't really mine at all.

Wipe away the details of this story and it's all of ours, isn't it? Maybe you didn't grow tits that early on. Maybe you've never even *been* to Miami. Maybe it was that your parents just weren't around that much and you were so overcome with extreme loneliness and craved affection so deeply that you tried to find it in hooking up with whoever was down.

Or maybe your parents were around, but they didn't bestow you with a curfew like all your other friends who had curfews (because, like, they were in eighth fucking grade), so the only people around to hang out with at the end of the night were high schoolers. And maybe one night those high schoolers let you snort a pale blue Adderall with them, and you felt like an invincible goddess who was so high up she could never, ever, fall down. So you kept snorting the pale blue Adderall until you finally discovered cocaine—and we all know that once you discover cocaine, you're no longer a kid. Your girlhood is officially pronounced dead on the spot. It's tossed out the proverbial window of the proverbial skyscraper. SPLAT onto the pavement.

Or maybe you were born into the Wrong Crowd™. Maybe your dark eyes and wicked sense of humor rendered you the female leader of the Wrong Crowd™ in the eyes of everyone's stuffy fucking parents, so you stopped resisting your unshakably bad reputation, and instead decided to play the part you were cast in.

Maybe your parents were addicts. Nothing will snatch the blooming youth flowers out of a girl's orbit like having parents who are addicted to drugs or alcohol. There are a million and one reasons as to why you grew up too fast, and I can't even imagine what yours might be.

But here's what I *do* know.

We share a special bond, you and I. Your therapist, your boyfriend, your girlfriend, your non-binary partner, your fuck-buddy, your coworkers, your shiny new adult friends, your blood family—they might not understand the wild ramifications of growing up faster than the speed of light. They might not be able to grasp the depth of the internal damage that's done to the girls who were once twelve going on twenty-seven. Of what it feels like to be robbed of those last few precious years of being carefree and rosy-cheeked, a smart-mouthed and athletic child. But *we know* how it feels. And the masses might laugh off our horror stories of youth, write us off as nothing but troubled drama queen sluts, but *we know* there is really nothing funny at all about growing up too fast.

I truly believe, in the deepest pit of my gut, that the most incredible time of our lives is when we're *girls*. Solid, true, bright-eyed, and bushy-tailed, eight, nine, ten, and eleven-year-old girls who are unafraid to talk sass to the cool boys; girls who recklessly sit in the mud and make fabulous mud pies; girls who dive boldly into pools and stay in there so long their fingers get all puffy and wrinkly; girls who conduct seances and sing their boundlessly joyful hearts out in the school choir; girls who laugh so hard milk flies out of their nostrils. Those girls are the true superstars of this sick world. They're in that sweet spot, the brief place where one is blazingly intelligent, empowered by their independence (*Mom, look! I made peanut butter and jelly sandwiches for everyone! Alone!*), long-legged and teeming with electric energy, and not at all, in *any* way, shape, or form, affected by the opinions of boys. Boys! Gag!

And then we change.

We stop getting attention for being the fastest girl in our class to run the mile, and start getting attention for giving hand jobs to Jimmy beneath the bleachers during recess. For showing Andrew our bare tits in the bathroom at Evan Goldberg's bar mitzvah. Everything suddenly revolves around *boys*. Your entire self-worth becomes completely wrapped up in being gorgeous for *the boys*.

And guess what? Hot girls don't lie down in the leaves and risk getting DIRT in their perfectly flat-ironed hair. Hot girls don't laugh until milk flies out of their nostrils (in fact, they don't laugh at all, really). Hot girls don't stay up all night giggling with their girlfriends. Hot girls stay up all night sucking face and smoking weed with their boyfriends in sad suburban basements. The very moment we're deemed objects for boys to play with is the very moment the dreamy little girl with stars in her eyes is put to rest.

Us girls who grew up too fast became objects at ten or eleven or twelve. We changed earlier than the other girls. It's confusing. And most painfully, it's lonely.

Girl, I know how much you deeply missed being seen as a kid during that time. And I want to tell you this: You might not have looked like a kid but you were still a motherfucking *kid*. I was still a kid when the Miami incident happened. A kid with curves and boobs. A kid who started getting plastered all the time. The only thing that blurred out the freaky flashbacks that haunted my soul late at night was getting so tanked that I passed out into a blank, dreamless sleep. Blackouts became moments of reprieve for me. If my brain was shut down, I didn't have to wrestle with the shame I felt all the time.

For most of my teens and all of my twenties, the thing that felt the most like love to me was a cold glass of champagne resting between my trembling fingers. (Hunger shakes, because I skipped dinner for five years.) Because when I was buzzed, I felt protected. Nothing could touch me. Nothing could hurt me. I became an invincible queen because I had a bodyguard lurking around me at all times. A savior who made me feel *strong*, a savior who made the insults and hurt and sad memories bounce off my body, a savior who made sure I was completely numb when dark shit went down.

Isn't love synonymous with this kind of protection? Aren't lovers supposed to make you feel safe like that? Aren't they supposed to always be there for you no matter what you do? So then, aren't drugs and alcohol sort of the same thing as love? Probably not. Scratch that—definitely not. But it sure feels that way sometimes.

Since I was robbed of those American Teen Dream, made-for-TV moments—like a tender deflowering of my virginity at the senior prom, or a sober first kiss under a star-spangled nighttime sky after the homecoming dance—I've always felt a little bitter about sex and love. For a long time, I couldn't have an orgasm with anyone I loved. To be honest, I don't think I know a single girl who grew up too fast who hasn't had a hard time getting off with someone she *actually* cares about. It makes sense. If in the most malleable moments of our lives, our sexuality felt dangerous and shameful, it's hard even as adults with loads of Prozac and therapy to remember that *making love* is even *a thing*. I mean, like, ew.

Most of us girls who grew up too fast tend to view men, all men (except the lovely gay ones with whom we are spiritually connected to), as the enemy. Whether their behavior has warranted their bad reputations or not is entirely irrelevant. If I see a man walking down the street and the street is vacant except for him and me, I will cross over to the other side of the street with my head held down. I will clutch the pepper spray inside my snakeskin bag so hard that my knuckles will turn white. Because *surely* that man is a rapist.

And really, the biggest, deepest issue I've found among girls like me is this: We can't tell the difference between a *kind person* who authentically wants to get to know us and an asshole who is *using us*, so we immediately decide a person is an asshole and we push 'em away. Better to be safe than sorry. We've been sorry before, and it sucks to be sorry. We're more guarded than the queen of motherfucking England. After all, being intoxicated strips you of your intuition. And when your intuition has been ripped off like a Band-Aid, you're an open wound vulnerable to everyone. And everyone feels like a threat. Everyone.

I always feel a little on the outside when I meet a new group of women who talk about how they spent the golden days of their youth running through the freshly cut grass playing, like, softball and, I don't know...*tag*? How do you talk about your childhood with normal women without traumatizing the whole room?

But despite all of the designer baggage we carry everywhere we go, we're still the most awesomely underrated type of human beings on the planet, you and I.

I'm sick of this cultural fetishization of the "innocent girl." The girl who waited until she was married to lose her virginity and was so Bambi-eyed and innocent she actually *believed* the dude when he said the white powder stuck inside his left nostril was from a powdered donut. Movies always celebrate this kind of girl. The sweetheart in the diner apron who captures the cold heart of the heavily tatted-up bad boy.

It's high time someone put us bad girls, us easy girls, us druggie girls, us overdeveloped girls, us depressed girls, us crazy girls, us slutty girls, on a fucking pedestal of our own! Because us girls who grew up too fast might have some pretty vile-looking scars, but we're beautiful. We're magic. Our early dark life experiences made us wiser than the rest. It gave us the ability to spot red flags when the other girls were blinded by the newness of teenage lust and booze. It gave us killer instincts that no one can ever take away from us. It rendered us life-saving heroes clad in skimpy crop tops and high heels and unapologetically red lipstick.

Like the time that toe-headed Becky took all those shots at the high school house party and no one else seemed to notice that she was passed out and choking on her own vomit in the kitchen—but because we've been watching this kind of shit go down *for years*, we noticed. And we knew she needed to get her stomach pumped or she would likely die. So we called the ambulance and went with her to the hospital, even though we weren't like *friends* or anything, and we DEMANDED that the doctors see her right away, and thanks to our aggressive attitude about it, the doctors pumped her stomach and saved her life. And Becky probably never even realized it was *us* who hauled her drunk ass to the hospital so she never thanked us.

Or when that girl from our dorm got date-raped her first week of college, and she intrinsically knew to come to us for help. She somehow knew that we would know what hospital to take her to, that we would know what STD tests she needed to take IMMEDI- ATELY, and that we'd hold her hand and keep her strong when she reported the incident to the police.

And when another sweet sorority sister, just a month later found herself in the throes of a bad acid trip at the frat party, she didn't go seek help from Catholic Lindsey from Alpha Beta Whatever to calm her down—she came to *us*. Even without speaking, our auras radi- ated a warm, non-judgmental sense of understanding. She could tell we have weathered worse storms than one lousy hit of dirty acid and that we are strong enough to steer her dark trip back into the light.

People tell us things they wouldn't dare tell others. They know that we are many things (loud, obnoxious, drunk, scandalous, intimidating) but we are not judgmental creatures. Us bad girls were never seen as the heroes of any story, so we never did anything for heroic accolades. We still don't do anything sweet or kind or selfless for praise. We do it because we learned this shit the hard way. And we don't want to see you hurt the way we've hurt.

My fellow girls who grew up too fast, I want you to know that none of this was your fault. I know it feels that way sometimes, and I know we've all done things we aren't proud of—but it's time to release yourself from the shackles of shame, babes. You did what you had to do at the time. I get it. But instead of letting the weight of regret drag you down into the ground, I want you to let your sordid past *lift you up*. Own your story. Be empowered by your story. As awful as all that was, it's granted you gifts that can truly make this world a better, more glittery place. Find some fucked up preteen and be the big sister to her that you so desperately needed when you were younger. No social worker or shrink in the stratosphere will be able to tap into the core of her complicated psyche quite like you, girl.

Be proud of the fact that you're not only still standing, but you're *sparkling*, and strut out into the streets with the confidence of the badass lady warrior you are. Your wealth of life experience is what makes you special. There is nothing sexier, more compelling, or more utterly useful to the world, than a woman with a past.

Everyone knows that.

It's time you learned that, too.

CHAPTER 3

PSA: Don't Take Adderall to Party

Song: "Pills" by St. Vincent

We're all in this crazy, wholly unpredictable, whirlwind of a life together, aren't we? We collectively screw up. We collectively learn. We collectively screw up again. We collectively learn again. And hopefully at some point we figure out how to make it out of the fire without searing our skin (and if even if we *do* get badly burned, we—at the very least—learn how to find beauty in those scars). However, there are certain life lessons I've learned the hard way. Shit, I would prefer you didn't have to learn the hard way. Namely, the shit that goes down on Friday and Saturday (and sometimes Sunday if you're a sucker for day drinking like yours truly). But as your self-proclaimed big sister, I feel it's my civic duty to warn you about all the dark energy that lingers beneath the pretty, twinkly stars on the weekends.

The week, for most of us, is pretty safe, right? We have jobs that require us to be sober, freshly scrubbed and cognizant at 9:00 in the morning. Maybe you religiously do hot yoga during the week. Or SoulCycle. And water? Oh, honey. You knock back at least a gallon of that shit a day. And you're always reading a slew of self-help books like, *You Are A Badass* and *How to Grow Up* and *Girl, Wash Your Face* as you travel to and from work on the train. You're a virginal saint during the week. Only to fuck it all up on the weekends.

Listen, you are *so* not alone. Almost every single woman I know has fallen down the same destructive trap, myself included. In fact, I have a tempestuous relationship with weekends in general. I love them, yet I fear the wrath of their recklessness.

I'll be on a strict ketogenic diet only to slug back sugary cocktails and binge eat pizza come Friday night. My friend will be manically worried about the GMOs in processed foods, eat exclusively organic and plant-based only to do a fat line of blow at 2:00 AM. My other friend will have blocked his toxic ex-boyfriend's number only to DM him on Instagram and wind up having relapse sex with him. Collectively we'll blow all of our hard-earned cash on booze and cigarettes and blurry late-night trips to ATM machines. We'll wake up with strange cigarette burns in our expensive denim jeans and we'll feel horrible about our lives.

Look: None of this shit would matter if the consequences of the weekends weren't so utterly dire. But the reality is, the consequences are actually...*horrendous,* if you roll with a hard-partying crowd like yours truly. They lead to major life setbacks and fill our precious bodies with shame. And harboring shame is toxic for the body. It eats away at our souls and zaps out our energy.

Since I'm a seasoned party girl who has fought long and hard to get her life together, it's only fair that I bestow you with a few unique quickie public service announcements designed to help you avoid weekend destruction, which will be randomly scattered throughout this book. Little nuggets of party-girl wisdom for you to keep in your pocket and touch like a crystal when you're about to spiral into the darkness.

Our first PSA is going to be focused on my ex-girlfriend. Her name is Recreational Adderall. I think it's best for you and I to both avoid hanging out with Recreational Adderall *at all costs* when partying during the weekend. Now, if you're in a prescribed relationship and only taking her for work or whatnot—I *do* think you'll have a better life without her, but this PSA is not directed toward you. I'm not a doctor. What the hell do I know.

This is directed toward anyone and everyone who pill-pops to have more energy whilst partying. And I *know* there are a lot of you out there.

Look—I get it. I work my ass off during the week. By the time Friday night rolls around I'm an empty vessel with nothing left to give. I long to crawl beneath the sheets of my bed and devour a juicy Gillian Flynn novel in my cow-printed pajamas. The last thing I want to do is adorn my lashes in heaps of mascara, take a long, expensive cab ride downtown and socialize (gag). But often I'm obligated to. It's a friend's birthday. It's another friend's art opening. It's bear night at the gay boy bar and I can't resist bear night at the gay boy bar, no matter how exhausted I am.

So I'll blast Lana Del Rey through the speakers, pour myself a hefty glass of wine, and adorn my lips with the brightest red lipstick to ever exist. I'll stretch a pair of sexy over-the-knee boots across my ample thighs. I'll whip out my baby pink vintage Chanel bag—the one with the beautiful long gold chain. I'll haphazardly toss my leopard-print coat over my shoulders, and that's it: I'm off to the races.

Say it's my best friend Ruba's birthday. She wants to party at some bougie hotel bar in Tribeca because she fancies herself an Arabic princess (as do I). I'll meet her there. I'll order a Sauvignon Blanc because I detest the smell of liquor. After six tiny sips, I'll begin to feel weary. A deep, dark fatigue will crawl all over my body like a bed-bug. It will latch on to the flesh of my back and will be too strong and stubborn to fight off.

But I have to rally. It's *her birthday* and you only turn *thirty* once, you know?

I'll tap someone—a boy probably—on the shoulder and ask him if he has Adderall. Of course, he does. He'll flash his freshly bleached white teeth and reach into his pocket. He'll hold his palm out proudly like he's presenting me with a shiny gold trophy. Only he's not. He's holding a pale blue pill. Ten milligrams of the drug we all love to hate and hate that we love, my irresistible ex: Adderall.

I'll snatch it out of his sweaty hand and swish it back with some cold champagne. It will taste sweet like sugar. And twenty minutes later I'll be passionately engaging with someone about something I know absolutely nothing about. Finance. Broadcast journalism. Soft-ball (if there are lesbians flitting about sports always comes up, and there are *always* lesbians flitting about in my world).

And because I'm on Adderall my tolerance for alcohol will have magically tripled! I can knock back drinks like I'm a two-hundred-pound man when really I'm a one-hundred-and-twenty-pound twink! And also, because I'm on Adderall, I'll feel like I'm fabulously rich and I'll buy shots for everyone at the bar! (I can hardly pay my rent!)

And because Adderall is an *amphetamine* I'll have zero appetite. That bitch steals your appetite as well as your soul.

Drinking like you're going to the electric chair, talking everyone's head off, taking shots and spending money—on an *empty stomach* no less—is a surefire recipe for epic disaster. Actually, if we want to get real, it's a prelude to a blackout. And blackouts are *awful*.

They leave you vulnerable to the worst kind of monsters—ones who prey on blacked-out women. They leave you feeling depressed and wracked with embarrassment the next day. They cause you to behave in a way that simply isn't *you*.

Look, here's the main issue I have with Adderall. Adderall disrupts your natural rhythms. If you're a slow talker by nature who chooses her words carefully, you'll suddenly be rambling nonsense at the speed of wildfire. If you madly crave carbs when you're boozed up, like me, you won't think about carbs at all. If you're the kind of person who feels buzzed after the first drink, you'll feel sober after the fourth.

But the truth is, you're not as sober as you feel, babe. And when the drug wears off (which it will) you'll suddenly be hammered. All those shots will hit your poor, dehydrated system at once. And it won't be pretty.

Also, let's not kid ourselves. Adderall is *speed*. It's not that different from doing coke. It's a drug like coke. Do you know how many girls have told me they "don't do drugs, they just do Adderall?" Look: I've tried almost every drug out there, and let me tell you, Adderall is one of the strongest substances, legal or illegal, that I've ever ingested. (It's also one of the most addictive.) And let us not forget that booze is a downer. Adderall is an upper. Mixing uppers and downers is fucking dangerous, OK? The combination of speed and a depressant can do a real number on your poor heart, and hasn't your poor heart been through enough already anyway?

I know that every single person on the planet appears to take Adderall when they go out, but I really don't think you should, little sister. Not only because of the reasons I've ranted about above, but Adderall also takes away the essence of who you are. At your core. It renders you a soulless version of yourself. It strips you of your charisma. There is a deadness in the eyes of girls who are hopped up on Adderall at the party.

Bottom line: You don't need it tonight. You're fabulous, even if you're exhausted! You're interesting and fascinating, even if you're too shy to talk to anyone (mystery is always sexy)! You're your best self when you are in your most natural state. I *swear* to Lana Del Rey.

If you're completely wracked with fatigue, listen to the temple that is your body. That holy space is telling you it needs some goddamn rest, OK? If you have a bad feeling about the night, that's your gut telling you something bad is going to happen and maybe you should stay home. Girls have the most powerful intuition; we can predict things long before they happen and we naturally have a good read on the energy of those surrounding us. These are gifts to be cherished. When we're keyed up we're speeding down the highway too quickly to notice that the car a few lanes over is recklessly driving and is going to cause a terrible, possibly deadly, accident.

(Seriously. Intuition, recklessness, and fatigue aside, Adderall tricks you into thinking you can handle another shot of tequila when you actually *can't*. And it's a fact that people who drink more alcohol than their livers can process, can reach blood-alcohol levels so absurdly high, they could go into a coma, experience organ failure, or die. This is not just about preserving your reputation. It's about preserving your *life*.)

And if you are tempted to use, imagine me at the bar with you. I'm wearing ripped black stockings and white over the knee cowboy boots by Jeffrey Campbell. I have gray circles resting beneath my eyes because I've had a long, hard week. But those circles look *chic*. They look even a little beautiful, maybe. They make you want to know more about me. And right as you reach into your large Marc by Marc Jacobs tote bag for a little pick-me-up-pill, I gently touch your arm. I look you in the eyes. My eyes *sparkle*. They sparkle in ways only the eyes of sober people can. Yours are sparkling too, and you can feel them glittering and gleaming around the room. We share a silent bond, you and I. Without speaking, we decide that you're not going to take that pill. We decide that protecting your sparkle is far more important than staying out until 2:00 AM. Your friends will forgive you. I *promise*.

CHAPTER 4

The Toxic Relationship with Myself

Song: "bad idea!" by girl in red

Imeet Ivy on Tinder because it's 2014 and everyone is meeting everyone on Tinder. After being cuffed in a relationship for the past few years, being able to flirt via cellphone is a giant thrill—a *high* and I can't get enough.

I am at work, swiping away, when Ivy's angular face pops up on Tinder. The moment my eye catches a glimpse of her I am struck with a feeling—a feeling I have never felt before. A dark rush? A chill? A dark but sexy vibration? I am not entirely sure. All I know is that Ivy's face staring at me through the screen has ignited a little fire up inside of me, a fire I want to jump headfirst into, even if I know it will burn the shit out of my skin.

Do you get hit on a lot? is her first question, which I know is, uh, a *weird* question to lead with.

No, I lie. I am a sex and dating writer in the thick of her twenties living in Manhattan! *Of course* I get hit on all the time. I'm not an *animal.*

Are you lying?

No. Why would I lie? The great question is why the hell am I lying and the hell am I entertaining this bizarre conversation from a bizarre stranger?

Three days go by and there is nothing but radio silence from Ivy.

I tell my colleague Alexia about the random strange interaction I had online with this mystery lesbian.

"Sounds like you dodged a bullet."

"You are so right." I say like I mean it, even though I don't. I am positively teeming with relentless curiosity over this rude Tinder lesbian. No one has ever spoken to me like that without even *knowing* me. I am used to the usual *what's up?* or *how was your day?* kind of back and forth that exists between normal people with boundaries who make polite digital small talk in lieu of prying.

On the fourth day, Ivy messages me. My hands trembled as I pick up my phone to see what she's written. Why are my hands trembling?

Can I take you out on a date? she has boldly typed. No smiley face. No emoji. No nothing. Just a bold-ass question after a three-day ghosting period.

Oh, how I want to be a bitch to her. I want to neglect to respond to her for at least *four days*, to beat her in her own game. Alas, before I know it I have typed back two words.

Fuck. Yes.

Who am I?

Meet me at Blenheim, the little bistro right across from The Cubby Hole bar, at 8 PM tonight.

Tonight? What if I am not available tonight? Who the hell is this presumptuous assho—

Sure, I type back before I can even finish my thought.

After work I rush home to the Upper East Side to figure out my wardrobe, which is super out of character for me. I usually wear whatever I wear to work on my dates (granted I work with twenty-two-year-olds and have no dress code), and spend my "getting ready time" pre-gaming with wine and salacious gossip with my friends. Nine out of ten times I arrive to a first date late and buzzed, rocking a stained crop top and smudged eyeliner. (Pro tip: Effortlessness always wins the race when it comes to dating.)

I agonize over what to wear. I try on a strapless silver mini dress, a designer classic fit-and-flair bought on consignment in the village. I feel too…*cute*. I stretch a pair of skinny jeans over my thighs and toss a boyfriend blazer over my torso. I feel too…*butch*. I throw on a white tee-shirt dress and over-the-knee suede boots. I release my hair from the shackles of the ponytail holder. I pout and paint my lips with gloss. I bat my lashes. This demure outfit feels…right. And demure *never* feels right. (Red flag. Red flag. Red flag.) I spritz half a bottle of an obscure designer fragrance I bought whilst buzzed at Barney's and dash out the front door. My heart races faster than the downtown-bound express train I take to Blenheim. Why am I so goddamn nervous? This girl seems whack-a-doodle. Why do I already have butterflies fluttering around my stomach? Are they butterflies? Or are they…maggots?

I arrive at Blenheim fifteen minutes early, so I sit at the end of the bar and order a Sauvignon Blanc. Just as my lips graze the glass, I feel a cold hand press firmly against my shoulder blade. I whip my head around, ready to smack a creepy dude in the face, when suddenly, my heart leaps out of its chest and splatters onto the floor.

It's Ivy.

Oh, Ivy! I want to write a poem about Ivy on the spot. For one, she has the craziest eyes I've ever seen. I don't mean crazy beautiful; I mean psycho crazy. Hyper-intense, blink-less, sociopathic eyes. Her lips are full and red, but not from lipstick. The kind of irritated red that adorns the mouth of someone who is constantly biting their lips out frustration—both sexual and situational frustration. Her hair is silver blonde and short, cropped close to her head. She is wearing a fitted button down that hugs her slim but sturdy frame, and black designer jeans that are tucked into pristine motorcycle boots. She smells like men's cologne and fresh lilies and spearmint gum. I don't know if I should run for the hills, away from this shocking-looking freak of a creature, or push her up against a wall and have sex with her right there in this tiny little West Village bistro, full of gay men and the fabulous women who worship them.

"Hi," Ivy says, the irises of her dark brown eyes dancing back and forth, hungrily eyeing my face as if I'm the last slice of pizza in all of New York.

"Hi," I squeak. I feel a tiny bead of sweat emerge on my upper lip. I wipe it away.

She raises her left eyebrow so high I think it might kiss the ceiling. "Let's grab a table," she says, licking her lips like a serial killer.

I nervously follow her to a table near the back of the restaurant. "*Leave. Leave. Leave. Leave. Leave. Leave. Leave. Leave. Leave. Leave. Leave,*" the wise woman (Sharon) who lives inside of me whispers. She is standing behind me, lurking, reeking of Clinique's Happy. She throws me a look of wild disapproval. I give her the proverbial finger and ignore her warning. Sharon is no fun. I need some adventure in my bleak life—and if anything, I can tell Ivy will at least make for a good story.

As soon as we get to the table, Ivy reaches over and grabs my wine glass, which I am clutching with all my might. She takes a healthy gulp. "Not bad," she says, as if it is perfectly normal to snatch a wine glass out of the hands of a girl you just met on Tinder and take it upon yourself to slug some back. I am speechless. This happens VERY rarely.

"I have something I need to get off my chest," Ivy volunteers, still holding on to my wine.

I begin to anxiously braid my hair. "Sure." I need my wine back, goddamn it!

"What's with all the jewelry?" she asks, pointing to my wrists—adorned with wooden bangles I bought on the street in Hell's Kitchen last weekend.

"What do you mean?" I ask, feeling defensive. I love my bangles. Excessive jewelry has been my signature look since Mary-Kate Olsen started rocking entire stores worth of accessories in the early 2000s.

"It's just…a *lot.*"

"*I'm* a lot." There she is! My old self is reappearing! I grab my wine out of her hands and take a triumphant swig.

"That's the funny thing." She peers into my eyes. I look away. I feel like she is staring right into the mushy vulnerable parts of myself—parts of myself I don't feel safe exposing to her. "I actually don't think that you're a lot."

I bitchily tap my long nails against my wine glass, as I'm wont to do when self-conscious.

Ivy continues. "I think you're a really nice girl." She says this earnestly. Like I am a bad egg being tossed into reform school and she is the nun-teacher who sees through my tough exterior.

I snort. I can't help it. I have just written an article about throwing up on a dick mid-blowjob. "Nice girl" isn't the phrase that comes to most people's minds when discussing me. (Though for the record, I'm VERY nice. There is a stark difference between being a "nice girl" and being "nice.")

Ivy flags down the waitress. "We'll take two more glasses of whatever the hell she's drinking," she purrs, eyeing the waitress flirtatiously, who happens to be blessed with an ass so big you could have a glass of champagne and maybe even a small cheese board on it. I watch Ivy gawk at the waitress as she walks away, her ass cheeks swishing back and forth like curtains in the wind. *What a fuckboy.* Ivy turns to me. She undresses me with her eyes. Slowly. I can feel every piece of clothing peel off my body and land on the floor.

My mouth begins to water. I scan the table for a glass of water but nothing is there, so I grab my glass of wine and down it as if it's water imported from the Fountain of Youth.

"Keep going." I murmur. "Tell me why."

"Why what?"

"Why you think I'm a 'nice girl.'"

"I can just tell. I know these things. You're a nice girl but you're... insecure."

I gulp. No. I. Am Not.

"Extremely insecure," Ivy observes.

"Um, so you think I'm insecure because I wear so many brace-lets?" I ask. I feel a sudden wave of rage wash over my limbs. An ocean of anger floods my brain. It feels like a relief. Rage and anger feel like freedom. *Screw this bitch! She doesn't know me. I will walk out of this restaurant right now and leave her with the fucking bill!*

"You try to cover up your insecurity by wearing all this—" She gestures to my bracelets. "And all of this." She gestures toward my face.

"What are you talking about?" I spit, gearing my body to stand up. For whatever reason I am glued to my seat. Held against my will. An Uptown hostage in a West Village bistro.

"All that makeup. What are you hiding from?"

"Oh, fuck you," I hiss. I am way above arguing with some butch bitch about how a girl can actually love red lipstick, *authentically*, not because she's trying to please the world with her prettiness. This is shitty internet, "think piece" bullshit. I get up and beeline to the bath-room. I look in the bathroom mirror. I feel the presence of Sharon behind me. I turn my head to look at her. There she is, draped in a brown peacoat that has clearly been purchased somewhere boring like Old Navy. "You have two options," she advises, lighting up one of her signature Virginia Slim cigarettes. "You can either get the hell out of this toxic situation, march out the door like a goddamn woman…"

"Or?" I ask leaning up against the bathroom sink, folding my arms like an angst-ridden teenager.

"Or, you can go back and end up in a dysfunctional relationship that will do irreparable damage to your self-esteem." She blows out a perfect ring of gray smoke, which surprises me. She's not a "perfect ring of smoke" kind of woman.

I giggle. "You are *so* dramatic, Sharon."

"And you are acting stupid." Sharon clutches her sensible Coach bag with her French-manicured hands and turns to walk away. Before she swings the bathroom door open, she stops and looks back at me. "Which is a damn shame. Because you're not stupid. Not at all." She slams the door behind her, disappearing into the mysterious abyss where our higher selves live.

I feel defiant. I feel unhinged. I feel fucking crazy.

The next thing I know I am sitting across from Ivy. *I'm going to tell her to go fuck herself and then I'm going to leave. Sharon doesn't understand the importance of a melodramatic exit!*

"You're wrong. I wear jewelry and makeup because I love it. So will you stop trying to read me?" I say.

"Prove me wrong. But Zara—" Just hearing my name in her mouth makes me tingle between the thighs. "Zara, I feel like I know you." She touches my arm. The little hairs stand tall in protest of her unsolicited touch. I take in the vision of her. There is an electric, unpredictable energy that seems to radiate out of Ivy's eyes. Has she blinked the entire date? Isn't not blinking the sign of a psychopath? Her finger presses into my flesh. "You're beautiful. Really. Beautiful."

Oh, how I want to roll my eyes! Oh, how I want to come up with a bitchy witty thing to retort back to her! I want to push her obtrusive finger off my arm. But I don't. I am not in control. I am *under* control.

"Want to get out of here?" Ivy asks softly. She pushes her leg into mine.

The next thing I know we're having sex. We're twisted up in her sheets, hot and sweaty, bare skin against bare skin. I'm fighting to get on top and she's fighting to get on top. We are two women wrestling, wanting to win. I pin her wrists behind her and she laughs. She's extremely strong—construction worker strong—and she flings my arms off of her as if they're spindly twigs blown off a tree by the tiniest gust of wind. Her breath is hot and smells sweet and I don't ever want this to end. I've never had this much fun during sex. I've never played so much during sex. The mind game, the power struggle, the weight of her body crushing me feels like ecstasy. Better than ecstasy, because I know there will be no sad chemical crash. No comedown. She gets on top and begins to kiss me. It's one of those kisses that has a beginning and a middle and an end. There is a story. An arc. We meet cute. We are kissing gentle and kind and shy.

Then we are frisky and fun. And then we're kissing hard and fast, like we only have six minutes to kiss for the rest of our lives and we're feverishly trying to drink each other in before the world ends. And then we go slow. Relishing those last few kisses. There is passion. Meaning. I'm working through years of trauma and hurt and disappointment through these slow, deep kisses. She stops and looks me in the eyes, and that's when I know I'm completely screwed. Now I know what my idiot friends mean when they say they're addicted to sex with their toxic partner. I've only had one taste of Ivy but I fear I'll crave her for the rest of my life.

The next morning, I show up to work in her sweatshirt and jeans. Everyone can obviously tell that I have gone home with someone the night before. No one has ever seen me in a sweatshirt or black jeans. No one has ever seen me glow sheepishly. I am teased the rest of the day. I can't help but grin the whole subway ride home. And I hate the subway.

"How was your date last night?" my roommate Courtney asks me. She is drinking a glass of red wine and has a towel wrapped around her head. She looks like a 1960s movie star.

"Best sex of my life." I answer, pouring myself a glass of red.

"Oh, you're fucked." Courtney says. She is always right about these things. I just nod my head and drink my wine and sext crazy Ivy until 2:00 AM.

For the next two weeks, Ivy and I can't get enough of each other. I detest talking on the phone more than anything in the world, yet I leap toward my cellphone when it starts to ring. I sleep over at her apartment every single night and break every single dating rule I've ever bestowed upon myself and the internet in the hundreds of dating articles I've penned. I tell her everything about my life. I tell her about the sexual traumas of the past—something I've never told anyone I've ever dated. I tell her about all the times I got bullied in middle school for having hairy legs. I tell her about my top-secret collection of all things Hello Kitty. I tell her about my obsession with mermaids and sea creatures in general. I tell her my fears and my dreams and all about my siblings and my family dynamic and my hopes for the future. She tells me about the abusive household she grew up in. About her alcoholic father. About how she wanted to be a guitar player but got sucked into sales because she grew up poor and is terrified of staying that way. She tells me about her nightmare ex who cheated on her with a guy. She tells me about all the times she's been burned by love. She tells me she loves me. I know it's too soon. I know in my bones that telling someone you love them after two weeks is mania, that it's not real, and it's just the oxytocin talking (women release a feel-good chemical called "oxytocin" after we have orgasms and it makes us want to be affectionate and loving toward whomever bestows us with said orgasm. It's known as the "love" hormone. Oddly enough, we release it after we breastfeed as well; it's part of what makes us want to nurture our baby). But I don't care. I want to ride this shit-show out for as long as I can because I know in my heart that at some point we will crash and it will hurt.

I tell her I love her back.

And that's when things start to get weird. As soon as "I love yous" are exchanged, Ivy starts acting like she owns me. Like I'm an expensive piece of property she's just invested her retirement savings into. And she's the kind of home owner that wants her lawn perfectly manicured. And I'm many things, but perfectly manicured isn't one of them. I'm messy. I wear fabulous clothes that usually have a rip or stain or tear in them, because I move through the world like a bull charging through a china shop. I am proud of this. I don't want to change this about myself. In fact, this what most people I've dated have found attractive about me. The wild juxtaposition of chic and scrappy. I'm starting to feel like Ivy wants to put me in a box, and my whole life's mission has been about encouraging women to tear out of society's boxes! I am ashamed that I'm letting Ivy dim out my sparkly light, so I don't tell my friends, and eventually start dodging their phone-calls.

"You look so stupid when you wing your eyeliner like that, babe." Ivy tells me as she watches me put on makeup in her bathroom.

"I love my winged-eyeliner. It's very Brigitte Bardot. She's the epitome of French sexiness!" I say, trying to convince her (of what exactly, I don't know).

Ivy walks over to me. She takes her thumb and wipes my wings away. I feel my identity start to erase itself. I hiss at her like a cat. She hisses back. And kisses me. Case closed. Wings clipped.

"Why would you wear a sequined mini dress to a casual brunch?" Ivy says, her brows furrowed in anger.

"I can wear whatever I want to brunch." I feel like a teenager arguing with my mother. Which isn't a healthy way to feel with your girlfriend who you have sex with.

"Come on, babe. You look so cute when you wear stuff like this." She says pulling a navy-blue boat neck romper out of my suitcase. "It turns me on," she says throatily, as she throws it my way. I feel myself shrink a few inches. I go from five foot six to five foot two. I put on the stupid romper and huff like a spoiled brat forced to wear ribbons in her hair to church on Easter Sunday.

One night I am wearing something *really* sexy. It's Halloween and the whole point of Halloween is dress as provocatively as possible, right? I am wearing a fabulously slutty Alice in Wonderland costume. It's so short it barely covers the short-shorts I'm rocking and it's so tight I can hardly breathe. I have a fetishy bow adhered to my head. My lips are deep red like cherries. I have false eyelashes on. I feel *hot*. I can't wait to see Ivy. I fantasize about the amazing sex we're going to have.

I nervously wait for her in my apartment.

Ivy knocks on the door and lets herself inside. If I could describe Ivy, it would be like that. *She lets herself in.* I jump into Ivy's arms. Her arms are stiff around my waist.

"What the hell are you wearing?" she asks, her pouty lips flattened into a paper-thin line.

"It's my costume." I say. "Don't you like it?" I bat my lashes at her like I'm a retro screen siren. It feels fake. It feels like the movie is about to end. They're going to call cut and the act will be over.

"You can't leave the house like that."

"Are you SERIOUS? It's *Halloween*, Ivy."

"You look ridiculous. Stupid. Cheap."

I feel a hot tear make its way down my heavily made up cheek. "Fuck you," I growl.

"Oh yeah? Fuck me? Well I am sorry that I'm a person who doesn't want you to get goddamn raped by some stranger! I actually give a shit about you. Why the hell would you dress like that after all the harassment you've endured? What, are you stupid?"

I hear my higher power Lana Del Rey yell, "CUT. END OF SCENE." I imagine her wearing heart shaped sunglasses, licking a lollipop in a bright red bikini, splashing around the pool of The Beverly Hills Hotel. I am stone-cold-frozen. "She just victim blamed you, ZARA. She crossed a line that CAN NEVER BE CROSSED. *She slut-shamed* you," Lana lectures. I am still frozen. "ZARA!" Lana is now yelling at me, splashing me with chlorinated pool water. It burns my eyes. Ivy punches the wall. She charges over to me like she's going to hit me. I hear Lana Del Rey sing the song "Ultraviolence"—the song where she talks about her her how her lover hitting her feels like a kiss. She sings it as a warning. Warning me that this abusive dynamic will crawl so deep into my psyche that I won't know the difference between a kiss or hit if I'm not careful. Ivy doesn't hit me, but she shoves me, and suddenly I wake up from the coma I've been in for six months. How did this turn into six months? Why does time move so quickly sometimes and so slowly at other times?

"I'm done," I say, slowly, tasting each word.

"Good," she says back. "We aren't right for each other anyway." She has tears glistening in her eyes. She lunges towards me and kisses me. She doesn't taste good anymore. She tastes like what she is: poison. I have sex with her anyway. Disconnected, angry, hair-pulling sex.

The next evening I meet with my friend Sam for dinner. I can't stop crying.

"You have to get out of this," Sam says. "I get a bad feeling from her. We all do."

"Really?" I ask her. "Why didn't you tell me?"

"You wouldn't have listened." Sam stabs her steak with her fork and sticks it into her mouth. There is something so primal about watching a woman eat meat. "Look at you. You don't look like you."

I look at my clothes. I'm not wearing the fabulous Zara drag I normally wear. Gone are the fishnets. Gone are the cheap wooden bangles. Gone is the glitter and the winged-eyeliner and the shocking lipstick. When a woman stops wearing her favorite loud lipstick in order to appease her partner, she's officially lost herself. I've officially lost myself. In my place is someone unrecognizable, in a cashmere plum-colored sweater and jeans. Since when did I start wearing jeans?

"I know."

"Your writing is different, too," Sam tells me casually, in the way only a close friend can. A close friend will casually tell you that you're acting like a shell of yourself without making a huge production out of it, which is one of my favorite aspects of close friendship.

This one hurts. I have worked so hard to write from a raw, real place, but I have been so afraid of offending crazy-jealous Ivy with my work. It's one thing to fuck with my style. Another to fuck with my *work*.

On the way home I check my phone. I have a plethora of text messages from Ivy. *Where are you? Where are you? Where are you?* I can feel her urgency over the phone. People like Ivy are psychic. They know when you're about to leave them, and they come up with a plan to keep you sucked into their orbit like a vacuum. The last text reads: *I'm sick. I need you.* I take a breath.

I'm sorry but I can't do this anymore. Please don't call me again. I'm done. I hold my breath as I type the sentence. But something weird is happening. I exhale. It feels almost spiritual. All of a sudden in my mind's eye I see...*the future.* Only there are two different paths. One path represents staying with Ivy. The path looks dark and murky and has a dead end in plain sight. The other path is my life *without*

Ivy. It's lit-up with strung lights that twinkle. It's smooth and full of wildflowers and palm trees and it keeps going. It goes on so long it looks as if it's descending into the sun. I now hear Sharon's voice in my head, which, unlike Lana's voice, lives inside of me, not above me. *You pick. A dead end. Or this beautiful life. It's up to you, Z*, she says, her voice flat and void of emotion. I decide to walk toward the beautiful path. I block Ivy's number. She will be my dead end. I know this more than I've known anything before. And for the first time in months, I honor my instincts.

I know the breakup is right, but the breakup still hurts. I call up my old therapist, Catherine, in Florida and request a phone session. To this day, I've never had a therapist as effective as Catherine.

"Wow. Sounds like you willingly walked into a house that was ablaze with fire," Catherine says in her mild southern twang. "But eventually it started to burn. So, you left."

"Yeah. It's weird, though. In so many ways she was the best I ever had," I say wistfully.

"How?"

"Well the sex was really…healthy. I've never had like, 'love sex' before her."

"That's interesting. You are only able to have healthy sex with someone who is wildly abusive toward you?"

Shit I forgot how *hard* therapy is. "*Wildly abusive*? I don't know about that."

"You said earlier she 'disapproved' of who you fundamentally are. At your core. Shamed you for it."

"Correct."

"Do you think you know why you actively lusted after someone who hates everything that everyone else seems to love about you?"

"No, Catherine. I don't." I'm annoyed. I want to be validated. Not challenged!

And that's when Catherine hits me with the best goddamn insight I've ever received in my life. So pay attention, little sisters, reading this book. I have a big sister witch vibe you need to hear right now, just as badly as I did in that moment.

"Maybe you're drawn to Ivy because her low opinion of you matches the low opinion you have of yourself."

I gulp.

Catherine continues. Her gentle voice almost coos through the phone. "And you think that if you convince her that you're good enough, you'll convince *yourself* that you're good enough."

Mic drop.

Once again, Catherine has rendered me shook. Once again, Catherine's words stay with me throughout a sleepless night. Once again, Catherine has helped me realize the truth.

Sometimes the truth takes years to figure out. Sometimes it takes a gazillion decades of therapy to really let a concept sink in. Sometimes you have to hike a crazy mountain in Africa to really *get it*.

But sometimes it takes an instant. Understanding the root of my addiction to this toxic relationship was easy. Maybe it's because I had years of prior therapy. Maybe it's just because the truth was so freeing and so simple. I mean, sometimes it's really *not* that complicated. Sometimes it's a short sentence uttered by a sweet shrink during a phone session—and BAM. You get it. Your life has shifted in seconds.

The truth is my self-esteem *sucks*. It royally sucks. It doesn't suck in the way that Ivy thinks it sucks. It has nothing to do with my clothes and not wanting to be "seen" or the piles of bangles clanking against my wrists or the slutty attire she thinks I wear because I'm desperate for a cheap hit of attention (and honestly, what the hell is so wrong about a woman wanting to get sexual attention? Why do we demonize a woman for owning her prowess?). It sucks deep down. It sucks like someone's self-esteem who has sex with someone who actively insults them on the first date.

Here's the biggest lesson I learned: I wasn't in a toxic relationship with Ivy. I am in a toxic relationship with myself. I wouldn't have let a toxic person into my precious orbit if I had a healthy relationship with myself, would I?

I was starting to realize that I had become convinced that my relationship with myself was amazing, even though it wasn't. After all, I am on meds! I have done years of therapy! I have a great job, a job I am proud of! What the hell is *wrong* with me that with all this work and self-esteem I had assumed I had finally truly cultivated wasn't real? Why was I still drawn like a moth to a flame, to a person who "disapproved" of my very existence?

That's the bitch about recovery. That's the bitch about "getting better." That's the bitch about doing work on yourself. The deeper you dig inside of yourself, the healthier you get, the more you realize that the lessons are not done. You peel back that gauze and treat the wound. The wound heals. You feel a great sense of triumph. Than the wound starts throbbing again. You realize that underneath the wound you healed was another wound, a deep tissue wound that desperately needs tending to. It's never-ending. But the more we keep caring for ourselves, the stronger we get and the easier it is to heal the core of who we are.

Here's the beauty of relationships. How we behave in romantic relationships, who we are attracted to, what we put up with, and who we want to have sex with, is the deepest reflection of what's *really* going on inside of us.

You know that impossibly gorgeous friend who dazzles the masses with her illustrious beauty? Not only is she supermodel stunning, she's *funny*. And *smart*. And makes a lot of money. She never takes shit from anyone! She's the first to call out a waiter for being rude. She's the first to slap a handsy bastard who is attempting to cop a feel at the bar. She's a fierce force of girl nature!

Yet, she always dates motherfuckers. Losers. Losers who don't appreciate her beauty and charisma and brilliant brain. You watch her crumble in their nasty, nicotine-laden hands. You wonder, how can a woman who has her shit together in every aspect of her life put up with these fuckboys? Maybe you've *been* that friend. Maybe you are that friend, right now.

I can't tell you why your friend is addicted to toxic relationships. I can't tell you why you are. But I *can* tell you this: It's not about who either of you are dating. This asshole doesn't have a magical spell over anyone because assholes don't attain an ounce of magic. It's about you. It's about her. Something inside of you is wounded if you find yourself weak in the knees in the face of toxicity and abuse.

For me, it was my low opinion of myself. Even though I was living a beautiful life and was starting to get the things I had worked so hard to bring into fruition, I still felt deep down like I was a fraud. I felt like I had no business writing. I don't have a college degree—what the hell am I calling myself a *writer* for? I still felt like the slutty friend no one would ever respect or bring home to their parents. For so long I felt shaky in who I was. Like I was going to be found out and exposed as a failure wrapped in a pretty pink bow. And Ivy validated all of my insecurities. Everything I feared was true about myself, Ivy assured me *was* true. But if I could convince her otherwise, I could convince myself otherwise, you see? That's why I was so obsessed with her. I was obsessed with finding true confidence. But she wouldn't ever give it to me. No outside person ever will, whether they're an angel or a devil. Even if an angel had appeared in front of my eyes, it wouldn't have healed my negative view of myself. No amount of angelic accolades would've convinced me I was *good* enough. Their compliments would have been merely words, words that bounced off me like a tennis ball to a cement wall. I would've probably pushed the angel away, because angels tend to be healthy creatures. And no healthy person wants to sit around convincing someone they're AMAZING.

But here's the beauty. Here's the beauty of *all* bad relationships. When you finally break free, when you finally get the courage to cut the cord, you're so vulnerable. And when you're vulnerable you're able to do the real work. You're able to ask yourself the biggest question of all questions: Why the hell did I let someone who treats me badly into my life? Why did I hold the door open and not just talk to my abuser, but become sexually intimate with them? Why did I choose to spend my free time with them over my loving friends and family? And when you're in the thick of figuring it out, you're going to do the most gut-wrenching- yet-wildly amazing work on yourself. And eventually you'll figure out the answers. And eventually you'll have clarity, the kind of clarity that frees you from the cycle of abuse. Things lose their power once you understand them, and when they lose their power, you heal. When you heal, you'll be in such a place that when the real love of your life comes waltzing through the doors of your inner-world, you won't freak them out because you're addicted to the toxicity. You won't push 'em away with your issues. In fact, I don't even think we attract the amazing people we deserve when we're sick. Sick attracts sick. Healthy attracts healthy.

And healthy is the goal. Because *healthy* is the real deal. The fleeting moments of blissfulness we feel from mind-blowing sex shouldn't be the ultimate goal because you'll never feel blissful all the time. You'll never feel happy all the time. That's why they're self-defeating goals. They're temporary highs you could waste your beautiful life trying to chase. Health and peace are accessed from within so they can last forever. They're sustainable because they are reliant on one person: You.

And love, *real* love doesn't need layers of hurt and manipulation and bullshit in order for it to be hot. It's hot and exciting and affirming on its own. Which is why it has legs to last. The ecstasy you feel when you have mind-blowing sex is so euphoric that it can trick your mind into thinking the person giving you these spine-tingling orgasms is the real deal. But it's not the real deal. It's a fleeting moment of an orgasmic high. Orgasmic highs come in doses—it's not something you'll feel all of the time, so don't even try. You will set yourself up for failure if you do. This is how people become addicts.

But before you go seeking the kind of health and peace that comes from within, you *must* cut the cord on this toxic relationship. And mend that broken heart of yours. It's going to be hard, but it's going to be OK. It's going to be better than OK. It's going to be transformational. You're going to find there is so much beauty in breaking up. When I broke up with Ivy, I was able to find the beauty in myself again. And this time the healing process didn't take as long as usual because Ivy wasn't my first heartbreak. A first heartbreak is so jarring it leaves you thinking you can't breathe oxygen without your ex. It's so emotionally traumatizing you're convinced you'll never love again. You'll never *feel whole* again. You'll never have sex *with meaning* again. I mean, if I'm being real, your first big-time breakup will leave your heart more black and blue than Evander Holyfield's eyes after the fight where Mike Tyson bit his ear off.

I know this from experience. For my beating heart was tossed into the ring and beaten bloody by a knockout named Lila.

CHAPTER 5

The Beauty of the Breakup

Song: "Nineteen" by Tegan and Sara

There is nothing, nothing in this cruel, cold world that will rock you to your core like heartbreak. In my lifetime, I've experienced two harrowing heartbreaks, both of which blew my house down, left me without a place to call my own, forced me to look at the broken parts and rebuild my life from scratch. That's the magic of a heartbreak. Everything around you shatters and breaks so you're working from a place of nothing. And "nothing" is freeing. Once you've lost everything, you can build your life from the ground up, fashioning it into whatever you want it to look like.

My first real heartbreak was with a woman named Lila. I had been the one to break it off with Lila because I knew in the deepest pit of my gut that our relationship was no longer serving me. We were two good people who hadn't done an ounce of work on ourselves yet, and we were dragging each other into the mud of our mutually untreated issues, traumas, and anxieties. Even though I had been the one to cut the cord, I was completely broken. I hadn't wanted to cut the cord—I had *needed* to cut the cord. I was turning into someone I detested, and in order to save myself, I had to abandon the relationship.

I cried into my pillow every single night. I stopped eating. I moved back in with my parents and Lila stayed in the beautiful apartment—the one with the Olympic-sized swimming pool that only cost us eight hundred dollars a month (total!)—alone. I sobbed for her loneliness and I sobbed for my own loneliness. Lila and I were completely enmeshed, our hormones were linked up, our primal scents had morphed into one, our bodies were not even our own bodies, they were one body, like a rat king. Have you ever seen a rat king? It's when a bunch of rats tails get all intertwined and tangled up together so they become one giant rat. We became a lesbian king, I guess.

And untangling ourselves from each other was a real son of a bitch.

When suddenly, overnight, you are not with the person with whom you've shared air for so long, you feel like you can't breathe. You've forgotten how to do anything on your own. The sudden, dramatic ending of intimacy is jarring as fuck, to say the least.

* * *

One night, I attend a holiday party that my sister is throwing. I know better than to go, for it's at this same party three years prior that I first met Lila. Knowing better has never stopped me from doing anything. Maybe it's my self-destructive streak, maybe it's because I like to rub the salt directly into the open sore, maybe it's because I have a flair for the dramatic, I don't know. I straighten my mass of newly dyed red hair (I love a break-over), throw on my favorite black jumpsuit from Nasty Gal, and saunter off to the party alone. Naturally, there is an open bar at the party. Naturally, I am in the throes of a breakup and in the most triggering environment possible, so naturally, I ask for a martini. I don't drink martinis. I *know* better. Ha. I suck back the martini like it's the last martini on earth.

Here's one of the many dangers of drinking whilst heartbroken: You're almost always drinking on an empty stomach. Something about having your heart ripped out of your chest and thrown outside the window of your fifteenth story apartment, watching it shatter to the ground as it gets repeatedly run over by a truck, can really make a girl lose her appetite, you know? And drinking without a baseline of food to absorb the alcoholic poison is a surefire recipe for a public meltdown at best. So imagine yours truly, who hasn't taken more than three bites of solid food in twenty-four hours, guzzling back straight vodka.

After the first drink, I'm desperately trying to flirt with everyone. I'm doing this because I have that false, buzzed confidence masking my hurt. It's very much like wearing a cheap dress from the mall; it looks kind of sexy, but if you were to even lightly tug on the fabric it would crumble into pieces, leaving you naked in a crowded room.

"Hi Maya!" I slur to a hot femme daddy I know from the gym.

"Hi Zara," Maya sing-songs back, not looking me directly in the eye. She looks sort of freaked out. Like I'm an unpredictable animal who could possibly bite her at any given moment. And I suppose I am. I'm surely radiating that off-putting "I JUST HAD MY HEART BROKEN!" energy, an energy that's both desperate and deranged, two wildly unattractive qualities in a person.

I stumble away from Maya. I decide to hit on a boy, even though at this point, I'm twenty-six and I've fully accepted that I'm not remotely attracted to boy-creatures (sorry boy-creatures). I don't care that I'm not attracted to boys, though. I'm not flirting because I want to get laid. I'm flirting because I want to be told I'm pretty, because maybe if I'm told I'm pretty I will forget about how sad and empty I am.

I notice Christopher lurking around by the bar. Christopher is the hottest guy in town. Every girl wants to date Christopher, but I have a hunch Christopher has always wanted to date me, namely because I'm a lesbian, which makes me unavailable. I strut over to Christopher. This will be easy-peasy, I think to myself. I teeter for a moment in my heels. So long as I don't fall on my face.

I tap Christopher on the shoulder. "Hi, Christopher." I once again slur, throwing him some (drunken) bedroom eyes. "I like to have a martini. Two at the very most. After three I'm under the table, after four I'm under my host," I manage to stammer.

"Nice, Dorothy Parker!" Christopher says. I'm impressed a boy gets my reference, so impressed I entertain the idea of kissing him on the mouth. Before I get the chance to nosedive head-first into his face and make a giant asshat of myself, Christopher lowers his voice. "How are you doing?" He leans in and gives me a giant hug. "I heard about your breakup," he whispers into my ear.

And just like that I am crying. Dripping wet, hot mascara tears all over the collar of Christopher's crisp white button-down. "I'm so sorry," I mumble.

"It's OK! Don't worry about it. Why don't you get a drink and I'll meet you outside for a cigarette?" Christopher says, pulling an American Spirit out of his pocket and tucking it behind his ear. "Let me just find a lighter. Meet you outside in five?" Christopher smiles and then scurries away. He can't get away from me fast enough. Nothing will freak a straight boy out more than a random bout of crying. (On the contrary, nothing will intrigue a homosexual woman more than a random bout of crying.)

Finally, my friend Matty and his boyfriend Brian waltz through the doors of the party. They are the sweetest couple you've ever met. They both have the brightest blue eyes you've ever seen, the most baby-soft skin, and the gentlest energy to ever be possessed by men. I am so relieved to see them I could start crying all over again. At this point anything will make me cry. Breakups are like that. A sales associate could tell you they don't have the dress in your size and you'll be reduced to a heap on the floor.

I don't even try to play it cool. I rush over to the boys with tears streaming in my (second) martini and blurt: "What the hell was I thinking coming to this party? I MISS HER. I MISS HER SO." *Sob.* "MUCH." *Sob. Sob. Sob.*

"Oh honey," my blue-eyed boys say in perfect unison, which is not rare for them. "It will be OK." They wrap me in their arms. They smell like Chanel Bleu and heavily applied hair product.

"Don't worry about that chick Miranda. I met her last night. She's nothing. There is nothing special about her at all," Matty says.

Suddenly the walls close in around me. I am suffocated. I can't breathe. Strobe lights flash in brain. Sirens go off. I want to ask who the hell Miranda is but it appears I've forgotten how to speak. I am blank. There are no words. Just sirens. Just strobe lights.

Brian shoots Matty a look that could kill a man. Matty looks at me and backs away. Once again, I am being treated like an unpredictable wild animal that everyone is trying to domesticate. Once again, I *feel* like an unpredictable wild animal.

"Oh fuck. You didn't know," Matty whispers, his blue eyes so soft I want to curl inside of them like a baby in a plush blanket.

You know when you're out on the town and it's about midnight and you see "that" girl? The girl who is screaming, howling at her ex-boyfriend in front of everyone? She seems completely unaware that she's making a scene—in fact, she almost looks primal, like a possessed woman channeling a demon? She's writhing around on the ground in a sparkly dress, she gives zero shits that she isn't wearing any underwear, she kicks the air and pounds her fist against the sidewalk. Her friends try and help her up but she violently pushes them away, blowing cigarette smoke in their faces, sobbing and screaming, her face puffy and streaked with black eyeliner, lipstick smeared across her face. "FUCK YOU!" She bellows every couple of minutes. "FUCK YOU FUCKING FUCK! GAHHHHHHHHHHH."

And maybe you'll be smugly enjoying your artisanal cocktail on the outdoor terrace of the hipster bar, turning your nose up at this shit show. "Can you believe how this woman is behaving?" you'll say to your friend.

Your friend will furiously shake her head and stick her pinkie right up in the air. "I know. It's unbelievable. What a crazy bitch."

The two of you will laugh and clink drinks and feel so grateful and holy and pure that you're not crazy bitches. You're not flinging ash in your ex's face in a sparkly, too-short dress. You're not screaming at the top of your lungs at your friends. You're not making a scene. You're just two adult women enjoying a seventeen-dollar cocktail.

Yeah. I've been the smug yuppie who rolled her eyes at the crazy girl rioting over unrequited love in public before.

And then, I *became* that crazy girl.

We never think we'll be the crazy girl until we've been hurt or wronged by a lover. I've seen the most even-keeled women lose their minds over love. Conservative women who work in finance and go to temple end up slashing tires and writing deranged tweets in the face of heartbreak. No one is safe from crossing the line. Heartbreak strips us of our polite window dressing and reveals us as the animals we actually *are*.

After that night, I forever stopped judging the crazy girl. In fact, I realized, she's not crazy. She's grieving. And grief makes us do crazy shit.

The next morning when I wake up it feels like the whole thing was a bad dream. This happens a lot when you're freshly heartbroken. The first few moments of waking up, you roll over and expect to see your beloved by your side and BAM, reality hits you like a fist in your most delicate hour.

I can't remember what exactly I did that night, because I'm pretty sure I blacked out in the middle of the whole thing, but I do have some distinct flashes. I remember feeling so angry I am pretty sure I foamed at the mouth. Like I had rabies. I remember making a thousand and some phone calls to Lila, in which I left voicemails so threatening, if anything were to ever happen to her, I'm certain I would be blamed in a court of law for her demise. I remember sobbing. Throwing my phone. Breaking a glass. A part of me thinks I don't remember much more because my brain shut down in order to protect me from the extreme embarrassment I brought upon myself that night.

If breaking up is "hard to do," well then, finding out your ex is happily dating someone else less than a month after you've called it quits is like running a marathon after a cocaine bender. In the days after that night, I am constantly sickened by the vision of this new little bitch sleeping in my bed. Yet as sick as imagining the two of them together makes me feel, I can't stop fixating over it. I can't stop obsessively stalking this new side piece on social media. I can't stop talking about her to everyone and anyone who will listen. My ex blocks me from Facebook. I feel like I've been pushed off a mountain by the person I trust the most. *I loved you for three years only to have you BLOCK me on Facebook?* The pain cuts so deep I don't know if I will ever recover.

The transition of navigating life with a partner into navigating life as an individual is jarring. Ever so suddenly you have no one to share menial moments of achievement with. No one to text: "Babe, my bitchy editor told me my essay was strong today!" I love my friends to death, but I can't ever imagine texting Ruba or Owen or Eduardo about something like that. Your toothbrush no longer shares a shelf. It sits all by itself, the toothpaste-stained shelf far too big to hold something so small.

When you're sharing a life with someone, they become a part of you. And when they are gone, you walk around the world feeling as if a piece of you is actually missing. You suddenly have this giant hole that needs to be filled. And that's when things get really interesting.

Lila had filled up all the space in my life. I like to think of my life as a small studio apartment. If there is a giant couch sitting in the middle of my small apartment, there isn't room for that chic velveteen chaise lounge I've been lusting after. It's one or the other when you live in a small space. Lila was the giant couch. And now the giant couch had left. My apartment needed something else in it, because the couch had been the grounding force of the space. It rooted me into the room. It was the place where I stretched my legs and curled up with a book on a rainy night. The place where I lazily stuffed chips into my mouth on a hungover Sunday. The place where I napped with my pets. The place where I propped my laptop onto my thighs and wrote my heart out.

Before I knew it, I was searching for something else to replace the couch. I was tempted to find another person to replace the couch, but dating as a lesbian in small town Florida is rough. It was like looking for that chic velveteen chaise lounge in a Bob's furniture store. And that's when something extraordinary happened.

"Do you have any interest in being in a play?" Mya, a local artist whom I adored and admired, asked me in earnest one afternoon. We were catching up, grabbing a coffee. Mya was my mentor and I'd known her for years. She knew me when I was a professional theatre and film actress. She knew how devastated I was when I walked away from the industry, too broken from the onslaughts of sexual harassment and body-shaming to continue to drag myself to any more auditions. She knew that I detested the industry, but that deep in my heart I still loved and worshipped the craft. And because she's slightly psychic (all good mentors should be slightly psychic), she knew that I was in a place in my life where I needed an outlet as badly as I needed air. Hearing the word "play" was the first time since my breakup that I had felt a tiny light of hope flicker inside of me. I smiled.

"Of course I have an interest in being in a play."

And within a few weeks I was cast in a play with two amazing men I hadn't really known before. Instead of drinking my face off and weeping to bartenders all over town, I was now spending my evenings in rehearsals. Instead of Facebook stalking Lila's new girl-friend, I was now spending my free time memorizing lines. Instead of feeling hollow in the couch-less studio apartment that was my life, I now had a beautiful new painting to gaze into! I hadn't even realized I didn't have art in my studio apartment, because the couch of Lila had distracted me from the lack of other things in my life. And art was a huge lack for a creative soul like me. That's the thing, kids. You might not even *notice* that a huge, important aspect of your life is going wholly unfulfilled because your relationship is taking up so much space that you can't even *see* what might be missing. I hadn't realized how much I missed being creative. I didn't have space to miss anything because my heart so fully belonged to Lila.

The more I dove headfirst into the rehearsal process, the better I felt. It wasn't just that rehearsing was a distraction from my pain. In fact, being creative forces you to confront your emotions, for there is no creativity without *feelings*. Seriously. You draw from the well of whatever you're experiencing when you're being actively creative. I tapped into the pain and channeled it into the pain my character felt. I released the hurt, the betrayal, the brokenness through fucking art! And even though I've studied acting and theatre at the best institutions and conservatories in the country, my breakup was the best acting training I'd ever had. You will never tap into your raw brilliance until you've been heartbroken. Do you think Alanis Morissette could've written *Jagged Little Pill* if she hadn't had her beating heart smashed into a million little pieces by that douchebag David Coulier? (Sorry, David, I'm sure you're a really nice guy but I'll always be team Alanis. *Full House* has nothing on "You Oughta Know"). No, she could NOT have. She probably didn't even know she had an album like *Jagged Little Pill* burning inside of her. David Coulier probably took up so much space that she was entirely unaware of her insanely amazing ability to turn pain into words and music that resonated with millions of people worldwide. Thank god she had her heartbroken. Screaming along to Alanis with the windows down is the best, most inexpensive kind of therapy a woman can have.

And in hindsight, thank Lana Del Rey I had my heart broken. Because I would have never said "yes" to doing a play when I was tethered to another person. I didn't have time. I had a job and a girlfriend there wasn't space for prancing around a black-box theatre six nights a week, you know? And while doing that play, I reconnected to myself again. I began to remember how empowering it is to have something that brings you an insurmountable amount of joy that doesn't involve another person. I began to remember that I *am* absolutely capable of feeling intoxicated and ecstatic on my own. And little by little, that built up my strength. It stripped the power away from Lila's grip and put it back in my hands. It stung to not have her in my life, but I now realized that I didn't need another person to make me whole. I needed hobbies. I needed passions. I needed creativity. I needed achievement harder to accomplish than hitting the one-year mark with another person.

The night we performed the play, we slayed. As I got up for the curtain call, tears welled up in my eyes. They slowly slid down my face and into my mouth. I could taste their saltiness. They were *my* tears. I wasn't crying over *anyone*. I was crying because I finally had something no one could ever take away from me. The next person I fell in love with, I now knew, could absolutely leave me at any time. Fuck, she could die! A dark thought, but people unexpectedly and tragically exit this earth every minute of every day. But no one could take my passion for theatre away from me. In fact, no one could take *me* away from *me*.

I really began to cultivate a relationship with myself after that. It really sunk in that the only relationship I would ever be in for life was this relationship. That I had to fall in love with myself harder than I'd ever fallen in love with anyone else. I gave myself my full attention. I explored interests I had never explored before. I began to write just for the sheer joy of it. Began to talk to people, random people in bars, some I made friends with. I didn't hold back in therapy. I talked Catherine's ear off twice a week and the subject was always the same: me. I had neglected myself in my relationship to Lila. I didn't know where she ended and I began. I didn't know if she was the reason I didn't care for sushi, or if I actually didn't care for sushi. Turns out, sushi is my favorite food in the world, a food I worship fervently. I hadn't realized that because my partner wasn't into it, so I had rarely indulged. I treated myself to sushi once a week after that. (Still do.)

I dyed my hair red. I know it sounds so cliché and trite to change up your look during a breakup, but I think it's so goddamn FUN and you need to have as much fun as possible when your heart is broken. Fun reminds you that being alive is joyous. Life is meant to be joyous. I hadn't dyed my hair in years because Lila loved my long, dark hair. But now I had no one else to think about when I made a choice about my appearance, so I went all out. I got a pound of hair extensions that fell past my hip-bones. Every time I looked in the mirror I felt a rush of autonomy. If you think being in love is a high, wait till you try doing whatever the fuck you want.

Every time I looked in the mirror, I was reminded that I was a badass bitch who could carve out a life for herself. There was no longer a co-writer in my life. I could write the script. And that was fucking amazing.

The beauty of the breakup is that you've lost the most important, validating, safety net in your life, and you're suddenly tossed into the middle of the ocean. Of course it's scary! It's dark. It's massive. You're not used to trusting your gut on which direction to swim in. But eventually, because we're resilient-as-fuck human beings, you get used to the water. It doesn't feel so cold anymore. You start swimming around. You trust your instincts. You see things you've never seen before. Some of it you like, some of it you hate. You start to learn about what you do like and what you do hate. You go on adventures you would've never gone on. Suddenly, you become aware of all these choices you have. There is no compromise. It's you in the water and there is no life raft, so you become wildly efficient. You stop fearing the aloneness of the open water. Because you know how to survive. And you only know how to survive when you truly know yourself.

The beauty of the breakup is that when the worst thing possible happens to you, and you lose the person you loved more than anyone (even yourself), you come down with a glorious case of the "fuck-its." Oh, you want me to be in your play? Fuck it, I don't care, I'll do it. Oh, you want me to go on an impulsive weekend to the Hamptons with you? Fuck it, why not? Oh, you think I'll look good with an asymmetrical bob? Fuck it. Who cares if it looks like shit. I've got bigger fish to fry than dealing with than an unflattering haircut, babe. MY HEART IS FUCKING BROKEN.

The fuck-its are amazing and fleeting. So enjoy them while they last. We take the most gorgeous risks when we're saying "fuck it" to life. We realize that we're not precious little flowers that can be so easily crushed. No, man. We can skydive. We can take an improvisation class and not die of embarrassment. The worst thing that could've happened, *happened*, so why not move to that city and pursue your dream career? If it doesn't work out, you'll be fine. When you have a breakup, you realize your strength in the fuck-its. All the shit you would've been too afraid to say yes to isn't remotely scary anymore. If you can stand up with a heart that has a giant slash through the middle of it, you can do anything.

The beauty of the breakup is that we don't have the anesthesia of another person anymore. Putting up with the job that you DETEST is a lot easier when you have somebody else's arms to fall into at the end of the day, isn't it? Living in this godforsaken small town that totally isn't for you isn't so harrowing when you know you have a dinner date every single weekend. We don't feel the discomfort of our lives when we have a person there to anesthetize our feelings of discontent. But when they leave us, we are forced to sit in the unsettlement. We are forced to feel how much we hate our jobs and our towns and the ways in which our lives are taking shape. And feeling bad, ugly feelings of detest for our lives is wonderful. Because it makes us change shit. You might've always stayed in that no-good town if you hadn't been dumped, babe. How depressing is that? Now that you're free you can go move somewhere you actually like. Maybe it's California. Maybe it's New York. Maybe it's Tahiti. Fuck, maybe you'll realize you're happier when you're in motion, and you'll live a life on the road. And you know what? Maybe you will stay in that no-good town, but you'll discover a whole new world there, a world you never knew existed when you were tethered to your ex. Doesn't matter. What matters is that you're learning how to live a life that you love.

And the most stunningly beautiful part of a breakup is this: You'll dig so deeply into yourself during this breakup that you'll attain a truly real sense of who you are. And if you play your cards right and start to truly get to know yourself, you'll start to love yourself. And when you love yourself truly, you'll get into a future relationship for the right reasons. Not because you're filling a void. Not because you're trying to make living in the city you loathe easier. Not because you're bored or lonely or sad. You'll get into a relationship because you love the person. Your life is good without them. Your life is like a bowl of amazing, mouthwatering penne vodka. Your partner is the parmesan cheese. The penne vodka is amazing without parmesan. But the parm adds a lovely little kick that adds to the dish. But if you run out of parm one day, you won't panic. Because the pasta that is your life is sensational on its own.

CHAPTER 6

PSA: Beware of Validation Sex

Song: "Lover I Don't Have to Love" by Bright Eyes

What is validation sex? I'm glad you asked. Here's a clear-cut example:

Let's say a few months ago you had your heart ripped out of your chest after the love of your life dumped you, seemingly out of nowhere. And let's say *today* is the first day you haven't cried on public transportation in *weeks*. You're actually feeling pretty amazing today. Your boss gave you a compliment. The guy who works at the bodega gave you your coffee for *free*. The winter air smells sweet like flowers. There is a lightness inside of you that's been shut off since the breakup. Just as you're basking in how damn well you're doing, you decide to scroll through Instagram. Innocently. Just, to like, *see* what everyone is up to, you know?

And as you mindlessly gaze into a sea of aspirational pictures from the slew of fashion bloggers you religiously follow, your stomach drops into your knees. Your spit gets thick in your mouth. You feel like you're going to vomit. You have a sudden onset of full body chills. The bad kind. The kind that are hot and cold at once. You blink to make sure you actually *saw* what you think you *saw*. As you open your eyes to double check, you quickly snap those lids shut.

Because *you did* see what *you thought* you saw. Yes, a random girl you happen to follow (you went to sleep-away camp together in fourth grade) has posted a picture of herself lovingly gazing into your ex's seafoam-colored eyes. The caption reads: "I found love when I least expected it."

Your ex commented with a heart emoji.

You run into the bathroom and dry heave for exactly forty-five minutes. Nothing comes up because you've officially been rendered empty inside.

As you walk home, the air no longer smells like flowers. It smells like shit. The sun has hidden behind a massive gray cloud. The kind of cloud that looks pregnant with a brutal, lonely rainstorm. The kind of rainstorm that takes down beautiful trees. The light gleaming at the end of the tunnel has been replaced by steel prison bars. You're never getting out of here. You'll feel this way forever.

When you get home, you kick off your shoes and look into the mirror. Mascara tears make their way down your forlorn face. You feel ugly. Hideous. Fat. Riddled with acne! Full of fine lines.

So you do what anyone in your position would do. You pour yourself a giant glass of blood-red wine.

The wine feels like velvet as you pour it down your sad little throat. You suddenly feel gorgeously *warm* inside. Like someone has lit a fire inside of your cold heart. You want more of this feeling, for it's a peaceful reprieve from the heartbreak that's been holding court in your bones. So you decide to put a pair of false eyelashes on. It gives you false confidence. You drink more wine. You toss some dark red, vampy lipstick into the mix. It's by Chanel. *Purr*.

You slide into a pair of sexy skinny jeans. You smoke a cigarette inside your apartment and stare at yourself in the mirror again. Even though you've draped your body in the lushest decor, you still feel like garbage. So you drink more wine. You drink until you can kid yourself into thinking you feel hot. You drink until the nasty voices, the voices that tell you that you're not pretty enough, you're not smart enough, you're not *thin* enough, you're not *enough*—are set to mute. It's replaced by a vapid valley girl upspeak voice that tells you "you look sexay!" The voice tells you, "Go out and get some ass!"

So you go to the bar, alone.

You strut over to a small high-top table by the window. You're wearing dangerously high heels. Your teeth are stained a deep maroon from the wine but you don't know that. You smile as if your life depends on it. And as soon as you finish ordering a martini, this sexy, swaggy, androgynous creature taps you on the bare skin of your exposed shoulder.

Their name is Jordyn.

Jordyn doesn't make eye contact. Jordyn gives you a bad vibe. Jordyn talks only about Jordyn and doesn't ask you a single *question* about yourself.

But Jordyn is hot and claims to have a ton of twitter followers. And your stupid, uncool ex didn't even *have* twitter. Jordyn says you look gorgeous. Jordyn says your ex is an idiot for leaving you. Jordyn's breath smells like something has rotted inside of their mouth, but you decide to go home with Jordyn to prove to yourself that you still "have it." That you're still desirable. That you can still *pull*, babe.

Jordyn's apartment reeks of stale socks. Jordyn's bed doesn't have sheets. Jordyn pulls you in close and when you kiss, it feels instinctively, gutturally, viscerally *wrong*. You don't want to fuck Jordyn. Your girl alarms sound off. You silence them by sticking your hand down Jordyn's pants. After all, Jordyn says you're pretty. And you want to be told you're pretty. That's what you want more than anything in the entire world, deep down inside. To be pretty. You're very ashamed of this. You secretly worry that wanting to be pretty makes you a bad feminist, but this whole debacle with your ex has validated your deepest fear of all fears: that you're unattractive.

You know that if you have sex with Jordyn, who has all the twitter followers *in the world,* you might prove that you are actually wrong about yourself. You might be pretty after all.

The sex isn't awful but it's cold and meaningless. There is no passion. There is no foreplay. There is no oral sex, even. You don't have an orgasm but you fake one. You fake a giant, lust-ridden, over-the-top, porn-star orgasm that puts Meg Ryan in *When Harry Met Sally* to shame. You fake it because you hope that maybe you can *lie* to yourself. If you put on a glittery orgasm show, maybe you'll fool yourself into thinking you had one.

Which proves that you don't need your ex.

Which proves that you don't miss your ex.

Which proves that even though your feelings are hurt (crushed is actually a better way to describe it) you can still cum like a rock star!

Your ex may steal your heart, but not your orgasms. Hell no, bitch.

After the sex is over and you lie in that sheet-less, disgusting bed with this vile-smelling creeper you don't even *know* and stare into the cracks in the ceiling, you suddenly fight the urge to cry. There is a lump the size of America in your throat. Your swirling brain is reduced to one thought, and one thought only: You need to get the hell out of there. *Fast.*

So you make up a lie and you scan the floor for your underwear and find it and scrunch it up into a tiny little ball and toss it into your purse and you call a cab.

And in the cab ride back to your place, you stare at the buildings and the swaying trees, and snow is starting to fall on the pavement, and you just want to crawl into a hole and never come out. You want to peel off your skin and run for the hills, skinless. You want to weep into a bag of Doritos and never stop weeping as long as you live. You want to tear the flesh off your body and send it to the dry cleaners.

Shame. Shame. Shame. Shame.

You can't shake off the shame.

Not because you had sex. You *love* sex. You stopped feeling bad about having lots of sex years ago.

You're ashamed because you had sex when you didn't want to have sex. You had sex to prove something to yourself and that tarnishes the pure, primal, humanistic joy of *sex*. You let someone touch you because you felt ugly and you hoped their touch would somehow make you feel less ugly.

But all it did was make you feel *icky*. There is no sophisticated word for how you feel. It's just, *icky*. And that ickiness cannot be washed off in the shower. That ickiness makes you isolate yourself for the rest of the weekend. Instead of dealing with your feelings, you attempt to numb the relentless ick-factor with shitty TV. And wine. And cigarettes. And fast food. And weed. And when Monday comes rearing its ugly head, you don't want to face the world.

But you do because that's what us girls do. We deal. We trudge into the office and work hard despite the fall of Rome happening inside our hearts—because we're survivors. And we do end up being like, *totally fine*. (I promise you. We've all had validation sex and it hasn't damaged us in the long run.)

However, I want you to try and avoid the validation sex if you can. Because validation sex doesn't ever make you feel confident like you hope it will. It might make you feel *validated* for a brief moment in time, but validation is a lot like cocaine. It makes you feel strong and cocky for ten cheap minutes and then is followed by a soul-scorching crash to the bottom of the ocean floor. Anything we use outside of ourselves as a way to feel temporarily better always makes us feel extraordinarily worse when the high wears off. And the high always wears off.

And as your lesbian big sister, I want you to feel good about yourself. I don't want you to be bathing in a giant pool of self-destruction if you don't have to.

So if you're feeling untalented, sad, ugly, heartbroken, like a desperate loser, like a total fraud—don't have sex with another person in hopes to quell these dark feels. Feel these dark feels. Write about these dark feels. Talk about these dark feels. Because when you do, they lose their power, little sister. I *promise*. All these negative thoughts and emotions thrive off of us avoiding them. When avoided, they begin to realize their power to intimidate us, and that gives them a great elitist rush of superiority which only feeds their nasty agenda. But standing up to the dark feels, telling them you're unafraid to get in the ring with them, that makes them skitter away in cowardly fear, like every other bully.

So if you're about to text some asshole you detest just because you want to be touched and told you're worthy of life, imagine me sitting at the edge of your couch. I'm wearing one of those old-school Juicy Couture sweatsuits. It's *purple*. It has rhinestones bedazzled all over it. My hair is in the highest ponytail you've ever seen. My lips are glossy in a vulgar way. I look like a fashionable eighth grader from the early 2000s. I'm chowing on salted popcorn. I wink at you. You wonder if my lashes are real or fake. I tell you they're real. I tell you about the amazing serum I've been using them that's making them grow like weeds. Then I tell you that tonight we're going to have a *slumber party*. We're going to talk about everything that's going on with you and I'm going to share my own shit as well.

And we'll curl up in bed watching old episodes of *Sex and the City* and we'll feel as if weights have lifted off of our heaving chests.

And we'll wake up feeling free, babe. Because we *are*.

CHAPTER 7

Talk Mental Illness to Me

Song: "A Better Son/Daughter" by Rilo Kiley

Do you want to know what my favorite topic in the entire, cruel, cold world happens to be? Mental illness. *Purr.* I adore talking about mental illness more than I adore talking about sex.

What meds are you currently on, babe? What meds *have* you been on? What meds slaughtered your sex drive? What meds gave you trippy dreams? What meds changed your life? What meds made you feel more unhinged than Britney Spears on her worst day in 2007? What's your official diagnosis? What do you suspect is your *actual* diagnosis? Have you ever taken a stab at cognitive behavioral therapy? Transcranial magnetic stimulation? The controversial Ketamine therapy? Oh, you *have*? Talk dirty to me.

Tell me all about your panic attacks! Tell me all about your last bout of mania. Undress the intricate layers of your mental illness, until you are the rawest, most exposed, stunningly sexy version of yourself.

I mean, who wants to talk about the Kardashians when we could talk about major depressive disorder, generalized anxiety, body dysmorphia, and borderline personality?

It's just so goddamn liberating to talk about shit that's deemed "taboo" by society, isn't it? That's why I started writing about sex so early on in my career. It felt exhilarating to speak freely about something I had been made to feel so fucking ashamed about my entire life!

When I first started writing about my sex life on the internet, I was met with equal parts shock and equal parts approval. (And death threats, of course, but only by middle-aged white men rotting in their parent's basements.)

"You're so bold! So fearless!" the masses sing-songed to me everywhere I went. They would giggle, cock a big eyebrow right in my face and murmur something like, "I love that piece you wrote about the threesome that turned you into a lesbian!" It was all very fun and lighthearted (until I started writing about sexual trauma, but that's neither here nor there).

In all honesty it *was* a little bit scary to write about sex at first. Like I always say: Sex is *vulnerable*. It's vulnerable to do and it's vulnerable to discuss and it's vulnerable to write about. But because I'm a woman who just can't *help* but push the boundaries (sound familiar?), once I got comfortable writing about sex, I grew very bored with writing about sex. And for me, there is no greater discomfort than feeling comfortable, you know? Probably explains my lifelong habit of leaving a city the very moment I start making friends and finally learn my way around.

So, I did what I always do when I'm in the dismal throes of a creative rut. I sat in my apartment with the air conditioner blasting at arctic temperatures, clutched a glass of Sauvignon Blanc, smoked a few proverbial cigarettes, and asked myself the classic question: *What am I the MOST terrified to write about?*

As I stared blankly into space searching for an answer, my eyes landed on a neon orange prescription bottle tucked discreetly behind my porcelain vase teeming with a dozen virgin white roses. (Does anyone else obsessively buy fresh flowers when their lives are crumbling in order to provide themselves with a falsified sense of togetherness?) It was my new bottle of Prozac.

I had just switched over from Lexapro to Prozac. For whatever reason, the combination of Prozac and booze didn't uh, *jive* so well together in my system. In fact, just three days prior I had blacked out at a work event (in front of my boss, shoot me between the eyes please) and had woken up in Harlem Hospital on Lenox Avenue and 135th Street with an IV hydration bag stuck into my left arm and the flavor of vomit hanging out in my mouth. I was wearing a beautiful pink and white Calypso dress my mother had given me. It was covered in bile. I didn't know how the hell I got there. (I still don't. Nor was I ever charged, oddly.) All I knew was that it was one of the scariest experiences of my life and I was still cloaked in a blanket of humiliation and shame over the whole ordeal. Not just because of the blackout. Because of the root of the blackout. My *depression*. The pills I had to take in order to deal with life.

That's when it hit me. I was terrified to talk about stuff like *this*. Blacking out due to psychotropic drugs. Having to take psychotropic drugs because your brain is broken and you can't stop fixating on the texture of tinfoil without them. (Shout out to my fellow OCD friends. I *see* you.) Major depressive disorder. Crippling anxiety. Being wracked with an unshakable, relentless sadness that no amount of SoulCycle classes can stave off.

I was afraid to write about mental illness because it wasn't sexy. And above all else, I wanted to be seen as *sexy*. I know it's not very woke of me to me admit that, but it's the truth. In fact, my sexuality was my greatest power. When you're writing about sex every single day, you become so deeply connected to that part of yourself. You ooze an intoxicating primal musk that follows you around everywhere you go. As a natural-born attention whore, I lived for the hot rush of being objectified. And as someone who had experienced so much sexual trauma at such a young age, it felt really good to flip the script and take the power back.

If I were to start writing about being a mentally ill human being, would people still want to read my articles about lesbian sex? Would I become too human to be deemed sexy? Isn't part of being sexy being mysterious? All these fears circled around my head like my own private tornado.

But when push came to shove, the need to challenge myself and connect authentically with my readership won the race. As much as I wish that sometimes I could be that perfect, sexy, one-note "brand" social media experts and talent agents always tell female writers they *need* to be in order to be successful in their careers, I Simply Can Not Do That. The need to be real with all of you is a visceral impulse that lives far outside the realm of my control. And mental illness is a huge part of my life. So *screw it.*

I wrote my first piece about mental illness for *Elite Daily* in July of 2015. It was called "What It's Like to Be Happy On The Outside, And Hopelessly Sad On The Inside." In hindsight it was a very melodramatic, unprocessed bit of prose, reminiscent of a teenage Tumblr blog—but damn it felt so freeing to come clean.

I didn't really expect anyone to read it. Who the hell wants to read about a girl and her toxic relationship with that bleak asshole Depression?

As soon as the piece went live, I could not *believe* the response I got. Within a few days, I had hundreds and hundreds of DMs from girls all across the world.

Thank you so much for talking about this. I feel less alone.

I never would've expected someone like you to be dealing with depression. I deal with it too. Thank you.

You put to words what I feel inside.

In a bizarre way, it felt healing to me. I felt like I had gone on the master cleanse and flushed away a lifetime of toxins. After all, nothing is more toxic to the body than harboring shame-ridden secrets. And now that I knew I wasn't alone in my sadness, I didn't feel ashamed anymore.

I began to write about mental illness all the time after that first essay. And the more I wrote about it, the more I realized how many people's lives are affected by it in some way. Party girls who don long, false, fluttery eyelashes and rock sky-high stilettos and are on the guest lists of the most exclusive clubs in Manhattan—they suffer from depression. High school cheerleaders with "perfect 10" bodies and brassy blonde highlights and popular football-playing boyfriends silently suffer from deadly eating disorders. Finance bros who skulk along Wall Street in their shiny leather shoes and work one hundred hours a week and take their Instagram model girlfriends to the Hamptons on the weekends suffer from obsessive-compulsive disorder. Your boss, with her extraordinarily neat office and no-nonsense demeanor and unscratched BMW, suffers from anxiety. Pimply teen boys with giant headphones resting on their sloping shoulders who sit too closely to you on the subway suffer from incessant panic attacks. The stone-faced bouncer who never smiles at you even though you see him every Saturday at the same dive bar in the West Village suffers from bipolar disorder. Parents are mentally ill. Prisoners have mental illness. I know *dogs* who take Prozac. Throw a stone on any street anywhere in the country and you're going to hit someone who suffers, in some way, from mental illness.

So why the hell is something so common so stigmatized? Why the hell would we ever feel so deeply ashamed and isolated about something that, according to NAMI (National Alliance on Mental Illness), affects 46.6 *million* people a year in the US alone?

Because we don't think it's *sexy*? Because we're not allowed to be nuanced creatures who are both hot and mentally ill at the same time? Because we fear we won't be hirable? Or dateable? Or thought of as strong? I have a newsflash for you, honey: Those of us who suffer from mental illness are some of the strongest, sexiest, most talented bitches I've ever had the pleasure of crossing paths with. You can't be strong or sexy or talented without being deep. And mentally ill people are deep as fuck.

I've gotten in trouble by the ever-annoying PC internet police for saying this before, but I don't give a shit, because I believe it in the deepest pit of my mentally ill gut: Those of us who deal with depression, anxiety, OCD, what *have you*—we're the special ones. I believe we were born feeling so deeply because we're tapped into a frequency that "normal" people are not tapped into. We absorb the pain and the trauma of every passerby on the street. We're empathetic. We look at the world differently, we see thousands of shades of gray where everyone else sees only two colors: black and white. Why do you think so many brilliant creatives have battled the demons of depression their entire lives? They saw things that other people could not see. They were able to express the human experience in a way that only a person who is present and alive and awake can. And to be present, alive, and awake is to be *sad* sometimes. The world is a screwed-up place. And when you're an open wound walking around, the sadness of the world is going to seep into your system and occasionally make you sick.

My depression and anxiety, in a strange way, have been the most beautiful gift I've ever been blessed with. It's given me the ability to connect with people on a deeper level. It's taught me to never, ever, ever, ever judge anyone, for anything (except maybe people who have "Live. Laugh. Love." plaques from Ikea on their walls) because I know how easy it is to slip between the societal cracks. I know how close I teeter over that thin red line that separates the sane from the insane. I know that if I didn't have medication and therapy and supportive people in my life, I would likely be homeless. My mental illness has opened my eyes to things I would have never been able to see before. And while it's excruciating and ugly and a straight-up nightmare so much of the time: I wouldn't change a thing. And if owning your mental illness translates into "glamorizing it" by the rigid standards of the humorless PC police, that's *fine* by me. If telling the truth is glamorous, then I'm the most glamorous bitch alive!

That's not to say suffering from mental illness is *easy*. In fact, my depression, anxiety, obsessive-compulsive disorder, and eating disorders are by far the most challenging parts of my life. They're what gave me the sick impulse to slice up my arms with a pretty pink razor blade in high school. They've driven me to self-medicate with deadly substances—opiates, benzodiazepines, uppers, booze. They've made me hermit inside of my apartment for weeks and weeks at a time because the anxiety was so severe I was sure that if I stepped outside into the sunlight I might actually fall dead of a heart attack. They've made my head fixate on disturbing images, images that get stuck in my head and play on a never-ending loop—images of abused animals, images of abused children, images of war. They've made me stick my own fingers down my throat and vomit up an entire box of cereal. They've driven me to contemplate *suicide* over eating a slice of pizza. They've made me so severely blue, that I stopped feeling anything at all—I was void of all emotion—except for this dull forlorn disconnect from the rest of the world. They've cost me money that I don't have—thousands of dollars in therapy and medication and drugs. But even with all the heavy baggage they've caused me to lug around, I've made peace with my mental illness.

Here's the tricky thing about depression, in particular. Sometimes depression is situational. Sometimes we are depressed because we've had our hearts ripped out of our chests, or we're stuck in a job that sucks the soul out of our skulls, or we're scared to come out of the closet, or we've just lost a loved one to sudden death. When something catastrophic happens or we're not in alignment with what we're supposed to be doing with our lives, it's normal to feel depressed. It's normal to have a deep, heavy sadness that feels like it's crushing all the bones in your body. It's normal to want to throw the covers over your head and never face the ugly realities of the outer world again. Part of being alive is to feel unshakably sad sometimes. Part of living with an open heart is accepting that sometimes assholes will creep their way into that sacred space and abuse the hell out of it. Part of allowing ourselves to love means sometimes that person we love the most will leave us. Unexpectedly.

But sometimes depression *is* chemical. Sometimes nothing is wrong in our lives—in fact, everything is going perfectly FINE (on paper). But still we wake up every single morning with a dead heart and a body dragged down with the heaviness of dread. Sometimes we feel so utterly guilty for being so utterly depressed because people have like, "real problems" and we don't have "real problems," so what the hell is wrong with us? Our friends and family tell us to write gratitude lists and go to the gym and meditate, but no matter how much effort we exert into our self-care routine, we *still* have lost our will to live. So we shut up about it and accept that this our baseline. Sad is our baseline. Depressed is our baseline. Anxious is our baseline. This is just the way it is.

I think that both situational and chemical depression is real. One is not more valid than the other. Both are absurdly painful and we all deserve gleaming medals for making it through the day! But either way, these depressive episodes rarely heal themselves. We need help. *Professional* help.

Which is why I believe that the best investment you can make in your life is a good therapist. It doesn't matter how much money you make, how many times you fall in love, how "lucky" you are, how many times you "win"—if you don't have your mental health, you don't have shit. If don't take care of your mental health you'll get sick. Not just mentally sick, physically sick. You will get headaches. Your body will run itself down. You'll feel tired and weak all the time. You'll get dizzy spells. You'll won't feel *well*. And life is too damn fleetingly short to not feel well.

I know what you might be thinking. Therapy is for the mega rich. It's for the uber privileged private school kids. It's for intellectuals who grew up on the *Upper West Side*. It's for non-functioning looney toons. Losers without friends to talk to.

Girl, I *get it*. I used to feel this way too. My family is British. We don't "do" feelings and we certainly wouldn't be so *daft* as to *pay* a stranger to talk about our feelings. But when I finally reached my breaking point, I got over my rigid Britishness. I dutifully did my research and was able to find a therapist I could afford and actually connected with. And it was sitting on that shrink's couch that I—for the first time—released stuff that I had been holding on to for years. And had I just let all that shit stew inside of me, I don't know if I would be writing this book. I would be sick. I would be so overmedicated I couldn't form linear sentences. I would be pent up with poisonous memories and unfelt feelings.

I would've eventually exploded.

And if *I*, the most non-confrontational, blithering idiot of a human being, can figure out how to vet a therapist, so can you.

Here is my official Big Sister Guide to finding a therapist.

1. Let's get real about your financial situation.

When I first moved back to New York City in 2014 I had a terrible panic attack one night all alone in my Upper East Side apartment. I called a woman named Monica who I was casually dating at the time. She was about fifteen years older than I was, and was the pinnacle sophisticated New Yorker. All sophisticated New Yorkers are plugged into the wellness scene, so I knew Monica would have some sort of therapeutic resource for a freaked out little lez like me.

"MONICA!" I shouted through the phone. My heart was beating so fast I felt like I had taken *meth* or something.

"Zara! Are you OK?" sweet Monica purred.

"NO, I'm having a PANIC ATTACK. Do you know a good therapist I could see tomorrow? I'm really SUFFERING!" I felt myself beginning to hyperventilate.

"Honey! Calm down. Yes, of course I do. I'll come over and take care of you and book you an appointment," Monica (a total power lesbian) assured me.

Daddy Monica came through on her promise. She came over, ordered a week's worth of Italian food, and booked me an appointment with a very prominent Park Avenue shrink. "She's one of the best in the industry," Monica told me, staring at my untouched plate of pasta. "She specializes in eating disorders."

The next morning, I threw my hair up into a haphazard mental illness bun (don't pretend you don't know what I'm talking about) and taxied to the shrink's office. Her office was so chic it looked like a fashion editor's office. A black Jonathan Adler vase with a white orchid sat on the glass side table next to her pony skin chair. The shrink was fashion editor-level chic too—in that seven-hundred-dollar silk sweatpants and ankle boots kind of way only the very rich and very thin can pull off. This shrink was nothing like my Florida shrink, Catherine. But I was refreshed by her sophisticated, urban prowess. (Also, I found her hot.)

For the next hour I poured my anxious heart and soul out to this fabulous, smart, female therapist. When the little timer went buzzing off, I actually felt so much better. I knew in my bones that this woman could truly help me get over this newfound bout of anxiety I was experiencing. Until.

My eyes zeroed in on the shrink's Cartier watch. "That will be four hundred and fifty dollars."

"What?" My throat went dry. My heart stopped dead in its tracks. I was overcome with a burning desire to vomit all over her pristine, orchid-adorned office.

"Four hundred and fifty dollars. I gave you a deal because Monica said you're in your twenties. I usually charge six hundred dollars." She smiled at me, a vacant, wealthy smile. Dollar signs suddenly came flying out of her eyeballs. I didn't know what the hell to do.

"Do you take credit card?" I squeaked, fighting back the urge to cry. I hardly had enough money for the subway ride home.

"Absolutely." The shrink pulled out her cellphone, which had one of those swipe credit card apparatus things attached to it. *I should really get one of those,* I thought to myself. What I would charge people for I wasn't quite sure, but I still coveted one.

I prayed to Lana Del Rey that my credit card, please dear Lana, didn't decline. Lana must've been looking out for me from the Hollywood Hills heaven I suspect she resides in, because my credit card magically went through. I imagined Lana sitting on a cloud wearing a flower-crown and cut-off denim shorts. "I'll let this one slide," I felt her decide as she pressed a pointy acrylic nail right up against her puffy, bee-stung lips and blew me a kiss.

The truth was, I was stupid for blindly agreeing to go to a therapist without asking the price per session. I mean, who does that?

Apparently, an anxiety-ridden party girl on the brink of a mental health collapse.

But now that I had re-experienced the intoxicating buzz of talk therapy, I was absolutely not about to give up. I searched and searched and searched and searched and searched and searched and searched the internet for a therapist that actually took my insurance. I got on ZocDoc (the best thing to happen to a generation that fears the phone like the phone has fangs) and set up an appointment with *ten* therapists in my network. It took time to scour for them, but I knew from experience that my mental health was on the line. After a little research I was able to ensure each therapist would have a copay of no more than forty-five dollars a session. I was a broke little writer paying for cocktails with quarters I'd find tucked inside the crevices of my couch—but I knew that even I could swindle a meek forty-five dollars per week.

Don't listen to what the other half might tell you. There *are* indeed fabulous therapists who accept health insurance. Do *not* do what I did. Be a grown-ass woman and make sure any medical professional you see takes your insurance before you start letting rich lesbians book your shrink appointments. We are not as helpless as we think we are. In fact, that should be our new mantra: *We are not as helpless as we think we are.* Write it down and tape it to your bathroom mirror.

If you don't have insurance, you need to accept that therapy is going to be a very real investment. But it's going to be an incredibly smart investment, one that will save you years of emotional blockage, trauma, darkness, failed relationships, job screw-ups, depressive episodes, self-sabotage, and anxiety. Also, saving for a therapist is not as brutal as you think it is! I am a reckless spender who would bathe in a fourteen-carat gold pool filled with champagne if I could. I would use a Chanel vibrator if they made one. I would definitely buy Gucci tampons if presented with the opportunity. I get what it's like to not even know how to budget for your rent, let alone a shrink. But again: We're talking about your mental health here. I always tell people to commit to **not** ordering in, **not** drinking your face off in a bar multiple nights a week, and **not** buying clothes for three months while you focus on your mental health. You can do anything for three months. And here's the really interesting part: You might actually *save* money while in therapy. An excellent therapist is going to help you navigate all the ways in which you're self-medicating—reckless spending included. When my mental health improved, I didn't feel the need to chase the temporary high of obsessive shopping anymore.

You don't need to spend $450 a session, but you'll likely have to spend $75–$100. Another great option is to find a therapist who recently finished school and is still building up her clientele. These therapists are almost always cheaper due to lack of experience and often better because they aren't jaded or burned out from the "industry" yet. There are so many more resources out there than you can imagine. There are digital therapists you don't even have to leave the comfort of your studio apartment to work with. Lots of therapists work on a sliding scale, according to your income. Also, we're millennials! Let's get real with ourselves: We don't know how to do many things, but we do know how to use a Google search bar. And you're one deep-dive Google search away from finding a therapeutic professional who could change the course of your life.

2. Go on SEVERAL consultations.

Vetting a therapist is a lot like dating. Sometimes the first person you swipe right on after a breakup ends up being a perfect match for you. You go on that first date and it's instant chemistry—you can't believe your luck! Sometimes the first shrink you see after a breakdown gets you to your core.

But more often than not it takes several failed dates and several failed shrink appointments to find that *one* person you connect with.

This why it's absolutely imperative to set up consultations with at *least* three to five therapists before giving up hope that you're doomed and will never find a shrink you'll ever feel comfortable opening up to. Finding the right shrink on the first try is akin to finding the person you're going to marry after one date in a brand-new city. Don't give up hope. Keep swiping. Keep dating. Keep setting up consultations.

3. Trust your gut.

If your therapist has all the credentials in the world, if they are *perfect* on paper and have the best reviews on ZocDoc that your eyes have ever borne witness to—but you still, for whatever reason, aren't connecting to them—you need to get out of dodge fast. And if you feel the slightest, *slightest* hint sexual discomfort, like maybe they're hitting on you, or maybe they hug you a little too long (no shrink should be hugging you without your consent), get the FUCK out of dodge fast. I wish we lived in a world where the threat of sexual abuse didn't extend to licensed professionals, but alas. We don't.

When I found the right therapist (Catherine), I knew it instantly. After about four failed trial sessions, I finally felt safe in a therapist's presence. Almost like I was back in the womb. I felt more deeply heard and objectively cared for than I ever had in my life.

If you're used to being in toxic relationships and you're addicted to hanging around malignant narcissists who verbally abuse you, you need to be careful that you don't fall into the trap of the nasty shrink. I once had a shrink who mocked me. Made fun of my personal style! Told me I was a "dangerous" person who needed to see her five days a week. Was convinced the cool razor blade rose gold necklace that Violet had given me as a gift meant I was definitely a cokehead. (I wasn't. At least not at the time.) Even though she was mentally abusive and definitely didn't get "me," I found myself faithfully doling out a crisp one-hundred-dollar bill each session. I not only chose, but *paid* to see a horrible human being on my own free will. That's how sick I was.

Thank goddess for my friend Eduardo.

"Why are you seeing such an evil bitch?" he asked me over dinner one night.

"She's probably good for me," I answered, gulping back my tequila.

"That's what you said about your ex. The one who kept telling you your body-type was 'skinny fat.' I think I'm sensing a pattern..." Eduardo advised, his shiny, dark eyes brimming with such blatant truthfulness I had to look away.

Eduardo's observation stayed with me. *Shit. I'm falling into the same dysfunctional pattern I've been falling into in my personal relationships. I'm actively seeking out someone who disapproves of me because I disapprove of myself so deeply that this abuse feels normal.*

I left the wicked bitch of a shrink a drunken voicemail, telling her I wanted to break up.

So, if you happen to find yourself drawn to this type of therapist, and there is a parallel between this shrink and your interpersonal relationships, you need to check yourself before you wreck yourself. I don't care how uncomfortable it is for you; I believe you should choose a therapist that's *kind*. You should feel supported and seen and respected in therapy. If kindness is outside of your comfort zone, your relationship with your therapist can be the first relationship that teaches you the importance of a stable, nice support system. In fact, my therapist was one of the first healthy relationships I ever had, and I'm so grateful to have been able to work through my discomfort with kindness, in a supportive, therapeutic environment.

4. Don't give up.

It's very easy to fall in "love" with a therapist after your first appointment. And then by, say, appointment *four*, you might end up detesting your beloved shrink. Why? Because shit gets real around appointment four. You might be tempted to run for the hills because you're staring down into the barrel of the truth. And the truth can look pretty vile.

Before you go rogue and think "screw this bullshit!" I want you to take a deep breath. Therapy is uncomfortable. Growing is uncomfortable. It's *hard*. It hurts. You will be triggered during therapy—after all, that's kind of the point. It is totally normal to be tempted to fly out the door faster than Usain Bolt and continue to live in denial and self-medication and repressed feelings. But here's the thing about temptation: You don't have to give in to it. No one ever died from feeling tempted. Millions have died from giving into it.

In the beginning of your therapeutic journey, you're often merely hanging out by the water. And then your therapist will begin to encourage you to stick your toe right into the cold waters, where your real issues live. It might feel impossibly chilly and scary, and you might want nothing more than to remain on dry land. You might find yourself angry with your therapist for pushing you so far out of your comfort zone. But you have to cross this body of water in order to get to the other side. And luckily you're doing it with a professional who is guiding you. She shouldn't be pushing you into the water without warning—she should be holding your hand gently, traipsing into that unfamiliar territory with you. That doesn't mean it won't be terrifying. There are goddamn leeches in that lake, bitch! But do you know what's even more terrifying than leeches? Staying on this side of the island. Never being able to get to the beautiful, sparkly, free side that lives across these murky waters you're about to cross.

But please don't give up the moment you start to feel new feelings. Therapy doesn't work like a Xanax works. Xanax treats the symptoms. Xanax is a pretty pink Band-Aid that temporarily covers up a nasty-looking wound. But we all know Band-Aids aren't designed to last forever. You have to treat the wound that's infecting your body if you don't want to remain sick. And treating a wound takes time. An infection doesn't just go away just because we want it to go away.

* * *

So now that we've discussed all things therapy, let's get down to the sexiest mental illness topics of all. *Meds.* A nervous breakdown in my early twenties (more on that later) led me to finally throw up my hands and take a stab at antidepressants. I had resisted taking them for the past decade out of a vehement fear that antidepressants would somehow numb me and rob me of my most cherished posses-sion of all: my creativity.

But I had reached a breaking point. I couldn't leave my flat in London because the energy of the city gave me sensory overload. I began to fixate on and obsess over the texture of the exposed brick in my studio apartment. Something about the squiggly lines indented in that rusty-looking brick shook me to my core. In fact, even thinking about it now sends a shiver down my spine. Even my beloved roses began to creep me out. They looked evil. Pretty soon anything with a geometric pattern, anything tinfoil, and anything with dots scattered across it made me want to crawl out of my skin and run for the hills, skinless.

I didn't know I had OCD, and that it could be treated with medi-cation, because no one ever talks about this shit—so naturally, I assumed I was losing my mind, was completely bonkers, and would never again live a normal life. I didn't tell my friends because A) I didn't have many real ones, and B) I was completely embarrassed about the fact that I was tripping balls, squares, and triangles not from acid, but from the texture of the brick in my apartment. When I started to have regular panic attacks at the beauty counter where I worked, I knew it was time to get help. I couldn't afford to get fired for going batshit at my posh department store job. I didn't have a ther-apist at the time, so I went and saw a regular doctor a family friend recommended.

"Alright, darling, why are you here?" my impossibly sexy English doctor asked me. She had large breast implants and was wearing a skin-tight body-con dress that teased the tops of her (very shiny) knee caps. Her legs were crossed and she was wearing black patent leather heels. I instantly trusted her.

I told her everything. "I am going insane," I blubbered to her, wiping mascara tears off my bloated cheeks.

"Darling." The sexy doctor smirked. "I regret to inform you that you're not losing your mind. You're depressed. You have anxiety! I suspect you have a bit of the ole OCD too. I have an excellent medication that will really help."

"But what about my creativity? I'm an artist! I need to feel!" I dramatically bellowed, imagining myself as one of those lifeless catatonics, sitting in front of the TV chain-smoking cigarettes with dead eyes, like in the movie *Girl, Interrupted*.

Sexy Doctor laughed—likely unaccustomed to us overly emotional American girls. "It's not going to do that. Look, you might have a chemical imbalance. Try it for six months." She looked at me with her smoldering eyes. "You know, I take it," she purred.

Sold!

I went home with a prescription for Lexapro, and I swear to Lana Del Rey exactly three weeks later I felt completely different. Here's the best way I can describe it: It was as if I had been living in a dark room my entire life, and suddenly someone had opened the shades and all this light poured into my world! Because I had been immersed in this hell my entire life, I had no idea I had been subsisting in the darkness. You don't know you're in the darkness until you experience what the light feels like. Suddenly, getting out of bed wasn't hard. I stopped obsessively staring at the texture of the brick. I was elated by the sun. I wanted to live.

Wow, I might actually be able to live a normal life, I thought to myself. I had isolated myself in my depressing apartment for months and suddenly I was able to pick up the phone and make plans with friends. I wasn't numb, in fact, I was experiencing a vast array of feelings I hadn't experienced in years. Lexapro felt like a miracle drug. And it was.

At first.

But little by little the nightmares began to creep back into my daydreams. Because I wasn't in therapy and I hadn't confronted the trauma of the past, the gauze of the antidepressants began to wear thin. Antidepressants can be incredible and life-changing for some of us, but like I said: No Band-Aid is designed to last forever. Just because you're medicated doesn't mean that you're exempt from looking into the wound and figuring out why it was there to begin with. There is no bypassing a trauma.

Since my head was glued on straighter than it had been before I went on *les* meds, I was able to make a rational choice. I knew I needed therapy. And when I finally got in therapy, I discovered that the combination of antidepressants *and* talk therapy was an excellent cocktail for me. If I wasn't on medication, I would've been far too depressed and weighed down by anxiety to even book an appointment.

But when I had been solely on medication, the monsters reappeared. They might not have come in the form of panic attacks, but they found their way into my world. They materialized in bizarre ways, too. I had night tremors. I broke out into cold-sweats incessantly. I acted strange when I drank alcohol. I picked wicked fights with my lover.

I'm a full believer that there should be no stigma in needing to take antidepressants or any psychotropic drugs. You wouldn't shame a diabetic for needing insulin in order to regulate their glucose levels, would you? You wouldn't shame a person with a broken leg for wearing a fucking cast? Of course you wouldn't—you're not a *sociopath*. So why would you shame anyone—especially *yourself*—for needing to take medication to manage your disease? It's called mental illness because it's an illness. If you're able to meditate yourself out of mental illness, that's awesome. But a lot of us cannot. And that's OK, too.

But even if you think you just have a chemical imbalance, it's wise to do more than merely pop a pill. I look at treating my mental illness as a giant spectrum of different things that work in tandem together. Nothing on its own has ever worked for me. Now, I do everything I possibly can. I meditate for fifteen minutes (almost) every single morning. I write gratitude lists in my planner daily, because studies suggest that gratitude can actually increase the dopamine levels in your brain. I drink gallons of water because dehydration makes me irritable and anxious even while amply medicated. I take probiotics and vitamins and go to yoga and do cardio and even dabble in the occasional sauna session. I try my best to eat a clean diet—the gut after all, is the second brain. If your gut is inflamed because you're eating trash, your brain is inflamed. I hash it out a couple times a month with a shrink. I watch my drinking (big depression trigger for me). I don't take speed of any kind anymore because the come-down of stimulants is enough to send me spiraling into the darkest depths of the blackest depression known to man. I try to wash my makeup off before I go to sleep at night, because waking up with a face full of foundation and crusty mascara-laden eyes makes me feel like a garbage person, and people with mental illness need to do whatever they can to avoid feeling like a garbage person. (Hence, the title of this book.)

But I also take a low dose of two different kinds of antidepressants. You can do all of the wonderful holistic things *and* take prescription medication, you know. I used to think you were either on Team Holistic or Team Big Pharma. But playing for just one side left me unsatisfied. So I started playing for both teams and started feeling good. Now I'm the pansexual of the mental illness world. I don't discriminate against anything that could possibly better my mental health. Shit, I meditate while medicated! And guess what? It works. For *me*.

And that's the main thing with mental health management: You Need To Do You. Everyone has a goddamn opinion. Half of society will shame you for needing medication and the other half will call bullshit on the fact that cryotherapy helps take the edge off your anxiety. Drown out the noise. No one knows you like you, OK, sister? Have an open mind, try everything that's safe, and when something works, stick to it.

Will I stay on meds forever? I don't know. I would like to try and go off them at some point in my life. But if I go off them and can no longer get out of bed in the morning, I will absolutely go back on them again. I will use all the tools and resources available to make sure I beat my depression in our life-long battle.

* * *

Meds or no meds. Therapy or no therapy. Meditation or no meditation. The biggest tip I have for managing your mental health is this: Look at your mental health as if she's a kid. Give her a name. My mental health is named Lola and I know exactly what she looks like. She is seven years old, scrawny and scrappy, but also pretty and charismatic. She's definitely a ginger who needs glasses in order to see the blackboard in school—you know the type. She has a constellation of freckles splattered across her button nose. Her knees are skinned from taking a plethora of reckless falls to the ground, but she's still got twinkly stars floating around her big green eyes. She's wild. She'll jump off the swing when it's as high as the treetops because she has this innate trust that she'll always land on something soft and pillowy to protect her. And while her innate trust in the universe and wildly adventurous spirit are what make her amazing, they're also what leave her at high risk for pain.

How would I parent a child like Lola? For one, I would want to protect her from falling and hurting herself, but I wouldn't shame her for having such a recklessly innocent spirit, either. I would keep a watchful eye on her. I would let her be her feral self, but make sure that I'm there to catch her when she flies off the trampoline and ends up crying with a mouth full of dirt and rocks. Because that's what adults do. We care for children. And Lola, *my mental health*, is a child. And I want to protect all children from the badness in the world—especially one that is so close to me.

After I began to personify my mental illness, I made a solid vow to never neglect Lola. Because while she is attached to me, she's also *separate* from me. She can run off with the wrong crowd if I don't reel her in. If I don't feed her, she could starve to death. And part of tending to her is actively NOT doing the things that threaten her safety. Like blacking out while drinking. Which usually comes after skipping dinner because I feel hideous and ugly. Or putting myself in toxic situations with people I have no natural connection to, which causes my anxiety to skyrocket and drives me to binge-drink in hopes of quelling the panic. Maybe if I stopped putting myself in those situations, I would be better at protecting Lola. Maybe if I fed Lola before I poured liquid poison down her throat, she would be nourished enough to stay *awake*. Maybe if I began to put her first, she would stay healthy. Maybe if I prioritized her over anything else, all the rest of the broken pieces would fall into place. My career. My relationships. My *confidence*.

So, have I begun to care for Lola after this dramatic life epiphany? Well, yes. Some days I do a better job than others (I'm a new parent! Give me a break!) but I'm trying and *mostly* succeeding. And personifying that part of me has driven me to care for her in a brand-new way. I nurture her. I am gentle to her. I don't judge her. Because even though she and I might not be always aligned on everything, we share the same body. We're in this life together. And the more time I invest caring for her, the better she'll care for me.

CHAPTER 8

Lez Talk About Sex

Song: "Seventeen" by Troye Sivan

It is the mid 90s and I am in the third grade. The Cranberries, 4 Non Blondes, Alanis Morissette, Pearl Jam, and R.E.M. dominate the radio. MTV actually plays music videos. The Meatpacking District in New York City is still dangerous.

And AIDS is the leading cause of death for people ages twenty-five to forty-four.

My mother is at the forefront of the HIV/AIDS crisis. To provide you with a bit of a context, allow me to describe my mother for you: Imagine it's 1970 and you're driving in a convertible down Sunset Blvd. You're stopped at a traffic light as you attempt to make a left turn at La Cienega. Staring down at you from a giant, three-story billboard is a blonde bombshell wearing a men's button-down shirt tied tight 'round her waist. She appears to be wearing no makeup. Her hair is parted down the middle and retro sleek. She's got a cigarette pressed between her fingers. You realize it's a cigarette ad. She's the perfect cigarette model—stunning in a powerful way. She's not delicate. She's sexy. Her eyes smolder and her razor-sharp cheekbones appear to be carved from stone.

That woman, the '70s bombshell of all bombshells, is the mother of yours truly (one of the many reasons I'm fucked up about food—my mother is a *model*). And what a force of woman she is! Not only is she a gorgeous model, but she's also a cheeky Brit, with lots of edge, lots of heart, lots of charisma, and fabulous style. Which means she's a natural-born best friend of the gays. Her best friend of all her best friends was a celebrity hair-stylist named Lyle. Lyle was also a cheeky Brit living in America.

My mother and her sisters adored Lyle. She tells countless funny stories about their adventures together, ones that eerily mirror my own life. For example: Lyle always had five to ten wigs on display in his living room, and before a group of them went out he would PLOP a wig right on the tops of all of their heads and off they would venture into the night, properly wigged and ready for anything that came their way!

My mother and Lyle traipsed through the wild jungle of young adulthood together, living everywhere from London to West Hollywood to New York City. They loved to dance deep into the night at Studio 54 and spend days lounging by the pool at The Beverly Hills Hotel (at least in my fantasy it was The Beverly Hills Hotel). They loved to go out, get dressed up, and gallivant around "the scene" they knew better than to take seriously.

There is an extraordinarily special bond that exists between unique women and gay men. It's almost romantic. We understand the deep longing of wanting to be *noticed*, of wanting to be *seen* so badly, while at the same time deeply fearing that one day everyone will find out that we're different. That We Don't Belong. And truthfully: We don't. We don't fit in with anyone, only each other, which is why we belong together, why we have a strange magnetic draw toward one another, and always seem to be in perfect sync with each other wherever we go. If you're a unique woman, you can be at the DMV on a hectic Saturday morning getting your driver's license renewed and somehow find the only gay man there, who is equally irritated (yet mildly bemused) by the rare sighting of "normal people."

The next thing you know, you'll be gossiping about *Drag Race* and Fire Island and oh, do you want to go to happy hour after we're done with this horror of place?

It should come as no surprise that my mother swam in a teeming sea of gay men (like mother like I daughter, I suppose). But what I like to call her "main gay" was Lyle. She had peed in a proverbial circle around Lyle. She claimed him as hers, and only a fool tries to snatch a gay away from a woman who's marked him as Hers with a capital H.

At one point sometime in the late '80s right after I'd been born, Lyle said something strange to my mother. They were having tea together, as Brits are wont to do, when Lyle suddenly said "There is a terrible disease going around the gay community. It's going to take a whole generation of us out."

"Oh, don't be ridiculous. What on earth could you *possibly* be talking about?" my mother scoffed, putting a giant dollop of Devonshire cream on top of her scone. (Again, the tea and Devonshire cream are likely a part of my illustrious imagination.)

"Trust me," Lyle said, his voice serious. The two of them sat there in silence. My mother had no idea what he was talking about, but she's a witchy woman, so she knew in her bones that something so dark and so ugly and so vile—that it was impossible to even imagine— was lingering in the shadows.

Lyle dies of HIV/AIDS in the mid '90s, when I am in the third grade. It kills my mother and her sisters. Little by little, they watch in horror as so many of their best friends deteriorate right in front of their eyes.

Even though I am a kid, I feel the weight of the death all around me. My mother is very open as to why "Uncle Lyle" has passed away.

I know that Uncle Lyle had contracted the virus by having sex. Trouble is, I don't exactly know what sex is. I know it is something that grown-ups do and it seems to be the motivation behind everything I see on TV, in magazines, and on billboards. I know that the reason businesses boom and crash and come into fruition is because of sex. I know that the world turns because of sex. I know that the reason my brother snatches discarded lingerie catalogues right out the garbage and stashes them beneath his bed is because of sex. I know the reason my sisters obsessively go to the tanning beds before their dates is because of sex. Sex. Sex. Sex.

But what the hell *is* sex? And why does the thing that seems to fuel every person over the age of sixteen inevitably come with a side of death?

Around this time, I discover masturbation. The first time I do it is right after I finish the book *A Wrinkle in Time* and I'm alone in my bedroom (I do it with a fragrance bottle, which is perversely ironic as my family is in the fragrance industry). I am blown away by that first smattering of a soft tingle, the escalation and explosion of pleasure I feel everywhere: in my fingertips, my toes, my ears, my face, my goddamn third-grade soul! As soon as that sweeping sensation washes over my limbs and dissipates into thin air, a giant wave of guilt crashes over me. I don't know how I know it, but I know what I've done is sexual. And I know that sex means HIV/AIDS. Which means dying and making my mother hysterically cry. I don't want to die, but most of all, I don't want to make my mother cry.

I tremble in bed that night. By the next morning, I am Living With Aids. I throw on my favorite velvet overalls and chenille, cap-sleeve turtleneck sweater and crawl onto the bus, overcome with a newfound sense of maudlin I've never before experienced. I am certain I only have a week to live. I envision the scene that will take place in my mind's eye, down to every last detail.

"I have to tell you something," I imagine confessing weakly, staring at my scuffed hot pink Dr. Martens boots (like mother, like daughter).

"Whatever it is, you can tell me, darling," I imagine my mother purring in her velvety English accent. She would be clutching a flute of champagne. She would smell like Jean Paul Gaultier "Classique" eau de parfum. She would be wearing a fabulous Norma Kamali dress with one shoulder, made of spandex. Her and my dad would be off to dinner soon and I only had a couple of hours left of life on planet earth. I had to speak up or I would never get to say goodbye.

"I have AIDS!" I would sob, running into her arms. In my mind's eye, my mother would look disappointed. She would hold me and collapse into sobs, but in her arms, I would feel her anger. *How could I be so selfish? Prioritizing pleasure over my family? After all she'd been through!*

I live with the guilt of what I've done all week long. Every time I sneeze I can feel myself slipping closer into the cold, scrawny arms of death. If I get a paper-cut, I run to the bathroom and wrap my finger up, certain the blood will infect my classmates and they too will die soon. It's one thing to destroy my own life because of my selfish sexual desires, but I can't kill my innocent classmates. When the dog furiously wags his tail and licks my face when I hop off the school bus, I savor every lick, every joyous jump. There probably won't be dogs in the afterlife.

By the time Friday morning comes around, I feel like a shell of myself. I feel deeply ashamed. I feel afraid. Most of all, I feel guilty. Guilt is the greatest bitch of a feeling. It's useless. When you feel guilty, you feel paralyzed. It doesn't spark a desire to become a better person, it sparks the desire to hide beneath your blankets. It's a particularly harrowing, confusing feeling for a child.

After school on Friday, I take a chance. I don't know why and I don't know how I muster up the courage to ask my mother this humiliating question, but somehow Lana Del Rey was on my side and before I know it they words are flying out of my mouth.

"Mom, how exactly did Uncle Lyle get AIDS?" I ask, my cheeks burning. I wish I can somehow reel the words back in with a fishing rod.

"Oh, darling! He got AIDS from sex! You do know what sex is, right?" she chirps, excited to educate me on the nuances of adulthood.

"Yes, *duh*," I lie.

"It's when a man sticks his penis in a woman's vagina in straight couples, like me and dad. For gay men it's different. A man sticks his penis in another man's bum." (I swear to Lana Del Rey this is exactly how she describes it.)

I feel—suddenly—like a giant beam of holy light is bursting through the living room. Butterflies swarm around the light, fluttering their beautiful, ornate wings. Angels appear and begin to sing a song of freedom! I feel stars burst out of my eyes and catapult into heaven! I am free! Masturbating is definitely not the same thing as sex! I am healthy, babe! I am healthy and young and ready to live my goddamn life!

And even though I feel such a great sense of relief, a heavy weight off my chest, a large luggage set dropped off at airport security—I am *still* a third-grade girl who associates sex with HIV/AIDS. I still associate sex with death. Nevertheless, I become obsessed with sex. I mean, sex is so powerful that people risk their lives to have it! Sex must be the most incredible, mind-blowing act in the world, huh? I become one of those children who incessantly watches softcore porn through the static of the TV. The moans, the screams of pleasure, the fact that it is so controversial people can't even watch it clearly, is so unbelievable to me. I find a copy of the Madonna *Sex* book in my parent's library and stash it under the bed. I pull it out at sleepovers and show all of my horrified friends (who are especially traumatized by the image of a grown man in a leather collar gnawing at Madonna's platform-clad foot).

By the time I reach the fourth grade, my mother—likely sensing my fear and curiosity—further explains sex and HIV/AIDS to me. She makes it very clear that if you use a "condom" you are pretty safe. She makes it very clear that sex is nothing to be ashamed of, and that it is a "beautiful" thing. She makes it very clear that HIV/AIDS is a devastating epidemic and that certain people are wildly homophobic and judgmental toward people who are positive, and that I should always be an activist and educate my peers. I take her words very seriously. I tell everyone in my fourth-grade class what a condom is. If anyone makes a gay joke, I snap. I am a pretty bossy, loud kid and I use my bossy, loud platform to become the youngest little AIDS activist in the affluent suburb of Westport, CT. Already some of my friend's parents have barred me from hanging out with them—but I don't care. I am ahead of my time.

* * *

It's the early 2000s and I'm in the eleventh grade. Gone are the angry girls strumming their angry guitars—the bad babes who ruled the '90s music industry with their rebellious prowess—and in their place is a bizarre mix of musical artists like Nickelback, OutKast, J.Lo, Linkin Park, and 50 Cent. Teen girls live and die in Juicy Couture velour sweatpants. Sometimes we tuck them into our UGG boots, which we religiously wear even though the boys say they're super unsexy. Lindsay Lohan and Mischa Barton and Paris Hilton are all alarmingly thin. Hollywood is hopped up on Adderall, actresses are always snapped by the paparazzi looking amphetamine-astonished and bug-eyed, clutching their sugar-free Red Bulls with their Von Dutch trucker hats strapped to their bobble-heads. We're obsessed with *Laguna Beach: The Real Orange County*. Rhinestone tiaras and Chihuahuas are all the rage. Hair extensions are just starting to become mainstream. Girls from LA talk in baby voices and get famous for leaked sex tapes. The opioid crisis is in full swing, though we don't know it. Nearly three-thousand people have recently died in 9/11 and everyone is mentally unraveling.

And this particular evening I'm stoked because my parents are out of town. They've gone away for the weekend to escape the Florida heat and have left me alone with the house to myself because I'm *sixteen* now, so I can like, *totally* handle it. I decide to throw a party.

Then it's three a.m. and the party has begun to wind down. There are six of us sitting on the floor of my back porch, lighting up bongs and drinking rum. We're listening to Aphex Twin and we're all completely wrecked out of our minds. We're talking about capitalism and college and music—we're really basking in the art of being a suburban teen. Just shooting the shit and dreaming of the future.

Little by little everyone excuses themselves to pass out some-where in my house. Before I know it, it's down to three of us. Sitting next to me, cross-legged on the floor and smoking rolled-up ciga-rettes is Pierce. Pierce is huge, giant really. He's at least six foot three and built like a brick shithouse. His hands are larger than my face. He's gentle and bohemian, around his thick neck rests a hemp neck-lace and his beard is no joke. Even though he's hippy-dippy he's pretty attractive, and loads of girls lust after him because he's got that alpha male energy. You know that even though he's a self-pro-claimed "pacifist" he would destroy any fucker who dares to mess with you—which they won't because no one messes with a girl who has a boy beast by her side. Sitting next to Pierce is a girl I've only recently started to hang out with. Her name is Taylor. She goes to a different school than I do, and might be the hottest girl I've ever seen. She's rail-thin with legs up to her ears, hipbones so sharp they could kill a man, and faded denim eyes. I'm wildly intimidated by her. My heart pounds so loudly when I'm alone with her, and I'm not quite sure why. All I know is that I want to be around her, but at the same time want to run away from her. She scares me and intoxicates me at once.

Because I've sucked back my body weight in liquor and because I've taken a few bong rips, I'm more relaxed than usual around Taylor. Pierce keeps leaning his body closer into my body and I can feel his warm breath against my bare shoulder, and it doesn't bother me, but it doesn't exactly entice me either. I notice that his arm is slowly making its way around Taylor's skinny shoulders too. Before I know it, I digest that he has one arm around me and one around Taylor. All of a sudden, the energy is getting very sexual. It's heating up. I envision a window slowly starting to fog up. Taylor crawls over Pierce's lap and kisses me right on the mouth. She slips her tongue into my mouth and I am completely present for the first time in my life. I am not thinking about the fact that Pierce is gawking at us, not being able to believe his luck that two hot girls are going at it right across his lap. I am not thinking about the fact that I'm making out with a girl either. I'm in my body. I'm acutely aware of each shiver making its way over my skin.

Pierce begins to rub my back and Taylor pulls away from me, looks me in the eye playfully and begins to make out with Pierce. All of a sudden it hits me: I'm about to have a threesome! Holy shit! What a *rite of passage*. The three of us stumble into my bedroom giggling, making out. When it was just Taylor and I it had felt more sexual, but now that Pierce is in the picture, it's more innocent. We're just kids experimenting. We can't even take ourselves that seriously. We're high off the fact that WE'RE ABOUT TO HAVE A THREE-SOME! Something we've only ever seen in that movie *Wild Things* with Denise Richards and Neve Campbell. The moment we enter my bedroom Taylor presses me up against a wall and passionately kisses me. "I have a huge crush on you," she confesses after about two minutes of making out. "I have a huge crush on you too!" I squeal. I squeal because only at *that* moment do I realize I have a crush on her, and I'm thrilled to have finally been able to identify the rush of adrenaline she triggers in me. I don't get this with boys, even though I wish I did. I am giddy. High. We kiss again.

"I have a crush on both of you," bellows Pierce. Oh, right. Pierce is there. I have forgotten about Pierce. Something about the way giant Pierce looks standing in front of us is so endearing. He looks like a puppy eager to play with the grown-up dogs who want nothing to do with him. You can tell he means it when he says he has a crush on both of us. Taylor and I exchange a smile and I grab Pierce's family-sized hand and lead him to the bed. We all take turns making out, our legs intertwined. And then Taylor and I get lost in each other again. We forget about Pierce again. I feel crazy. I can't believe how good girls feel. I have heard friends who have hooked up with girls describe it as "soft" but there is nothing soft about Taylor. She's like a sexy razor blade. She kisses me not like I'm a delicate flower, but like I'm an equal. She's far more confident than any boy I've ever been with. I am far more confident touching her than any boy I've ever touched. We just seem to understand each other's bodies. We have an intrinsic sense of what feels good. We aren't two dopes hoping for the best, which is what most of my sex life with boys has been like. In the words of Angelina Jolie in the movie *Gia*, when asked about sex with a boy: "I could've done that with a German Shepherd!"

I can't tell you how long Taylor and I roll around in my bed for. It feels like hours and seconds at the same time. A little voice in my head keeps whispering: *This is what it's supposed to feel like. This is what it's supposed to feel like. This is what it's supposed to feel like.* My hands slip down her skinny jeans.

The next thing I know sunlight is streaming through the blinds of my bedroom. Pierce is nowhere to be seen. My head is pounding like a heartbeat. My mouth feels like the Sahara Desert. I'm tucked beneath Taylor's arm. She is sound asleep and looks like a rock star even when sleeping. I have a flash of seeing Pierce slump out of the room, like an emo Basset Hound being ignored as the kids prefer the company of the kitten over the dog.

"You had two genders in your bed," Sharon (the wise woman who lives inside of me) whispers. I see her in the corner of the room, standing awkwardly. She's smiling, holding a cup of coffee. It has the skyline of New York City on it. At least, the former skyline before the Twin Towers got taken down by the terrorists. There are brown lipstick stains on the cup. She *would* wear brown lipstick. "And you preferred *one*." She winks and walks away.

* * *

It's 2009 and I'm twenty-something years old. I live in Los Angeles, where I'm trying desperately to pursue a career as an actress. Michael Jackson and Farrah Fawcett die on the same day. Obama is sworn in as the 44th president of the United States. Kanye West hops on stage and snatches the microphone out of Taylor Swift's hands right as she's accepting an award at the VMAs. *Rolling Stone* magazine puts Britney Spears on the cover; it's a maudlin black and white close-up of her and the caption reads "Britney Spears: Inside an American

Tragedy." Cropped leggings and waist belts and gladiator sandals are at the height of fashion. Beyoncé is Sasha Fierce. Things feel very light and hopeful for the first time in a very long time. I am stoned as hell with my boyfriend inside of his San Fernando Valley studio apartment that his parents pay for.

"Can I ask you something, Z?" my boyfriend says, his chocolate brown eyes cast downward.

"Of course," I say, my cheeks turning hot. I have a feeling this is going to be a tough conversation and I'm too high to deal with anything, except perhaps devouring the bag of Flamin' Hot Cheetos resting in my lap. I fight the urge to take the bag right to my lips and chug them like booze.

"Are you not attracted to me anymore?" he asks, his head still facing the floor.

I feel my heart crack. I love this boy so much. He's the sweetest, loveliest, most beautiful person I've ever met in my life. I want to crawl inside of his chest and live there forever. No one has ever made me feel more safe. There is an authenticity to this boy creature that I've never seen anyone else possess. He doesn't speak with subtext. He speaks the truth.

But I don't want to have sex with him. I can't tell him that. So I lie through my freshly bleached teeth: "Of course I want to have sex!" I say a little too loudly, a little too hysterically.

"We haven't had sex in months, Z."

"I know. I'm sorry. I am really not feeling good about my body right now," I say, which isn't necessarily a lie. But to be fair, rarely have I ever felt good about my body and it hasn't stopped me from getting down and dirty.

"It's OK. It just...makes me feel disconnected from you." Finally, the boyfriend looks at me. He looks like Bambi.

Zara, you're a fucking selfish bitch. Get over yourself and at least blow him or something. Actually, that's a great idea! Give him a goddamn blowjob! Just shut your eyes and think of England and get it over with. I am high and my mouth is dry, but I decide I absolutely must give my boyfriend a blowjob. I can't stand seeing him reduced to this vulnerable little sexless fawn. I'm the problem. There is something wrong with me. This boy is a perfect, pore-less specimen. Something inside of me is broken for not wanting to have sex with him.

I put my hair up. I take the bag of Flamin' Hot Cheetos off of my lap and place them on the table. I eye-sex them for a moment, imagining how hot they would taste in my mouth. I take a deep breath. I make a big show of batting my lashes at my boyfriend. I give him over the top sex eyes—it's very vaudevillian. I unbutton his pants. His breath gets heavy.

"I love you," he whispers.

"I love you too," I answer. I mean it. I softly moan in "pleasure" as I get on my knees. I don't mean it.

Just do it and get it over with. Suddenly my spit is thick and at the forefront of my mouth. My stomach lurches. *You're just high. You're not going to throw up. You're just stoned. You get weird when you're stoned which is probably why you shouldn't get stoned anymore.*

I begin to dutifully blow my boyfriend. My eyes start to water immediately. My head is spinning around in circles. I feel Flamin' Hot Cheetos crawling up my throat. They feel like foamy spiders. That's when I wretch. I pull my body away from him and make the loudest retching sound. So loud I have no idea my body is capable of making such a *sound*. It almost sounds theatrical, comedic, but there is nothing forced about my wretch. I feel my eyes get really big. Stretched open wide in astonishment over this involuntary gag. My chest heaves. I vomit. All over his dick.

"Did you just throw up on my dick?!" my boyfriend asks, his voice is more shocked than angry.

I did indeed. "I'm sorry. I'm so sorry. So, so, so, so—"

"It's OK. It's—" my boyfriend starts laughing. Laughing so hard tears are rolling down his face. For a second, I am angry! This isn't funny. And then it hits me. It is funny. It's really, really, really funny. I laugh along.

The next morning, Sharon pays me a visit. I am driving home from his house in my yellow MINI Cooper, the windows are down and I'm blasting Tegan and Sara. I'm singing along to the lyrics like my life depends on it. Sharon is sitting in the passenger seat. She lights up two cigarettes and hands one to me. "Thanks," I say.

She chuckles. "Remember when you had two genders in your bed and you just wanted one?" she asks me.

I do remember, but I don't tell her I do. I just stare at the freeway endlessly sprawling out in front of my eyes. Where does the freeway end?

"You know, the body knows when you don't like something. And throwing up is usually an indicator that you don't like something," Sharon continues as she ashes out the window. The ash flies right back into the car and lands on my face. I furiously blink it out of my eyes. It's sticking to my eyes like a contact lens.

I crank up Tegan and Sara, realizing for the first time how truly fucking gay I am.

Sharon stays with me the entire car ride home. I am shocked to learn that she knows all the lyrics to all the Tegan and Sara songs I blast.

* * *

I am still in my twenties and totally head over heels in love with a woman eight years older than me. She's brown-eyed and beautiful, tiny but cute as fuck, and she has that light beaming out of the crown of her head, that powerful light that makes everyone want to be around her all of the time. She won't sleep with me in the beginning of our relationship even though I'm begging for it. She says she wants to get to know more first. That she knows that this is more than just a hookup. I am wildly offended.

"Are you sure you're attracted to me?" I ask her, my body trembling for her touch.

"Are you freaking kidding me? I am so attracted to you." She gives me this lust-ridden look that confirms that she *is*.

We are falling in love. I can tell we are falling in love because every time I see her we strip a protective layer off our bodies and the more I see of the real her, her without a filter, the more my heart aches to see more. Even though I'm falling for her, I don't feel like I'm ever going to hit the ground. I am suspended in the thin air, and it feels so good to not feel my feet rooted into the earth (even though yoga teachers always tell you to "ground yourself"—the yoga teacher must've never been in love before), it feels so good to float, I want to float for as long as possible.

One night we're hooking up in her very grown-up bed in her very grown-up apartment in her very grown-up neighborhood. I am wearing this silky maroon jumpsuit that keeps sliding down my shoulder. I stop pulling it up. I stop thinking about what I'm wearing and what I look like. I don't think I've ever felt so…in my body before. We are kissing and it feels different, unlike any other kiss I've had before. We kiss like we've known each other forever, like we were born to kiss. She kisses me with so much tenderness it starts to freak me out. I feel exposed, and sex before now hasn't made me feel exposed. When I feel this vulnerable during sex, I am immediately reminded of all the times I've felt this way in the past, and those were all terrifying experiences. I feel out of control. I decide to take control of the situation. I get on top. I start making a big show of being sexy, running my hands through my hair, giving her sex eyes, being a master tease. In rushing through the process, trying to get her hot, I stop focusing on my own pleasure and just focus on making HER feel good. This whole thing is becoming a performance and I feel like I'm slaying the role of being a sex goddess queen tease vixen. She pulls away. I feel the stab of rejection pierce my heart. I am ugly. I am gross. She doesn't want me. I knew it.

"Baby," she says softly. "Relax. Let it happen. No need to rush."

"What are you talking about?" I am flustered and my ego hasn't been bruised, it's been broken in two.

"Shhh. Let it happen," she says. Her eyes are mild—like Emma Lazarus describes the Statue of Liberty's eyes in the sonnet "The New Colossus." (I think of this in the moment because I'm weird.) She touches my shoulder gently and looks me in the eye and I know that she knows why I'm so guarded. Why I'm putting on this ridiculous porn show. She's not going to let me get away with it, because she can see that this act is not the real me and she's interested in the real me. I don't know if anyone has ever seen me like this before. I take a deep breath. Because the intensity of her loving intentions are so goddamn fucking intoxicating, I give in. I take a deep breath.

The next thing I know we're having *love sex*. I guess some people could call it "making love" but for whatever reason that term makes me want to gag—it sounds like something a creepy dude high on ecstasy would whisper into your ear when he wants to get in your pants. Plus, we're not making anything. We have sex. But there is, like, love involved. Which, I suppose, means we're having *love sex*.

I let myself feel her touch. I usually blackout when someone starts to tenderly touch me, because it's all too real and too much. I only am in my body when someone is aggressively touching me because aggressive, rough sex makes me feel in charge. It feels kinky. I want sex to be kinky because kinky isn't soft or sweet and doesn't stir up the intimate feelings I've spent a decade trying to avoid.

But I have given in and she's got her fingers interlocked with my fingers and we're kissing and it's gentle but it feels...hot. In fact, it feels more amazing than any of the wild sex I've ever had and I've had a LOT of wild sex. I never want it to end. We are sweating and moving slowly and treating each other like we're sacred beings. I am getting to know her life story as we're having sex. I am showing her my life story as we're having sex. I am lost in the moment—for once, not one bit of me is hanging out in the rafters staring at the scene.

After, we cuddle. I hate to cuddle after sex. She kisses my eyelids. It's the sweetest thing I've ever felt, and I'm melting like an ice-cream cone, I'm mush.

I stay up all night completely in awe over what just happened. The idea that sex isn't about ego, the idea that sex isn't just about pleasing the other person, the idea that this raw, real, authentically passionate sex actually exists, and that I, Zara Barrie, am capable of connecting with someone during sex blows my mind. I fear it will ruin my sex life. Now that I know love sex exists will I ever be able to fake it again? I gaze at my sleeping lover. I don't know if I'll ever know the answer. But I do, finally, understand the power of sex and love when they're intertwined. It's the first time I feel safe and excited at the same time, and it's such a beautiful feeling I want to seek more of it. And is wanting to seek sex with someone who loves me really such a bad thing?

"No, it isn't, Zara," Sharon whispers to me. She stands over me and pats me on my head. "My work here is done. At least for sex," she adds before flying away. I've never seen Sharon fly before.

CHAPTER 9

PSA: Don't Starve and Drink

Song: "Hunger" by Florence + the Machine

Look. If anyone gets it, it's *me*.

Let's stop trying to be heroes for one fucking second and let's get real as fuck. Down and dirty with the ugly truth. Let's shamelessly make *love* to our dysfunction. At least for the duration of this chapter.

I suffer from *major* body dysmorphic issues.

I'm sure it's rooted in internalized misogyny or the patriarchy, but that's not what this chapter is about. This is about the self-inflicted danger and humiliation I've bestowed upon myself trying to diet (starve) when trying to party (get drunk).

You don't need to eat dinner. You'll be drinking. So many calories in booze, babe. You can't eat AND drink. You must choose one or the other. And you're choosing to drink. So listen up, you lush bitch. No food for you, you over-indulgent bitch. I would repeat this to myself, like a mantra as I adhered giant globs of mascara to my eyelashes.

I would stand in the shower clutching the ample flesh stretched across my thighs. *You're disgusting. No one is going to be attracted to you because you're disgusting. No dinner for you. No dinner for you. Dinner is for skinny people. Not you.*

I would stand naked in front of the mirror pinching loose flesh. *Better wear the most slimming dress in your closet with that bloat.*

I would slither into a taxi, my dress wrapped around my body like a hospital bandage, my stomach screaming for food. My brain screaming at my stomach to shut the fuck up, my spirit silent when I needed her the most. *This dress is already tight. You can't fit food.*

I would order a vodka soda, the most boring drink to ever exist in this cruel, cold world, but vodka soda doesn't have as many *calories* as my real love, Sauvignon Blanc (*there's so much sugar in wine, bitch*).

After a sip, I would feel the soft vibration of a buzz. When your stomach is devoid of nourishment, the booze has nothing to hold on to, it's got nothing to cradle in its flailing arms, so it creeps its way into your spine the moment it touches your tongue. After a glass, I would hear myself slur. The hunger would start to feel actually painful. I would eye sex the nuts sitting in all their salty glory on top of the wood-planked bar. *Don't you dare. You're already puffy.* I would resist the salty wonder nuts. Instead, I would toss back another basic tasteless, soulless vodka soda. It would taste like khaki pants.

After the second drink I would be slurring *and* stumbling but totally unaware that I was hungry. For better or for worse, booze sometimes numbs your need for necessary human impulses like the desire to chew food.

And the next thing I knew, I would be doing something I hadn't *planned on* doing. Like calling a toxic ex. Or making out with someone with breath reeking of poison (the kind of poison that comes from *within*). Or falling asleep in a taxi, which is sort of like playing Russian roulette. With your life.

Or crying.

In fact, if you give a hungry woman alcohol, it will almost always lead to mascara tears cascading their way down her sad, wasted, sunken face. Not that crying is anything to regret, but a drunken, public cry doesn't serve you the way you in which you want a good cry to serve you. You want to *feel* yourself cry, you want to be *sober* when you cry, so you understand it and appreciate its beautiful release. A wasted cry session in front of a crowd of fuckboys who likely don't give a rat's ass about you and are going to exploit your drunken vulnerability by rolling their eyes and gossiping at the sight of your sacred tears—that's not a release, babe. That's self-destructive. And eventually leads to post-drinking shame spirals, which I *never* want you to have because shame spirals take a fucking toll on the soul. Shame is toxic. Shame is disease. Shame leads to more starving and more self-punishment and more self-hate.

What I'm really trying to say is this: Eat dinner tonight! Even if you're *not* drinking. We're grown-ass adult women—we're not tiny baby fawns who can subsist on a handful of grass in an entire day! We were made to eat dinner in the evening. Like a *fully realized* dinner, not a slice of *gluten-free toast* with no butter. Dinner makes us feel warm and cozy inside, it nourishes us so we can have bright brains and light up the goddamn world, it grounds us in its fabulous ritual, it blesses our bodies and helps our hearts unwind after a long, tough day. You'll never feel beautiful, *truly* beautiful when you're hungry. You might feel concave—but let's stop confusing feeling empty with feeling pretty. So eat the pasta tonight. Eat the thick slab of salmon. Eat your vegetables. Eat the veggie burger. Eat the chocolate lava cake! Actually, I retract that. It's not up to me to tell you *what* to eat. I'm just here to tell you, little sister, that you *need* to eat. The silver lining? When you eat, you'll actually have fun at the party. Because you can't have fun when your body is starving, starving, starving. And in a society that does whatever it can do to rob us of fun and render us miserable and vacant, having fun is a badass act of rebellion. And you're one rebellious bitch! Stop acting like a conformist. It's *so* not who we are.

And if you're struggling to get through your meal tonight I want you to imagine me sitting across the table from you. I've lit candles on the dinner table and they're flickering so brightly, it's lighting up our faces. I gently touch your hand. I fucking smile. In perfect unison, we both take a bite of the most delicious food we've ever tasted. It tastes like *sex*. Together we savor every goddamn bite because it tastes so good and we deserve to taste good things. We wash our food down with a glass of wonderfully cheap, sugar-fueled champagne. We feel full and hot and ready to plunge into the night. We'll exchange crying for laughing and emptiness for wholeness. *Real* wholeness.

CHAPTER 10

The Body Wants What You Give It

Song: "Nighttiming" by Coconut Records

One morning I found myself in Las Vegas, Nevada, standing dead center in the casino of the Hard Rock Hotel at seven in the morning on a Monday. Before we go any further, let me disclaim: I detest Vegas. I might be a natural-born party girl but there is something inherently dark about Vegas. Maybe it's because in Vegas I see shit that's too real, you know? I'm the kind of party girl that prefers to intoxicate herself in the company of champagne and dark lighting. Flickering candles and a five-star menu. I like to mask the darkness lingering beneath the surface of the party with a bit of bourgeoisie glitter. I like to pretend that no one is addicted or running from anything or self-medicating—because we're in a chic restaurant somewhere civilized like, I don't know, *East Hampton*. Vegas is too raw. People party beneath bright lights at seven AM. I don't want to see your pores as you slug back booze in the harsh desert sunlight. I don't want to see the lines of dehydration in your face beneath the fluorescent lights of the casino. I don't want to see the deadness in your eyes as you pump a slot machine full of tokens. (Note: I *do* understand that it's all the same shit. Substance abuse is substance abuse is substance abuse, regardless of the "ambiance." It's just easier for me to be in denial about the dark reality stewing inside the party when the party looks *pretty*. Sigh. And that's because I, Zara Barrie, can indeed be a superficial millennial fuckgirl at times, a personal truth that I'm not exactly proud of but am working through in therapy.)

I avoid Vegas at all costs.

So what the hell was Vegas-loathing Zara doing in the Hard Rock Hotel in the wee hours of the morning? She was clutching a cup of coffee, prepping for a day of panels at a convention centered on lesbian fan fiction (don't ask). My girlfriend Meghan had tagged along with me for emotional support (I belong many places, but a lesbian fan fiction convention is not one of them) and we were both red-eyed and sneezy because Vegas tends to make a lot of people red-eyed and sneezy. Suddenly, my eyes zeroed in on a bleach blonde bombshell of a girl in her early twenties, just a hair younger than me. She flew out of the elevator like a bat out of hell, puffing on a cigarette and slurping back a cocktail like her life depended on it (you could tell—it did). Strapped to her tiny face were giant sunglasses, and even though she looked like a hot mess as she teetered around in filthy ballet flats and tiny white denim shorts, she was beautiful. She had hot girl energy. She stubbed out her cigarette on the carpeted floor like she owned the place. Only hot girls act cocky while sporting filthy ballet flats. Perfect examples: Amy Winehouse and Cat Marnell.

I peered at Meghan, who was also clutching a cup of coffee and gazing at this morning-cocktail-sippin' babe. "Damn," Meghan sighed, sticking her free hand into her sexy wax-coated black jeans. "Isn't it a little early for a drink and a cigarette? And who the hell smokes in an elevator?"

I felt myself growing wildly defensive. "Babe, we've *all* been there. Come on! Plus, it's Vegas! You can do *anything* in Vegas."

Meghan raised her left eyebrow and stared at the girl. Her eyes went soft. "Just because you can doesn't mean *you should*."

Meghan *did* have a point. It's not exactly ideal to be chugging booze and sucking back cigs on a Monday morning. Mornings are meant to be pure. Virginal! Sixteen ounces of spring water and fresh air. Something made me feel deeply depressed as I looked more and more at the girl, who in my mind I had firmly decided was named Kendra. I felt sad for the colossal hangover she was about to endure. I felt sad for the spiral she would inevitably have once last night's cocaine wore off. I felt sad for her pending liquor shakes and amphetamine sweats and shame shudders. I felt sad because she was clearly going *through it.* A girl who is drinking at seven AM on a Monday is going *through it.* Yes, it's Vegas, and yes people party like they're going to the electric chair in Vegas. But normal people, when in Vegas, party till about three AM, and pass out in their hotel rooms in a full face of makeup. Normal people don't need to drink at seven AM. That's when it hit me: Kendra wasn't drinking for fun. Kendra was drinking because she needed to drink. No one *wants* to drink at seven AM. You drink at seven AM because your body needs alcohol to stave off the withdrawal. Normal people, who drink recreationally, don't have alcohol withdrawals.

If there's one thing I've learned, it's this: Nothing is ever about what you think it's about. If I dug deep inside of myself and unearthed the truth, I realized I wasn't wracked with a sudden onset of severe depression because of this Kendra character. I was wracked with depression for my younger self. In fact, Kendra *was* my younger self. I've partaken in benders so severe that I needed a drink in the morning. I've taken in so much poison that my body got used to the poison and needed more poison in order to feel human. And those were dark times. Times I never, ever want to revisit. But alas, here was Kendra reminding me that the past never stays in the past. It creeps up into the present from time to time, and whispers, "Never forget where you came from, bitch." Kendra was my shadow. The side of me that follows me around no matter how hard I try to shake her off. If I turn my head back and look at her long enough, I just might become her again. And that's a deep-pitted fucking fear of mine.

Later that night Meghan and I treated ourselves to dinner at a fabulous restau..ant on the strip. Even though I wasn't on any kind of drug/drinking bender, and was completely in love and in a stable, healthy relationship—I still couldn't shake the icky feeling of my drug-addled past. In my head, I was no longer my healthy New York self with a steady job, I was a girl living in Florida teeming with toxins, craving more and more toxins. I was someone who had no respect left for her body and treated it like a trash bag. I felt like all the work I'd done to get healthy over the past few years was fruitless and that I was a fraud and belonged with Kendra, chain-smoking at the slot machine. By dessert, I started to believe I was Kendra.

"Why do certain people crave toxic shit more than other people? Is it a self-destructive tendency? Is it a death wish? Why do some people lust after health and others lust after the deadly?" I asked Meghan, as if she was an oracle that held all the answers to the world, which she might be.

Meghan twirled her linguini clams around her fork. "The body wants what you give it," she said casually, as if she hadn't just dropped one of the most profound statements I've ever heard in my entire life.

The body wants what you give it. The body wants what you give it. The body wants what you give it.

Suddenly everything came into clear focus. Kendra's body craved cigarettes and booze because she fed it cigarettes and booze. My body used to crave cigarettes and booze because I fed it cigarettes and booze. When I ate nothing but one pop-tart a day in the thick of my high school eating disorder, that's all I craved. I, the girl who loves pasta more than anything on the planet, the girl who was born obsessed with really good fucking food, only wanted pop-tarts. At first, it was tough to live off of only pop-tarts. But after a while, that's what I wanted. So that's what I gave myself. When I became obsessed with downing a gallon of water a day, my body began to yearn for a gallon of water a day. If I didn't flood my body with water, I felt as dry as the Sahara Desert. As dry as Vegas in the summer. But when I popped Adderall into my lips every day I never thought about water, despite the acute dehydration that goes hand in hand with speed. My body didn't want goddamn water. It wanted pretty blue focus pills.

The body wants what you give it.

And now that I didn't drink my face off every single day, I didn't care as much to drink my face off every single day. When I first cut back, hell yes, it was hard. Hell yes, I wanted a goddamn martini every evening. But I began to feed myself good, whole foods instead, and pretty soon, that's what my body asked me for. Me, the cigarette-smoking, wine-guzzling girl who lived off of one pop-tart a day for over a year—suddenly began to crave salads, and bananas, and wild salmon, and luscious bowls of pasta, and mineral water, and blackberries, and dark aphrodisiac pieces of chocolate, and voluptuous oysters, and crispy kale, and plush avocados, and sexy pieces of shrimp plucked out of the ocean that morning. The idea of a pop-tart sounded disgusting to me. I wanted real, healthy, organic, fabulous food. Who. Was. I?

The more I became aware of what I put into my body, the more effortlessly healthy I became. I no longer had to make this giant effort to eat balanced, healthy meals. My body wanted what I was giving it, and I was giving it balanced, healthy meals.

The more I thought about it, the more I realized that the whole "the body wants what you give it" theory isn't just about food or drugs or drinking. It's not just about processed garbage and organic produce and *carbohydrates*. It's about relationships. It's about social media. It's about sex. It's about anything and everything in your life.

Have you ever felt addicted to having sex with a terrible, toxic human being? Someone who belittles you and treats you like garbage? Your friends don't know what the hell is wrong with you, and quite frankly you don't know either. But it feels out of your control. Completely. Like there is a twisted magnetic draw that is pulling you directly into the bed of this fuckboy/fuckgirl/fuckperson. Your body craves them. You know they're chipping away at your self-esteem and your self-worth but you can't seem to ever say no to their sexual advances.

Maybe you think it's because the sex is mind-blowing! Or because deep down inside you love them! And if only you could break through their "tough" exterior surely something sweet and loving would existence underneath.

I'm here to tell you that you don't love them. The sex probably isn't even that mind-blowing. And if they act like fuckboys, they're most definitely fuckboys. **YOU WILL NOT CHANGE THEM.** Your body simply wants them because that's what you're giving your body. Your body has been poisoned by them, and the trouble with poison is it tricks your body into thinking it needs more POISON to survive. That's why poison is so deadly. Poison begets more poison.

However, if you were to stop exposing your poor body to this toxic creature long enough your body might quickly realize that you were simply *addicted*. And once you get through those few months of withdrawal and you start feeding your body healthy shit in the form of kind, good people—your body is going to start to feel *good*. Authentically. Effortlessly. You will no longer have junkie cravings for toxic people. You're going to, on a cellular level, crave wonderful, sweet, kind genuine people. And the only way to attain a semblance of peacefulness in this whirlwind of a life is too surround yourself with sweet, kind, genuine people.

And you'll begin to recognize the difference that being around only healthy people makes in your life. When one area of your life gets super healthy, it bleeds into the other areas too. Your mood will lift and your confidence will soar.

So when you're literally trembling for a person you know in your gut is doing nothing but vampiring the energy out of your body, rather than giving in to the craving, try doing the *opposite*. It's going to be hard, kicking any addiction is fucking hard (just read any rock and roll memoir from the eighties). Yeah it will feel uncomfortable. But when you've been addicted to a toxic person, doing something kind to yourself should feel strange, for it's unfamiliar to your body now. So pick up your phone. Go hang out with that friend who floods you with genuine compliments, the friend who authentically cares about you and your happiness, the friend that provides you with that beautiful rush of inspiration for you to be the most lit-up, electric, peaceful version of yourself.

Let's talk social media. Do you ever feel like social media is your demise? I know I do. I'll go through phases where I spend hours upon hours of my fleeting time on planet earth scrolling through meaningless Instagram photos of strangers I've never met. Time I could've spent writing something beautiful. Or catching up with a friend. Or having sex with my girlfriend. Things that fulfill me and make me feel human. But because I've been feeding my body nothing but aspirational images of influencers posing with green juices, I crave these demeaning, fake, empty, altered images with every fiber of my being—no amount of them can satisfy me. And guess what? Scrolling my life away doesn't serve me. It pulls me out of the precious moment. It kills my motivation. Makes me feel fat, ugly, less-than, like *I'm not going anywhere with my life*. It slaughters my gratitude and makes me feel jealous. And nothing makes me want to give up more than feeling jealous. It's one of the ugliest emotions. Yet despite all of this, because I've been immersing myself in social media for multiple hours a day, I want MORE of it. Even the girl who hates cigarettes will become addicted to pointless, deathly cigarettes if she smokes them for a couple of weeks straight. But once she kicks the habit, she'll wonder why the hell she ever subjected herself to all that nicotine and tar.

So what do I do when I find myself stuck in the throes of a social media addiction? I put my damn phone in my underwear drawer and walk my dog for thirty minutes, device-less. My anxiety will spike and I will break into a cold sweat for the first ten minutes. "I JUST WANT TO SCROLL SCROLL SCROLL SCROLL BITCH!" My body will scream, going into full withdrawals. I will let these feelings wash over me. And they do precisely that. They wash over me. And after that thirty-minute walk, I arrive back at my apartment, completely present, completely in awe of the city that I live in, and so inspired to create that I don't even want my damn phone anymore. I want to live and be present, and I realize I'm doing neither when I'm resentfully scrolling through fake pictures of fake people living fake lives.

What about work? If you show up long enough to a job that's snatching your soul out of your skull, a job that's not in alignment with what you *really* want to do with your life, your body falls into the rhythm of your work environment. You'll start to feel safe at work. And once you start to feel safe and complacent in a job, it will get harder and harder to motivate yourself to leave. And before you know, you'll have neglected all of the extraordinary dreams that filled your beautiful head as a kid, and you'll begin to be one of those people who just goes through the motions. Which is terrifying. We both know that isn't you. All it takes for you to make a change is for you pull yourself out of your comfort zone—start looking for other jobs, going on interviews, putting yourself out there—when you do that, you'll remember who you are again and what you really want. We're all just creatures of habit, aren't we?

After really sitting with this concept I began to look at what in my life was serving me and what wasn't. What foods did I crave that made me sluggish, unfocused, and sick to my stomach? What foods made me feel vibrant and energized? What if I ate more of *those* foods, and cut back on the food that made me feel like complete and utter shit? What habits did I have that made me feel insecure and anxious? What if I limited looking at social media to just one hour a day, and didn't mindlessly scroll my life away, but rather went to specific people's accounts, ones that lift me up? What if I entirely stopped subjecting myself to images that make me upset and bring out the worst in me? What if I didn't look at my phone until noon, because when it's the first thing I see in the morning it sends me spiraling into anxiety? Who says I can't do that? What if I stopped drinking so much? And stopped taking Adderall entirely? And instead began to go to the gym because, holy shit do I feel like Wonder Woman when I hit the gym?

When I implemented the habits that made me the best version of myself and rid myself of the ones that made me sick and weak and sad and envious—my entire life transformed. Going to the gym used to be torturous for me. I always loved the endorphin high I received after the gym, but getting there felt like I was dragging my body to prison. Until I started going consistently. I didn't put pressure on myself to dive into something hardcore like SoulCycle every single day, I just started to walk on the treadmill to a killer playlist for thirty minutes in the morning. After a few weeks, I couldn't wait to hop on the treadmill and rock out to the gut-wrenching sad girl ballads that make me feel connected and sane in this mixed-up world. And *girl*. I'm not a natural work-out person. I had to really give it to my body, in order for my body to want to work-out.

I also looked at aspects of my career I loved and examined the ones I hated. I love writing. I love writing personal essays specifically. Writing them was scary and exposing but I felt passionate and alive and creative while writing them. I didn't write them often because I was so used to churning out third-person listicles. I was so used to writing mind-numbing listicles that I began to dream in listicle format! Talk about the body wanting what you give it. I started to push myself to write the pieces that connected with my audience and made me feel like I was making a true impact on people. The more and more I shared my truth with the masses, the more I craved it. And pretty soon that's all I did. And before I knew it, I had built a career on *sharing*.

It sounds frighteningly simple, and that's because it is. Obviously, there are things in life we all have to do that we don't want to do. But there are plenty of things we don't want to do, that we do, out of habit, that we don't *have* to do. We don't have to take shots of tequila every time we go out. We don't have to stay in the relationship that's alienating us from our friends and making us weep into our pillows every night. We don't have to stalk our exes on social media. We don't have to mindlessly consume food that makes us groggy and foggy and feel generally terrible. We don't have to stay in a work environment that's disconnected from our ultimate goals. We don't have to go to dinner once a week with the friend that makes us feel like an irrelevant piece of shit.

And we can replace all of those things our bodies crave, things that are bad for us, with things that light us up. If Kendra hadn't been on a bender for the previous three days, she wouldn't be craving a ciggie and a drinkie in the wee hours of the morning. And a ciggie and a drinkie in the morning doesn't serve any of us. It's no way to start the day. Ask Kendra what *she* thinks. She's not doing that shit by choice. But Kendra can change. Kendra can shake off the hangover, sweat it out, resist the urges that plague her soul and replenish her body with goodness. And goodness will beget more goodness. And pretty soon Kendra will want the goodness. Putting goodness in her body won't be a choice, it will be a need. Her body will ask her for it. And though Kendra might not be perfect and she might slip up from time to time, she'll know that all she needs to do is replace what is making her feel lousy with what's making her feel wonderful, fabulous, expansive, in her flow, in her groove, and in alignment with the extraordinary girl she is. She doesn't need to judge herself for her occasional slip-up, but she can let it be a reminder that if she keeps indulging in the darkness the darkness will follow her. If she steps into the light, she'll no longer have to search for the light. Because she'll live in it.

The body will sometimes want to crawl into the dark caves of toxicity—sometimes out of nowhere. Or after the death of a friend or a devastating breakup. But here's the beautiful thing about crossing over the side: The light always welcomes you back if you've made the journey out of the hole and into the light before. Remember that. None of us are too far gone. None of us are damaged goods. The light is all love, and love will never judge you. You, my little sister, *produce* the light. The light is you! So you know where the light is, I don't have to tell you. And remember: Doors are open all around us. All you have to do is walk through them.

Whenever I feel like inhaling the dirt and the poison, I think of Meghan sitting across from me at dinner in the overly raw, over-exposed city of Las Vegas, Nevada. I think of her casually saying "the body wants what you give it." And then I remember that I *live* in my body. And I want to live somewhere really fabulous, so why then, don't I give my body fabulous things so that it craves even more fabulous things, and before I know it, I'll have a fabulous fucking life?

CHAPTER 11

Drugs, Music Festivals, and Creepy Men

Song: "Coachella" by Lana Del Rey OR "Wet Blanket" by Metric. Personally, I recommend reading the chapter twice to both songs. You'll get something different out of it!

It's festival season. That seemingly ~carefree~ time of year when spring's natural treasures gorgeously bloom and the promise of a blissful summer effortlessly lingers in the air. Ever-so-suddenly, our Instagram feeds are positively teeming with expertly filtered images of girls. *Festival girls.*

Golden-skinned, twenty-something beauties—long skinny legs haphazardly tossed inside ankle-grazing booties—pose against vast open desert backdrops, their sun-kissed "beach" waves tickling the exposed flesh of their delicately tattooed backs. They wear tribal print crop-tops with matching shorts and flash peace signs as they smirk into a camera lens, the sun beaming on their exquisite faces. They top off their universally loved, viral photographs with whimsical captions like "Festival Magic."

Who doesn't want a little taste of that *festival magic?*

"I wish I was going to a festival this summer. It seems so life-changing!" I overhead an adolescent girl whine to her friend on a downtown-bound train.

"I know. All the girls look so pretty and thin in the pictures. I bet their lives are perfect. I bet festivals are the most fun things ever," the friend moaned back in solidarity, her disenchanted voice deflating like a pin-pricked balloon.

I felt like crying. Why was I so triggered by a couple of punk kids daydreaming about music festivals on the subway? And that's when it hit me: I was triggered by the not-so-carefree memories of my festival past.

See, a festival can be a magical experience. A festival has all the ingredients for the perfect bohemian-dream recipe: The best musicians of a generation! Sunshine! Moonshine! Young energy! Dancing!

But festivals also have an underlying darkness to them, a darkness that no one seems to want to unearth. A darkness you can't quite see through the static screen of a social media post. A darkness that I, and countless girls I know, were shocked to witness when we blindly twirled into our first festival.

We thought we were in for three days of nothing but dancing and sharing joints with so many cool, like-minded people. No one warned us about the dangers lurking beneath the seemingly carefree surface.

And we left those festivals shattered and confused, each harboring a scary memory that we tucked away deep inside of ourselves because we were embarrassed and ashamed. We didn't want to be the freaks, the "no fun" bitches, the sensitive killjoys, the only ones who didn't have the time of our lives. So we took a vow of silence, like the generations of girls before us.

I'm sick of sending out dishonest messages to girls in order to keep up some tired myth that raves and festivals are bohemian safe spaces, places that foster free love and connection to all that's right in the Universe, nothing more.

Which is why I'm going to candidly discuss the dark side of the festival. Maybe you're one of the lucky ones, and you've been to a dozen festivals and have never come in contact with their dark side. Maybe you're like me and you have.

Or maybe you're going to a festival for the first time—in which case, I say: Go and have this electrifying experience, but also, you deserve to know what you're truly in for. First off... Be VERY wary of wolves in sheep's clothing.

And behind bandstand number two are a fleet of:

Creepy Dudes That Don't Deserve to Be There.

Where there are drugs and where there are pretty young girls, there are creepy dudes. Creepy, bad, dirtbag dudes who suck the magic out of raves and festivals with their blood-hungry fangs.

I'll never forget the first time I noticed it. It was the eve of my nineteenth birthday and I was at an electronic music festival in Florida. I had just swallowed an alarmingly bright pink colored pill that a guy with hair longer than mine had assured me was "pure ecstasy."

I stood barefoot in the grass and looked at the stars, as I patiently waited for the tidal wave of serotonin to wash away this bad feeling I couldn't quite shake. To my left, four of my closest friends were rolling their faces off.

"I FEEL AMAZING RIGHT NOW!" Bria, a red-haired pixie belted into the swampy air.

"You know what will make you feel really amazing?" the long-haired boy who had given me the pill asked, his voice like gasoline.

Bria didn't say anything. She just beamed into the distance, her vacant eyes twinkling like Christmas lights.

"A massage," he purred. I suddenly noticed deep-set wrinkles engraved across his greasy forehead. He had to be at least thirty-five.

What is he doing hanging out with a group of teen girls? I thought to myself. I prayed to the god I didn't believe in that the ecstasy would kick in soon, because the scene unfolding before my sober eyes was too much to handle without the soft filter of drugs. Brian's hands crept all over Bria's skinny body. Her eyes rolled back into her head.

"Bria!" I nervously sing-songed. "Let's go smoke a cigarette!"

Suddenly an unfamiliar arm snaked its way across my waist. "I'll give you a massage," slurred an unfamiliar man's voice. The hairs on the back of my neck stood up, alarmed.

"Bria! Let's have a cigarette!" I said, laughing maniacally, because I didn't know what else to do, and no one prepares girls for the creepy faux-bohemian breed of older man that pretends to be enlightened and guru-like but is really just a bona fide sexual predator in a hemp necklace.

"I feel amazing! I don't want a cigarette!" Bria giggled as Brian pulled her inside an army-green colored tent. I wrestled out of the stranger's grip and found a place to smoke in peace.

The drugs kicked in shortly after that, but they didn't manifest in my system blissfully. Maybe the pills were cut with something dirty, or maybe it was my newfound awareness that that sent me into a bad trip, I'll never know. Either way, I spent the rest of the night hiding under a blanket, hyper-alert to an ugly reality: This festival was full of monsters.

The next morning Bria was uncharacteristically quiet. Her silence impregnated the air with a forlorn heaviness.

"What happened?" I asked.

"I don't know," she responded, her eyes searching the car desperately like she had misplaced something really important. "Like, I actually don't know."

There is nothing in the world more jarring than not knowing what happened the night before. Waking up with the feeling that something happened that you didn't consent to (you can never consent to anything when you're high), but not being able to place faces on bodies or navigate the difference between a feverish dream and the night's reality—that's terrifying. The uncertainty of nights like that still haunts me to this day.

I wish, I wish, I wish that music festivals and raves weren't teeming with no-good entities who take advantage of youth and beauty and innocence, but I would be lying through my big-sister teeth if I glossed over this unfortunate truth: Predators don't deserve to be at any festival or rave or concert or party. But they're there.

So. Whether you're falling down drunk, flying high in the sky, or stone-cold sober, I want you to remember this: You don't have to trust anyone, even if he has access to a VIP area. Even if he seems woke and claims to know more about feminism than you. Listen to your gut. Alert your friends when you're overcome with a bad feeling. Call 911 (I'm not kidding) and contact the police right away if anything sketchy goes down with any dude. I don't care if he's famous, I don't care if he has a lot of social media followers, I don't care if he's your friend's boyfriend. No amount of social clout gives anyone the right to touch you, harass you, taunt you, or pressure you into doing anything. Always remember this: "Maybe" equals FUCK NO.

It sounds so simple, but hell, I wish I had known that when I younger. I wish that Bria didn't have to reckon with what might have happened at the festival that had promised to be the most magical night of our lives. I wish that the memories of my late teens and early twenties weren't tarnished by so many nights exactly like that.

Druggie Energy Is Intense.

Whether you participate or spectate, masses of people at music festivals take all kinds of drugs. And drugs are a complicated animal. They're wildly unpredictable and affect everyone in wildly different ways.

Some people might take that pill or snort that powder and have the time of their lives. Other people might take the same pill or snort the same powder and walk through hell and back. Drugs pull out the most extreme emotions that exist deep down inside of a person and fling those complex feelings into the energy and ambiance of wherever you are. You might see someone at a festival crying their eyes out, convinced someone is trying to murder them. In the next corner you might see someone who is so gleefully happy, they're dancing on clouds.

If you're a sensitive person who can't help but absorb the feelings of those around you, this can be a total mind-fuck. Personally, I get super depressed when I see someone in the throes of pure drug-induced bliss. Something about the falseness of it all disturbs me to my core. I begin to think about how the girl will feel when she comes down, I'm saddened that she thinks she's happy when really, her body just has a cocktail of chemicals swishing through it, chemicals that are tricking her into feeling happy. On the contrary, when someone is in the throes of a bad trip, they're so raw and so naked—too naked to be wrestling with these gut-wrenching feelings in public. In both cases, I begin to spiral into panic on their behalf.

Festivals are a mosh-pit of many opposing, wild, drug-induced energies in a relatively small space. And if it rattles you, you're definitely not alone.

Here's my advice: Plug into the music when it all feels like it's too much. You're there for the music, remember? Crawl into your own safe little orbit, ground yourself, breathe, and laser-focus your attention on the performance. It's what I do now, and it majorly helps to calm me down when I feel overwhelmed by a surplus of druggie energy.

And if you can't shake it off? Go home, babe. Call your friend, your mom, an uber, and go the fuck home. I wish someone had told me it was that simple! That you don't have to stay for your friends. That you're not obligated to force yourself to jive with something that doesn't naturally jive with you. Tell your friends you're sick, offer them a ride with you, keep your phone on in case they need your help, but girl, *go home*.

Honor Your Girl Alarms.

All girls are born with an amazing internal alarm system that lets us know when danger is ahead. As you've read by now, I call them girl alarms. It's the feeling of your stomach being twisted up in knots, of your heart racing outside of your chest, of sweat drenching your body for no apparent reason. It's the voice in your head that suddenly yells "don't do it!" Honor your girl alarms by listening to their precious signals. If you listen to your girl alarms, you have a chance at experiencing the magic of the music and all that, without getting pulled into the darkness.

But, if for whatever reason bad shit outside of your realm of control happens, don't you dare feel ashamed. Speak up instead of stuffing your bad experiences down. The more we all speak up, the stronger our collective voice is, and together we'll snuff out the darkness of the festival, and maybe one day it will be full of light. Sort of like it is in the Instagram pictures, but *without* being digitally altered.

CHAPTER 12

PSA: Strong Women Own Their Mistakes

Song: "8 Ball" by Waxahatchee

When I was twenty-four I did a brief stint living in good ol' London. As you might recall, this was not a happy time in my life. I was severely, severely depressed and severely, severely traumatized and in complete denial about both my depression and my trauma. To say I was on a booze bender would be the understatement of the *year*, girl. I was drinking like I was being sent to the electric chair (almost) every single night.

Let me get one thing clear though, my dear: Blacking out was never my intention. It just *happened*. I wasn't eating much at the time and I had just started taking Lexapro, both of which are a recipe for disaster when mixed with booze.

One night my really cool model friend, let's call her Lacey, invited me to a really cool model's birthday party at a really cool gastropub in really cool Notting Hill. When Lacey invited me to the party, I was certain I would be able to drink like a normal person. It helped that Lacey wasn't a blackout drinker herself. Granted, she was a healthy, hydrated 5'11" and I was unhealthy, dehydrated 5'5"—but I didn't think so *critically* back in those days. My head was cloudy from both the manic depression and the excessive drinking.

I put on my favorite Marc by Marc Jacobs dress, a cute black and white shift dress with a Peter Pan collar that made me look and feel far more prim than I actually was. I was extra careful to iron out the kinks in my hair and I was sure to wear heels I could actually walk in. No stilettos on the Notting Hill cobblestone for *me* tonight. No making a fool of *myself* tonight. Tonight, I was just a normal girl going to a trendy party with a non-raging alcoholic nice-girl friend of mine.

The party took place at one of those very cutesy-looking pubs, the kind with a garden outside that's filled with wild English roses and smells like freshly rained-on soil. A sweet fireplace held court in the center of the restaurant, making it look more like a grand-mother's living room than a pub. (That is, if British girls did cocaine in this particular grandmother's living room.)

The birthday girl, the model, was seated in the back table with a bunch of other exquisite looking, impossibly thin, impossibly tall girl creatures. I felt very short and very squat and very Jewish next to these Anglo-Saxon amazons. The boys there were hideous, with bad teeth and bellies that shamelessly hung over their belt buckles, but you could tell they were very wealthy and very powerful by their unabashed confidence.

The vibe was not my vibe. I don't do well in cold, cool environ-ments. I need warm, wet, sloppy environments in order to have a personality. I felt out of place—a puppy dog with its tongue hanging out of its mouth tossed recklessly into a sea of sleek eels. I didn't even know this model princess, why had I gone to her birthday? Lacey was as sweet as always, but was stretched even thinner than she already is, and that's saying a lot for a model. She was surrounded by other tall beauts she'd known since she was sixteen. So, I did what I always did when I felt uncomfortable. I removed myself from the situation and went home.

Ha. We all know what I *really* did: I removed myself from the table, ran faster than a cheetah on the prowl in the dead the night and went straight to the bar. Where I decided it was a good idea, on a stomach with zero food, only Lexapro inside of it, to order a double vodka soda. If I couldn't be comfortable in this crowd naturally, I would drink myself into comfort! Which had always worked out so well for me in the past, so why on earth would it backfire tonight?

I downed one double and felt better, so I decided to order another to feel even *more* better. I could feel the alcohol lubricate my personality, making it ripe for the plucking. In the corner of my eye, I saw two girls in blazers giggle at me as I chugged my beverage like the American piece of trash that I was. In hindsight, I realize they were probably laughing about something that had absolutely nothing to do with me, but misery can make a girl wildly narcissistic. I stumbled to the table, where everyone was sitting, tamely drinking champagne as if it were English tea with the Queen. I was definitely more lit than anyone else there. This made me self-conscious, so when one of the puffy fuckboys asked me if I wanted a glass of champagne, I said yes. Of course I wanted a glass of goddamn champagne.

The rest of the night is a blur. I have flashes of stumbling. I have flashes of falling. I have flashes of slurring nonsense to a non-impressed Australian dude. I have flashes of a look of bright red embarrassment dancing across poor Lacey's face. And then the flash crystallizes and is so clear and so vivid it will never, ever escape my brain.

I'm not going to lie, this is not something I want to revisit, but it's imperative that I go *there*.

I emerge out of a blackout and my bare hands are covered in cake. A *birthday cake*. The rest fades to black. I come back into consciousness as someone, a man I think, is yelling: "Are you eating a birthday candle?!" Suddenly I taste stiff wax in my mouth. I realize I am, indeed, eating a birthday candle. I am met with the freezing cold sweats of acute embarrassment. I don't know what to say, but my friend Violet's voice comes bursting into my brain. *Deny, deny, deny, deny.* That's the advice she once gave me when was I worried I had an STD from a one-night stand and had maybe given it my new partner.

"I'm *not* eating a candle," I slurred, trying to fight back the sting of tears invading my sore eyes. I confidently chewed the candle in front of him, as if it were a regular piece of cake, no big deal. It was hard and waxy and tasted like poison.

Then I took off and ran out of the bar. I could hear Lacey yelling my name behind me but I was far too ashamed to look her in the eye. I was suddenly sober. Actually, I was hungover. Had I really stuck my hands into the cake? Or was that a figment of my imagination? I'll never know. But here's what I do know: If I was hammered enough to eat a birthday candle out of a model's birthday cake, I was most certainly hammered enough to ravage the cake with my bare hands.

The next morning when I woke up, I pulled the covers right over my head and lowered the blinds until it was pitch black in my bedroom. My heart was racing. My mind was racing. How could I ever go out in London again? I, Zara Barrie, had blacked out on my new antidepressants at a party full of very cool, very beautiful, very normal people. Not only had I blacked out. I ate. A birthday candle. Not Violet or Owen or Eduardo's or Ruba's birthday candle. A fucking model's birthday candle. Not only did I want to never ever face Lacey or London or Notting Hill ever again, I didn't want to face myself again.

The truth was, I had let myself down. I wanted to stew in my stupidity for the rest of my life.

And I did for a few days. I avoided Lacey's concerned calls. I hardly ate. I hardly slept. And then, good ol' Sharon showed up.

"Baby girl. Get out of bed," she chuckled, grinning.

"Why are you grinning? This is the most embarrassing moment of my life."

"I'm grinning because it's funny. Zara. You. Ate. A. Birthday. Candle. On Lexapro. Yes, it's mortifying, but shit, what a fabulous story it will make one day." Sharon slapped her stomach and released a giant, deep belly laugh. Her laugh sounded like a relief. It gave me permission to release myself from the shackles of shame. It was infectious. The next thing I knew I was hysterically laughing along-side her.

"I'll never drink doubles on Lexapro again!" I said, tears of laughter streaming down my face. I wiped a tear off my cheek and looked at it. It looked exactly the same as a sad tear. *How strange,* I thought to myself as I flicked it off my finger.

"Now Zara, you clearly screwed up and this is something you don't want to make a habit of, but where is all this shame and guilt going to get you? You made a fool of yourself. You didn't kill someone. You didn't intentionally try to hurt anyone. So, you ate a candle! Big fucking deal. I ate a live fish once," Sharon said, lighting up a cigarette as she always did when she was about to reveal something juicy.

"A fish?! Why?" I asked, imagining my childhood goldfish, Kisser, swimming down Sharon's plump throat.

"It was a dare. I was being hazed for my sorority. Plus, I had taken down ten gin and tonics."

"You were in a sorority?" I asked bewildered.

"Yeah and you ate a candle. We all have a past. It's part of what makes us so sexy! I'll let you stew on that, babe." Sharon gathered her coach bag and her Virginia Slim cigarettes and yellow BIC lighter and made her way out the door. Right before she left, she turned to me and said: "If you ever catch yourself taking yourself too seriously, remember...you ate a candle."

Before I had the chance to chuckle with her, she was gone.

The moral of the story here is that if you are harboring shame, if you're spiraling over what you did last weekend, or are steeped in regret over who you had sex with last night, or are wildly embarrassed about your mental illness, I'm here to tell you to get over yourself. I'm here to tell you that at least you didn't eat a birthday candle. I'm here to tell you that Sharon is *right*!

While there is nothing sexy about falling down drunk, there is something extremely sexy about a woman who is unafraid to own her shit. A woman who can hold her head up high, and say, "Babe,

I got plastered and I fell down last night. I'm on new psychotropic drugs—can you believe it? Oh well." Because anyone who is remotely interesting has embarrassed themselves at some point in their lives. My friend Dayna split her latex pants in front of a crowd of hot lesbians at her birthday party last year. Not only did she split her pants, but she was also *twerking* as she did it, and her entire asshole was exposed to a group of beautiful strangers. She looked at me and said, "I have to go home and kill myself immediately." But she didn't. She went out on the town and rocked the split pants and made everyone laugh as she dramatically retold the story, embellishing it with each fresh cocktail. My friend Beya farted during sex with the man of her dreams. A loud, wet fart that stunk up the whole room. When he asked if she had actually, *indeed* just farted, she said "It wasn't me!" even though it was just the two of them in the room and it was clearly *her*. She ended up not only confessing, but writing a viral essay to a mainstream digital publication about the experience.

So here's my PSA: Strong women own their mistakes.

Tape that onto your bathroom mirror. Memorize it. Live it. Get over your shame. The beautiful thing about screwing up is now you *know* better. I never ordered doubles on Lexapro again after that. Because I *knew* better. And in the words of the late Maya Angelou: "When you know better, you do better." So get on your knees and kiss the ground and thank the universe for your glorious fuck up. Laugh about it. Sing about it. Write about it. You're so hot when you scream about icky parts of your life from the rooftops. You're so dynamic when you don't just display your highlight reel to the outer world. You're so sexy when you talk about your ~turbulent~ past. And the more you screw up, the more you learn about how to *not* screw up. The lessons are all in the screwups. So let the shame go, girl.

And if you're still teeming with shame over what you did last night, imagine me, lying in bed with you. I have cake stains all over my dress. I have candle wax in my teeth. I'm clutching a bottle of Prozac like it's a goddamn trophy. But I still look sexy. Because I'm laughing about it. I'm taking my humiliation and using it as a tool to make you feel better. You realize how powerful that is. You realize it's time to tell your story to help other girls feel less ashamed about their shit, too. Because regardless of what you look like or how you grew up: All girls have shame. You're not special. You're just real AF. And I'd rather be real than special any day. Because real is refreshing. Special is fake and precious. And I don't fux with fake and precious, do you?

CHAPTER 13

Praying to Lana Del Rey

**Song: "Mariners Apartment Complex" by Lana Del Rey.
I chose this song because my partner told me it was
writing's song to me, and I believe writing is praying.
Yes, we are weird/intense lesbians over here.**

Let me tell you a little story about my first *ever* yoga class. It was my first day of art school in Southern California. I was a total train wreck with nerves! I was reared in the tri-state area, the land where the spray-tanned masses hurl swear words at strangers while speeding down the turnpike; the land where mouthy Italian Americans and opinionated Jews with thick, rich *New Yawk* accents are always trying to feed you spaghetti or matzo ball soup; the land of freezing cold winters and brutal sarcasm; the land where epic beauty parlors are perched next to Chinese food restaurants in suburban strip malls; the land of bridges and tunnels and subways and buses and taxis and metro cards, the land of the "buy one get one free," and the home of the baddest bitches you'll *ever* meet. To say I was out of my comfort zone in Southern California would be the understatement of the goddamn century. Have you ever *seen* a girl who spent her formative years on Long Island try to navigate fair-weather So

Cal? If you haven't, I highly recommend it. It's like watching an alien shop for food at Costco.

Even though Southern California was completely new to me, and even though I was a scraggly, scared-shitless eighteen-year-old who had been recklessly tossed out of her element, I was *so* excited. I was *so* excited to be at art school in this gorgeous state made of mountains and…what's that…*sunshine*? What is that *color* on those girls' bodies? Is that what a real tan looks like? It certainly didn't look anything like the streaked orange tan that reeks of Ritz crackers that I'd grown accustomed to. (Have you ever noticed that spray tans and Ritz crackers smell eerily similar?)

More than being jazzed about this new exotic California terrain and the authentic tans that came with it—I was ecstatic to be in art school. Finally! My entire life I had dreamt of going to art school, of being in a theatre conservatory where my days would be spent doing what I loved most: releasing all the feelings of resentment I harbored by expressing them on the safety of the stage. I was a melo-dramatic teenager, to say the least, with a head swirling with visions of late-night rehearsals over clove cigarettes and goblets of red wine. I even loved the name of where my beloved art school resided: *The Santa Clarita Valley*. Where I was from there were no valleys, especially ones with sexy Spanish names like "Santa Clarita." The tri-state prefers blunt, to-the-point titles for our worldly wonders, like the "Queens-Midtown Tunnel" and the "Long Island Expressway" otherwise known as the L.I.E. If you want to understand tri-state culture just take a look at the names of our bridges and tunnels and expressways and turnpikes. They don't screw around. The New Jersey Turnpike is *not* pretending to be anything that it's not: It's a fucking Turnpike in New Jersey, got a problem with that?

My first class at art school was called "movement." *Oh, move-ment! That sounds exciting! What does one wear to movement class?* I wondered as I combed through my collection of Dr. Martens boots and leather motorcycle jackets and Frankie B. hip-hugger jeans that rode so low I had to shave everything.

I settled on a velour Juicy Couture sweatsuit for my first movement class. Not only was it a Juicy Couture sweatsuit, but it also spelled out "J-u-i-c-y" in Swarovski crystals across the ass. Not only did it spell out "J-u-i-c-y" in Swarovski crystals across the ass, but it was also Barbie pink. Bubble gum pink. Bimbo pink. It was a sentimental outfit for my first day of school, for my darling mother had gifted me the sweatsuit to assure her precious daughter kept herself "warm" during the cool Valley nights. "The temperature really drops at night," she'd warned me the night before I left, handing me my brand new swaggy sweatsuit.

I arrived to movement class fifteen minutes early. A beautiful girl with legs for days was already there, warming up. I watched in awe as she stretched her long, willowy limbs across the floor, her eyes blissfully closed, her diaphragm expanding and retracting as she breathed in and out. She was wearing a black, skin-tight leotard paired with leggings. She seemed at ease in this strange space, a little black box theatre with a mirrored wall and a ballet bar. I would later find out that her mother was a famous actress. She exuded cool-girl actress offspring vibes, like she had been born in a theatre in the East Village. In sauntered a brunette male in slim fitted jazz pants and a tee-shirt that was cut-out at the collarbones, exposing his bare, exfoliated shoulders. One by one, student after student waltzed into the room. Everyone was in black, stretchy clothing. No one was in velour. No one was wearing pink—let alone Barbie, bubblegum, bimbo pink. I suddenly became very aware that I was the only girl in class who was wearing mascara and foundation. I suddenly became very aware that I was the only girl who appeared to be wearing hair extensions. Was I the only girl whose hair wasn't twisted into a neat bun? I looked around. I most definitely was. *Oh, why the hell didn't I think to bring a hair elastic?*

Suddenly our professor appeared. She was younger than I had imagined. Early thirties, I suspected, with arms so toned they gave Madonna a run for her money. She was wearing loose, tribal print harem pants and a fitted black tank top. She was braless and wore no jewelry, with the exception of a red string Kabbalah bracelet that loosely dangled from her wrist. Her skin was clear, her face free of makeup. I could feel my acne sitting on top of my face, taking up all the space it desired, like an entitled white male man-spreading on a crowded subway. She sat in front of the class with her legs crossed into a pretzel shape. Her knees rested against the floor. Her hands were clasped together in prayer. Something about the way she was silently sitting in front of an eager room of new students, her face so serious, her smile so smile-less, made me feel like I was being too loud even though I wasn't making a sound. I was used to warm Italian American women who greet you with a "WHAT'S YA NAME, HONEY?" followed by a cheek kiss that marks your face with bright red lipstick. You pretend to loathe your stamp of affection, but secretly you adore it because it's such a token of love and warmth. I so badly longed for a wet-cheek kiss from a loud New York woman. I longed to smell the familiar mix of cigarettes and Chanel No. 5 and bodega coffee. This room didn't smell like anything at all.

"My name is Gwen. And this movement class will be a Kundalini yoga and meditation class. This is an *ancient* practice." She studied the crowd of eager students, nodding her head in approval at a few, dismissing the rest. "Who here has never done yoga before?" she asked like it was a challenge. Like she was asking, "Who dares to solve the impossible math equation on the blackboard?"

I gulped. I bravely raised my hand.

"And your name is?" she asked, but didn't really ask. She commanded.

"Zara," I said loudly and clearly, trying to mask the rumble in my voice.

"Well, Zara. You're going to have to pay very close attention. This is a serious practice. One that requires extreme focus."

I nodded and stretched my mouth into an enthusiastic bare-toothed grin, trying desperately to show her I was excited to embark on this linguini—I mean, *Kundalini* experience.

Gwen looked me up and down. She wrinkled her nose. "Are you wearing perfume, Zara?"

I could feel my cheeks burn. Actually, it was eau de toilette not eau de parfum, but I knew better than to say that. So I settled for an uncharacteristic: "Yes, ma'am."

"My name isn't 'ma'am,' it's Gwen. And please refrain from wearing fragrance in my class. This is a scent-free space. There are people with fragrance sensitivities here, myself included." I felt a sharp pang of homesickness stab me right in the belly.

We began to do sun salutations, which is a sequence of poses done in repetition. I had no idea what I was doing. I prayed to the god I didn't yet believe in that my snug, stretch-less velour sweat-suit didn't rip in the crotch as I spread my legs open wide and hung upside down. I felt the scorch of Gwen's eyes burn through the cheaply made faux velvet of my sweatsuit as I clumsily stumbled my way through the sequence. She had us stay in downward dog for five minutes. By minute two my legs began to shake. By minute three they were shaking so violently I actually wondered if there might be an earthquake happening.

Gwen walked around the room giving feedback. "Love how deeply you're leaning into the discomfort, Stella," she cooed at the girl with the famous actress mom. *Was it just me or did she sound like a fangirl? Was a yoga teacher supposed to get star-struck? Didn't that go against the ethics of yoga?* Not that I knew for sure, but us tri-state girls have killer instincts. Blame it on the unpredictable weather and even more unpredictable characters we deal with on the crosstown bus.

Next, she gently touched the lower back of a curvy blonde who was breathing heavily. "Keep breathing. You got this. You're a warrior," she whispered.

When she made her way to me I felt hopeful that maybe I too would receive a gentle guru touch. Or sweet affirmation complimenting me on my breathing. Instead, she just folded her arms. My eyes were closed but I could energetically feel her fold her arms.

"Some of your legs might be shaking," she said as if she was addressing the room, even though she was clearly addressing me. "That's just your body detoxing from the nicotine and the coffee and the alcohol and the processed foods you've been poisoning your body with."

The fact that she had assumed I was a boozy, chain-smoker who lived off Styrofoam cups of coffee hurt less than the fact that she didn't even address me directly. It was as if I was too hopeless a cause, too far gone down the Verrazano Bridge, to be acknowledged by "high-frequency" Gwen.

After we chanted and said "Namaste" Gwen pulled me and a pretty blonde (why was there such an influx of pretty blondes in California?) aside. Her name was Jill.

"Jill," Gwen said, beaming. "Would you mind meeting with Zara privately to go over sun salutations? You have beautiful form and I think Zara could really benefit from working with you."

"Sure," Jill said thrilled to have scored the role of the teacher's pet after her very first class.

I felt like a failure. I felt like a misfit. I felt like a ridiculous piece of tri-state trash. I felt like a bubblegum Barbie bimbo wearing a pink Juicy Couture sweatsuit in a room full of black leggings. I *was* a bubblegum Barbie bimbo wearing a pink Juicy Couture sweatsuit in a room full of black leggings.

I skulked back to my dorm room. I had been so excited for *movement class*. I had felt so hungry to learn yoga. I had been curious about yoga for the past few years. I knew that it was somehow connected to spirituality and I had a hunch that I, Zara Barrie, the first girl in her class to grow tits and the last to earn her driver's license, might be, indeed, a *spiritual person*. I had no formal "spiritual training" but I had always felt this deep connection to something far greater than myself. I had always felt this sort of relentless calling to explore the world that lived beneath the surface of the earth. I had always felt like I had the ability to recognize and sense a force in the universe that wasn't visible or linear. I had been excited to examine this side of myself, and art school in California seemed like the safest place to do just that. Far away from my radical atheist brother who would bellow, "Do you believe in freaking unicorns too?" anytime I uttered anything remotely esoteric. On the East Coast, people mocked the spiritual yoga world.

I was starting to see why.

I buried my face in the pillow of the cot of my tiny dorm room, and decided right then and there that none of this was for me. If my yoga teacher rejected me after knowing me for mere minutes, surely the entire spiritual/wellness world would too. And as a Jewish American Princess, I had zero interest in subjecting myself to further humiliation and ridicule from a gentile rocking a Kabbalah bracelet.

The message Gwen had sent me was loud and clear: Girls who slather themselves in fragrance and didn't come flying out their mother's vagina knowing how to perform perfect sun salutations have no place in the new age. And quite frankly, if I wasn't to be taken seriously in my very sexy bubblegum, Barbie, bimbo pink attire, I didn't *want* to do yoga. Or meditate! Or eat clean. Or get down and dirty with the rest of that new-age bullshit. I shut the proverbial blinds to all things wellness and retreated back into my familiar world of cynicism and cigarettes and loud characters who have never even been to therapy, offer unsolicited cheek kisses and bake in tanning salons.

At least my people had a sense of fucking humor.

Ever since that class, I made fun of any friend that took a stab at veganism because, in my mind, vegans were all yogis with sticks up their asses (I was right about that one—which I can say with confidence as a current vegan). There was the new-age world and there was the party girl world. And the new-age world didn't seem to take kindly to girls who have a taste for sequins. It rejected all of us imperfect, (yet interesting) girls who enjoyed the occasional cigarette and the not-so-occasional cocktail. It wasn't for us girls who have ripped every pair of stockings we've ever owned, or us girls who swore and wore black eyeliner to the grocery store, and it certainly wasn't for loud girls. And honey—I'm *loud*. My brother says my voice sounds like a Jewish fog horn. Not only am I *loud*, I'm a wild animal let loose in a five-star restaurant! I don't know how to enter a room without causing a scene. Whether I'm tripping over my giant platform shoes, or stumbling into a side table, or knocking over an expensive antique, or breaking out into a loud, unstoppable bout of hiccups, I always seem to disturb the peace. Disrupt the *ambiance*.

Which is why I've always felt so at *home* in gay clubs. Not because I'm a lesbian. Because *everyone* is disruptive in the gay club and there is no peace to disturb. Queer people are so used to standing out and making the masses uncomfortable just through their very existence, that most of us start to think, "Fuck it. People are going to stare anyway. Might as well be my loud, freaky self!" A Barbie Bubblegum Bimbo sweatsuit would never be too extra at a gay club. I could wear all the fragrance of all the beauty counters at all the Bloomingdales across the globe and it still wouldn't be too much. If a yoga space in art school is scentless and zen, the gay club is the opposite of a yoga space in art school. It's teeming with rich smells and fabulous strobe-light energy.

The first time I went to a gay club at the age of thirteen, with my older sister Audra, I cried tears of relief. I wish I could say they were tears because I finally was accepting my sexual identity—that would beautiful and poetic—but it had nothing to do with that. I wept because a gay man wearing a tutu complimented me on my eyelashes for the first time. The gay club is the only place where you get complimented by strangers on the length of your eyelashes. I wanted to stay there forever.

As I grew deeper and deeper into my twenties I began to really get in touch with my intuition. My senses sharpened. My ability to predict the outcome of a situation was so spot-on it scared me. My anxiety intensified. I didn't know what to do with the great sensitivity that was getting more and more severe each day. I detested it. I stored it away. I threw on a party dress, slid into a pair of high heels, and drank a glass of champagne. I wanted to quiet my mind but I didn't know how.

Anything wellness-related repelled me. Who were these self-important bitches, clad in all white, telling me to go on their goddamn silent retreat? Who were these obnoxious, self-proclaimed gurus forcing me to take my shoes off, so I don't drag the dark energy of the street into their sacred space? I mean, if the dark energy of the street is that powerful—wouldn't it cut through the sole of my fucking shoes anyway? It seemed like each "high-frequency" person I came in contact with was nothing more than a glorified snob who thought they were better than everyone else. How can you claim to be so evolved when you spend all of your free time in a two hour, fifty-five-dollar meditation class in Malibu with a bunch of rich white women? Does being spiritual mean you have to be rich? Because all those astrology readings and all of that clean organic food and all of those stretchy leggings are *expensive*.

It was just a couple of years ago that I was browsing my favorite book store on the Upper West Side when I came across a book by an author I love. The book was called *How to Grow Up* and the author was Michelle Tea, the creator of Sister Spit. I know it sounds like woo-woo bullshit, but I promise I'm not embellishing or lying, in fact, I am a little embarrassed to even write this sentence: I was called to the goddamn book. Like I picked it up without thinking, shrugged, and traipsed over to the cash register.

I love to read more than I love a cold glass of champagne on a summer evening, and I strangely find a lot of my books just trolling bookstores and grabbing a book that seems interesting. I never read book reviews and only ever ask my friend Dayna for book recommendations (she's the only other person I know who will admit to loving trash romance novels and Sylvia Plath). I'm pure instinct when it comes to my book choices.

That night I curled up into bed and dove into *How to Grow Up*. I instantly connected with Michelle Tea. A queer punk with a wild past navigating how to evolve and grow up without losing her punk-rock ethics. Not that I identify as anything *cool* like a queer punk, but I at the time I was completely stuck in the identity crossfires of *clubby champagne swilling party girl* and *woman who lusted after something more meaningful than the glitter of the party*. I didn't want to neglect the glitter—the glitter had held and accepted me my entire life. But I needed some tools to help ground the shitstorm that swirled inside of me.

The part that struck me the most was when Michelle Tea discussed the whole higher-power thing. She explained that you don't have to believe in a traditional god. That your higher power can be anything you want it to be. In fact, Michelle Tea's higher power was Stevie Nicks! She *prayed* to Stevie Nicks. Just the idea of being able to pray to a badass rock goddess legend, a fierce force of a woman with a former Clonazepam addiction and the most iconic wardrobe, blew my mind. Tattooed, loud, flawed, talented, former-alcoholic, queer AF Michelle Tea prayed to Stevie Knicks.

The more I read of Michelle Tea's memoir, the more I realized that she fully makes up her own rules when it comes to spirituality. She too was a misfit in the spirit world, but she didn't let that stop her from doing all the witchy, meditative, manifest-y rituals her heart desired. Reading *her* punk rock take on the new age gave me permission to re-explore that world—this time on my own terms.

I needed my own goddess to pray to. I didn't even have to think for a minute who *I* would choose to be my higher power: Lana Del Rey. Obviously.

Since the moment I was exposed to Lana Del Rey I've been completely besotted with the reigning Queen of Hollywood Sadness. The thing I love the most about Lana Del Rey is that she's a wild juxtaposition. She wears romantic flower crowns and classic old Hollywood red lipstick, yet has "trust no one" and "die young" tattooed on her perfectly manicured fingers. In her music, she references Sylvia Plath and Walt Whitman *and* Rikers Island and cocaine. Her pussy tastes like soda, not just any soda—Pepsi cola. If pussy and Pepsi isn't a wild juxtaposition I, quite frankly, don't know what is. When I embarked on a spiritual journey, it sort of mirrored what Lana Del Rey embodies: being a woman that doesn't quite fit into a specific box. A rough-around-the-edges klutz tripping over herself, stomping through the hallways and making an insufferable amount of noise as her bangles CLANK CLANK CLANK against one another, seems a little out of context in the spiritual world. But fuck it—I had found my goddess and I was all in.

I began to pray aloud to Lana Del Rey in the shower every single morning. As the hot water hit my naked flesh I would just start talking to her. That's the thing they don't tell you about praying. There is no perfect way to pray. When you're praying to the goddess of your own choosing you can do whatever the fuck you want.

I didn't hold back in prayers. I used my shower as a time to articulate everything I was grateful for, everything that pained my heart, and everything I oh so wished and desired for the future. The beauty was I never planned what I was going to say when I prayed, I just said it. I let the words move through me. Having so much freedom gave me clarity and a deeper connection to myself. How often do we really express ourselves, without worrying about impressing others, or thinking about how smart and selfless we sound? What it is that we really want? How often do we actually *twist* our lips around the unabashed, goddamn truth? I didn't even realize I wanted the things I wanted until I said them aloud to Lana Del Rey, whilst naked and exfoliating in my shitty pre-war uptown shower.

I am not going to tell you that everything I said to Lana Del Rey came true. I'm not here to feed you any woo-woo bullshit, babe. But here's what I *will* tell you: Checking in with myself in the morning and giving myself time to just verbally release everything I was feeling, and allowing myself to explore what exactly what I wanted, made me strut out into the world with a clear, focused intention. Usually, I just had a gnawing feeling of dissatisfaction that I couldn't quite place. I knew I wanted more, but I wasn't sure what that more exactly *was*. Praying to Lana Del Rey in the morning was like having my own private life coach. I imagined her all pouty-lipped and flower-crowned, regal in that badass way only she can pull off, lovingly nodding her head as I worked through my life goals, as I explained how I was feeling versus how I wanted to feel.

In case you are wondering, Lana Del Rey is very different than the wise woman who lives inside of me, Sharon. Sharon is my gut. Sharon is the sensible, reliable creature that shows up when I'm about to really mess something up. I guess you could call her my "higher" self. Lana is more like an ethereal figure. When something beautiful and unexpected happens, I imagine it's Lana granting my wish. When I somehow avoid a head-on collision in a taxi or when the creepy guy following me home somehow decides to change direction, that's Lana looking out, babe. Lana is fantastical. Sharon is practical. I need both of those women in order to stay sane. Lana is my kite; Sharon is my rock. The beauty of making spirituality your own, is that you can create your own executive team of spirit guides all who serve a different purpose in your life.

Before you suggest I lock myself up in a mental institution, allow me to disclaim, honey: I don't actually believe the ghost of (the very much alive) Ms. Del Rey is lounging on a star way up in the sky somewhere, listening to me as I verbally vomit my deepest thoughts and feelings while I scrub my scalp (though it would be extremely lit if she did). The beauty of having an imagination is that you can use your imagination as a coping technique to help you when life gets rough—and honestly, when is life not rough? Unless you're hopped up on way too high of a dose of Paxil, shit's always going to feel a little rough. Life is always going to feel shaky. Even when things are working out perfectly fine. We're all nervously waiting for the other shoe to drop. We're all teetering between feeling like a queen and hating ourselves. One day we're thriving, the next day we're hardly surviving. Life is inconsistent if you're truly living it. That's why it feels comforting to have the ritual of prayer. And so many of us bad girls have cut ourselves off from praying or meditating because we don't like the dogma we've seen surrounding those things. Fuck the dogma! Pray to your idol! It's not about taking it so literally that you expect your idol to be *goddamn listening*. Rather, it's about releasing all that is pent up inside of you to an external energy. The universe. The earth. The air! The gods! Whatever! So long as all of your hopes and dreams and fears aren't stewing inside of you, it doesn't matter who is listening or what the energy you're praying to is. Plus, it's fun to pretend there is an entity greater than you protecting you. And maybe there is. Maybe it's not *Lana*. Maybe it's not a tangible god. Maybe it's something we'll never ever quite understand, but we'll just feel these proverbial wings wrapped around us, holding us, when we feel like life is testing us.

After I started praying to Lana Del Rey, I had finally popped my spiritual cherry and I was ready to dabble in yoga again. After much research, I found a studio in Chelsea, Manhattan that seemed to not take itself too seriously. The founder was a lesbian with spikey short hair, who used to be a notorious party girl and fixture on the downtown nightlife circuit. My class was filled with all kinds of people. Shirtless men in tiny shorts. Rocker babes in skull print leggings. Hippies of all ages. And yes, a few pretty blondes too. The teacher cranked up Nina Simone and Lou Reed during our sun salutations. She instructed us to scream and release all of our anger out at once. The class erupted in the most guttural, raw scream I've ever heard. The room shook. Like my legs in that god-awful class with Gwen ten years prior, but not like that at all.

I kept going back to that class. I ended my narrative that "girls like me don't belong in yoga." And here's what I learned in that beautiful studio: Yoga is for everyone. Meditation is for everyone. You have just as much of a right as the California native with the naturally blonde hair who's never smoked a cigarette or done drugs to be in that goddamn room. It doesn't matter how big or how small you are, it doesn't matter if you're a chain smoker, or an active drug user, it doesn't matter if you're hungover, or if you ate like crap that day. It doesn't matter if your legs shake or if you always fall over during tree pose. It doesn't matter if you don't believe in a higher power or if you secretly fear you haven't been correctly recycling for the past decade. Everyone belongs in yoga. So take up space in that room, babe. Breathe as loud as you want. Wear your rock and roll sweatshirt or your obnoxious bright pink sweatsuit. And if your yoga teacher makes you feel like you're un-evolved scum, tell her to fuck off and find a new one. Because do you know what the word "yoga" means in Sanskrit? It means *union*. And to this little unhinged party girl, the word union means to unite. To bring people together. All kinds of people. Not just people who have memorized the correct way to do sun salutations and look good in skin-tight leggings. Gwen might've been a certified yoga instructor and professor of movement (whatever that means) at a prestigious college of the arts in Southern California, but the bitch clearly didn't understand what yoga was. Because union is about connectedness, not divisiveness.

So, my darling girls, you don't need to be anything other than who you are when dipping your toe into the wellness, new-age, spiritual pond. As the great poet Rumi once said: "There are as many paths to God as there are souls on the Earth." So get creative. If there is one thing us bad bitches are, it's creative. Stretch your imagination and create a god (or goddess or non-binary entity) that perfectly understands you and your ethics. One that will forgive you, support you, and always be in alignment with you as you evolve as a human. One that won't give two shits if you stop believing in them or use their name in vain. One that has a sense of humor. One that fucking loves the shit out of you even when you do stupid things like fart in a guided meditation (It Happened To Me), or vomit on the bar after taking a shot of well vodka, or wake up in bed next to your ex.

Because if you want to get down and dirty with what I really believe, it's this: Your higher power doesn't live in heaven. She lives in *you*. She's the energy inside of you that makes miracles happen. Your higher self is your guide; your high power is the one who makes the magic happen while you're just trying to get through the day. She is a force that lives in your bones so no one can ever snatch her away. No matter where you go or what you do, there you are. And there she is too. You're never really alone. You've got Lana Del Rey with you. Or Stevie Nicks. Or Oprah. Or Megan Rapinoe (who would totally be my higher power if I wasn't so stupidly attracted to her!). Whoever you idolize more than anyone in the world can be your higher power. Because the light we see in our idols, I believe, is really the light we see in ourselves.

CHAPTER 14

PSA: You Deserve to Have a Good Time at the Pool Party

Song: "Everybody But Me" by Lykke Li

This public service announcement is going to be brief but it's extremely, utterly, direly important. But most of all, it's *specific*. This is for the girls who don't want to go to the beach or the pool today because they don't want to be seen in their bikinis.

Let's say you've been invited to a pool party. Your best friend Joanna lives in a bougie town on Long Island and her parents are away for the weekend. Joanna is throwing an epic pool party. All of your friends have decided to hop on the Long Island Rail Road and jet over from the city to the 'burbs for this fantastic party. It's all you've been talking about for weeks and weeks. This party has been the light at the end of the tunnel, your prize for working your ass off this week.

It's been a long, stressful winter. You've been pouring your soul into your career. You had a gut-wrenching breakup with the love of your life. You've been battling the demons of depression, in fact, you just started Prozac last week (it hasn't kicked in yet). The last thing on your mind has been going to *the gym*. The last thing on your mind has been prepping your limbs for bikini season (ick, can we please remove the term "bikini season" from our vocabulary?).

It's the morning of the party and you decide to try on your favorite bikini. It's a beautiful bikini. It's high waisted and bright pink with a bandeau top. You always feel sexier than the fiery pits of hell in this particular bikini. She's never let you down, not once. You stretch her over your body. To your horror, she fits entirely different than ever before! Her bottoms creep so far up your butt cheeks she's reduced to a thong (and you are NOT a thong girl). In the harsh light of your bathroom, she appears to highlight your stretch marks and cellulite. Suddenly you noticed that your stomach is bulging out the sides of your faithful bikini! You take in the sight of yourself and want to cry! You do cry. You break into deep, guttural sobs. The walls close in around you. The room grows smaller and your reflection in the bathroom mirror expands and expands and expands by the second. You rip the bikini off your body and run out of the bathroom feeling claustrophobic in your own flesh. You want to rip your flesh off your body. It's too hot and too thick for your unairconditioned apartment. You run over to your bed and cry softly into your pillow. There is no way you can go to the pool party! There is no way you can pose for pictures on Instagram next to *Joanna*. Joanna is a part-time yoga instructor with visible abs and sinewy arms. And then there is Luisa, your Brazilian friend. She has one those perfectly round asses that is so smooth it looks as if it's been retouched with an airbrushing app. She always shows it off in a thong, understandably so. And then there is Dayna who is so deeply tan and has just giant beautiful breasts, and such perfect hips and such toned legs—everyone is invisible when Dayna is flitting around in a bikini.

You *know* everyone will have their phones out and will be documenting the entire day on their Insta-story. You *know* the girls are going to want to get a group picture of the whole crew clad in bikinis. The thought of having to pose next to these perfect specimens with your pale, fleshy, pockmarked skin makes you want to scream. You'd rather have lunch with your ex-boyfriend and his ultra-wealthy, ultra-pretty new girlfriend than be on camera in your bikini. Plus, that boy Chris, the one who allegedly thinks you're cute, will be there. He won't think you're cute when you shatter his illusion by sporting this skimpy bathing suit, and you really need someone, *someone* in this cruel, cold world to think you're cute right now, OK? 'Cause you feel like shit. Chris thinking you're cute is the only thing that's keeping you together right now. Yes, you're a bad feminist, you know you're a bad feminist. Oh well. Another reason not to go to the pool party. Body-negative bad feminists have no business being at *pool parties*.

So, screw it. You'll stay home. Who cares that it's the most beautiful day of the year? Who cares that you haven't been out of the city in months and the thought of being in the comfort of a suburban McMansion sounds like heaven? Who cares that you've been looking forward to being in a pool—a sparkling, clean, bright blue pool—since Thanksgiving? Who cares that swimming is your favorite way to pass your time, and who cares that all the people you love will be hanging out together, drinking champagne and living their best lives? You don't deserve to do any of these things because you look shitty in your bathing suit. You must punish yourself for your lack of diet discipline and isolate yourself in your tiny, unairconditioned apartment! It will be you and the mice that terrify you (but you don't have the heart to kill). That's where you belong. Melting into nothingness on a beautiful mid-July day with the goddamn rodents.

You grab your phone. You furiously type out the words: "I can't make it. Sorry. I've come down with a sudden case of food poisoning." You're pleased with your lie; no one ever questions a girl who confesses to being in the throes of a diarrhea episode. It's not lady-like. But before you go any further, I suddenly appear in your doorway. I'm wearing an orange one piece. It's not overly bedazzled, it doesn't have a cool tribal print or a sexy cut-out or any of the other extra shit you'd expect a girl like me to rock. Nope, your lesbian big sister looks more like she's ready to swim laps at the YMCA than she looks like she's about to lounge at a glamorous pool party packed with sexy millennials.

"What are you doing here?" you ask, alarmed.

I aggressively grab the phone right out of your hand. "I'm here to tell you to knock it off!" I shout, as I savagely delete your perfectly crafted text message.

You stick out your lower lip in defiance. Your eyes get really shiny, the way they get right before you're about to cry. I sit down at the edge of your bed and look into your eyes so directly I cut through them and see right into your soul.

"Look, I get it. If anyone gets it, it's me," I say, softly now. "But here's the thing. First of all, you look *beautiful*." I watch you grimace. I continue. "But I'm not here to convince you that you're beautiful. This isn't about feeling beautiful. Because guess what? No one feels beautiful all the time. Models don't feel beautiful all the time. And it's exhausting to try and feel beautiful every goddamn day. Do you agree?"

You nod. You *do* agree.

"So, get over feeling like you need to feel like the most beautiful creature on the planet in order to have a good time. The purpose of this pool party isn't to strut around and take pictures in your bathing suit."

"Yes, it is," you say.

"OK, maybe it is for *some* people. But it's not for you. That's too empty of an objective for a girl like you, a girl with substance, brains, and imagination. The real purpose of the party is to enjoy yourself. Have a day in the goddamn sun! You're depressed because you haven't been in the sun since last August, you know. You're lacking in vitamin D—"

You start to chuckle.

I'm not amused. "And by D I don't mean *dick*. I mean *the sun*, asshole. You've been working hard. You deserve to take a dip in the pool, eat some snacks, drink some wine, and chill the fuck out!" I tear into my purse and take out one of those canned sparkling wines that are all the rage these days. I crack it open. I hand it to you.

You grab the sparkling wine out of my hand. You take a small sip. It's not great but you appreciate the gesture. "But I'm going to be around such beautiful girls. I don't think I can handle it."

"First of all, those 'beautiful girls' are likely waging their own wars against their own bodies. It's the first pool day of the season, everyone's feeling a little self-conscious. I hate to say this babe, but no one is going to be looking at you. Everyone is too into their own shit to notice anyone else. Do you obsess over all the minute flaws on other women's bodies?"

"No. Not really. I'm too self-absorbed," you say, sheepishly.

"You and everyone else. And also, let's get over this idea that we need to look perfect to have a good time. You don't. Do you think men are sitting here obsessing about their bodies? No. They aren't. They're thinking about the beer they're going to buy and pondering whether or not to bring a frisbee. Don't you think that the powers at be are trying to keep us women down by forcing us to spend all this TIME LOVING OUR BODIES? Men don't try to LOVE THEIR BODIES. Because trying to LOVE YOUR BODY every single day is as time-consuming and as toxic as hating your body every single day. Men don't waste time loving or hating their bodies. Society has taught them that they are more than a body. So they just throw on a bathing suit and jump into the pool. So get over it, put on your bathing suit, and jump into the goddamn pool. The sun is shining. The birds are chirping. You're young, you're alive, let's have fun bitch!" I say. I'm now standing on the bed aggressively looking over you. My hands are on my hips. I'm a boss.

"I guess you're right," you say. I can tell you're not fully convinced.

"You know who Diana Vreeland is, right?"

"Yes," you lie.

I know you're lying, so I tell you. "She's the former editor-in-chief at *Vogue*. She was fabulous. An icon! A force to be reckoned with. Let me read you one of her quotes." I pull out a notepad and flip until I find the right page. I begin to read the words of the great Vreeland. "You Don't Have to Be Pretty. You don't owe prettiness to anyone. Not to your boyfriend/spouse/partner, not to your co-workers, especially not to random men on the street. You don't owe it to your mother, you don't owe it to your children, you don't owe it to civilization in general. Prettiness is not a rent you pay for occupying a space marked 'female.'" I pause and let the words land on you. I rip out the page where I've scrawled the quote and hand it to you. "Stick this shit on your 'vision board' or whatever, and read it every day," I advise in my bossy, big-sisterly way. (For the record it has recently been exposed that it was not Diana Vreeland who said this quote, but Erin Mckean. Regardless, you get the point.)

"You're right," you say. "I don't have to be pretty or beautiful. I just need to have fun. Fine! I'll go!" You're whining but I can see the light back in your eyes. I gather my things to leave. My work here is done. Right before I go, you stop me. "Hey, Zara," you say.

"Yes, darling?" I answer.

"Why are you wearing such a plain, ugly one-piece?" you ask.

"Because today, I'm meeting some friends at the beach. And I don't want to worry about my string bikini coming undone in the waves. I want to boogie board, dude. I want to enjoy myself. Today isn't about strutting around in a *bikini*. It's about fun," I say winking.

"Huh," you say, taking it all in.

"Oh, and before I go—if you feel self-conscious, take a deep breath and talk to people. You have so much to say. Focus on stimulating your beautiful brain over your beautiful body, OK? We need stimulating conversation more than anything in this clickbait world, you know? You want to add the ambiance? Talk. Share. Listen," I lecture.

"Bye, Zara," you say, queuing me to go. I get the message. Sometimes I can be overkill. I know that. I stomp out of your apartment, ready to show up at the next girl's house who might spend a day locked up indoors because she's having a body meltdown. In fact, my day is so packed I probably won't make it to the beach myself. But that's OK. A lesbian big sister always puts her little sisters first.

CHAPTER 15

It's Okay to Be a Cold Bitch Sometimes

Song: "all the good girls go to hell" by Billie Eilish

Let me start this piece about being a cold bitch by letting you know that I am not, actually, a cold bitch. Most of the time. Most of the time I'm like a Cadbury cream egg. All you have to do is lightly poke my tough shell exterior and you'll find your hand immersed in warm, sticky goo.

However.

I've learned how to conjure up my inner ice bitch when appropriate and she's been a lifesaver to me in my darkest hours. Let's travel back in time, shall we?

It's the first day of my junior year of high school. A few days prior I had moved from Westport, Connecticut to Sarasota, Florida. I'm super pissed at my parents for uprooting me and have taken to chain smoking on our back porch (they pretend not to notice). I'm pining after my summer-camp boyfriend (yes, boyfriend) who lives far, far away on Long Island. He was girl-level pretty and sometimes even wore eyeliner.

And I deeply, deeply miss my friends. I feel as if my heart has been ripped out of my chest because my friends are not by my side. I mean, is there anything in the world more intense than high school friendships? The weight of a high school friendship rivals any love affair you'll ever have as an adult.

Anyway, the vibe is super different at my new Florida school than it was in the North East. All the boys are very early 2000s emo—shaggy short hair with bangs dramatically pushed off to one side (a look that makes teenage boys look like lesbians in their early twenties, which was wildly confusing to me). The girls are emo too; it's all dyed black bobs and baby doll bangs and menthol cigarettes and sad panda eyes.

I show up for my first day of school wearing pin-striped black pants that hang ultra-low on the hip. So low they reveal my new tattoo (an Oscar Wilde quote because I'm a pretentious-as-fuck teen). My backpack is full of Marlboro Lights because that's what Kate Moss smokes and I want to be Kate Moss more than I want to be a successful actress. I think menthols are, like, *trash* (I didn't know yet that all cigs are trash). I'm rocking cat-eye makeup and mega heels. I am East Coast *fancy* compared to these little baby punks. I tower above everyone too (probably 'cause of the heels). As I sheepishly skulk down my new school hallway I am suddenly overcome with the urge to cry. To weep. To sob! I look out the window which, for whatever reason, has steel bars like it's Rikers Island, not school. There are spindly looking palm trees peppered across the lawn. Where are the beautiful, strong, protective oak trees? And where is the crisp promise of fall lurking behind the lazy summer sun? The song "Out of Habit" By Ani DiFranco plays on a loop in my head. She sings about wanting her old friends and her old face and her old mind back and oh fuck this time and place.

Suddenly a girl comes strutting down the hall. She is tall like a model. Taller than I am, and she's in flats. She has diamond studs fastened to her earlobes, and I can tell by the way her lips are fixed into the shape of a spoiled smirk that her diamonds are real.

"Hi," she says breezily.

"Hi," I chirp. I notice a belly button ring creeping out of the bottom of her shirt. *My kind of girl*, I think to myself.

"Are you new?" She raises her (very) arched eyebrow. I noticed a Marlboro Light tucked behind her diamond-clad ear. *Purr.*

"Yeah. It's my first day. I'm from a suburb of New York," I say, which is technically true but insufferably pretentious. Connecticut just doesn't roll off the tongue like New York does, you know?

Her eyes scan my bare stomach. Her hands make their way to her hipbone (early 2000 girls and their razor-sharp hipbones!). One eye radiates seduction, the other aggression. Her left eye bats. I wonder if she's going to kiss me. Her right eye flickers. Or kill me?

She does neither.

"What does your tattoo say?" She studies my stomach like she's a seasoned buyer at a bougie department store and I'm a purse she isn't quite sure is fabulous or tragic.

"'And wilder and wilder grew her song,'" I tell her proudly. "It's from an Oscar Wilde short story—"

"I know who Oscar Wilde is," she snaps.

"Oh, cool."

"But that tattoo is disgusting. Sexual innuendo much? Are *all* the girls sluts in New York?"

Suddenly time slows down. It's my first day at a new school. And I am getting...bullied...by a bitch wearing diamonds. That's *not* how the story was supposed to end.

But like the late Robert Frost, suddenly I have found myself standing in the cross-section of two roads diverged in a yellow wood. Except there is no yellow wood, nor are their roads for that matter. Just a bleak public-school hallway that reeks of socks and Juicy Couture fragrance (mine). I have two choices: I can crumble. Or I can turn...to...ice.

That's when I feel the cold wash over me for the first time. It's not a conscious choice. I just suddenly feel my eyes *glaze* over. I am standing as still as a statue. I stare at the teen bitch with lifeless eyes. My arms fold against the fabric of my stretchy bebe top.

"Yes. We are all sluts," I purr, my icy voice devoid of emotion and expression. Something about my grounded stance and lack of reaction to her blatant provoking seems to rattle her. She shivers. She scurries away like a Manhattan rat crossing First Avenue in the daylight.

I stand there for second feeling really *powerful* for the first time. Instead of crying, instead of shrinking into myself, instead of shouting—I had...gone...cold. I didn't let that bitch get to me.

I was an ice queen.

I suddenly feel in control of my out of control existence. Yes, this Florida bitch could call me a slut. A teacher could humiliate me in front of my entire class. The boys could make fun of me for having small tits and hairy arms. I can't control the wicked, day-to-day nuances of high school. But I can control how I react to them. And based on the stellar results of my first stab at channeling my inner ice queen, I have a hunch that a cold, removed reaction throws bullies off their game.

Bullies aren't used to provoking coldness. They are used to invoking the sounds of screams and squeals, of manifesting tears and hysteria or scaring their victims into silence. They aren't used to *ice*. Ice girls terrify them. Because a girl who feels a gorgeously twisted cold rush of power swish through her body when being insulted is...dangerous. She's capable of *anything*. She'll kiss you then she'll slit your throat with her dagger eyes. Tear down her house and she'll rebuild it into something even more fabulous. In a second. Your efforts in wanting to hurt her are fruitless because she's an ice queen and ice queens don't get hurt.

For the record: A cold reaction is vastly different than *no* reaction. No reaction can read as weak. Looking blankly at the floor as a bevy of insults are being hurled your way shows a bully that you've shut down. And the goal is not to shut down.

The goal is to go *cold*. Cold is *cool*. It's *aloof.*

You heard what they said, yeah. But you're bemused by the idiocy of it all. Think of Kristin Cavallari back in her *Laguna Beach* days. You could tell she knew high school was one big joke that would all be over soon, so the drama didn't affect her. She watched it with detached amusement. It rendered her feared and never fucked with.

It's been over a decade since high school and I still practice the art of the icy bitch any time I feel intimidated or sense someone is trying to belittle me. It's been my faultless armor I can throw over my scantily clad body anytime I need. It has majorly helped to quell my anxiety because I know that no matter what happens, the cold girl I keep stored inside of my purse will take care of it. It's like you have a powerful, aloof, cool friend with you all the time, the kind of friend that you feel safe around because no one crosses her.

And truthfully, I don't have to channel the ice queen very often. Luckily, I've built a life that contains mostly nice people I can be giggly and mopey and vulnerable around. But when that greasy-faced fuckboy condescends me in the boardroom at work and I stare at him and fold my arms and slowly, smoothly clap back at him in front of everyone—I can almost see his dick *shrinking* inside of his pants (coldness shrinks balls). When confronted with a mean girl or an asshole director or boss, the ice bitch has my back. And once I unleash her on a specific person, I don't usually have to let her back out again with them.

No one fucks with an ice queen twice.

Now, I know that *like*, all these well-meaning women's publications are going to tell you to tell everyone HOW YOU FEEL and to honestly express anytime someone has HURT YOUR FEELINGS (WAH) but I'm going to tell you that I think that's bullshit. *And* sexist (most of those pubs are run by men). Like *why* are women always obligated to be OPEN WITH THEIR EMOTIONS? Do men in the workplace tell other men when their feelings have been crushed by a snide comment? No. They don't.

And we don't have to either.

In fact, the older I get the more I realize that our deep feelings shouldn't be revealed to everyone and anyone. I wish we lived in a world where it was safe to shout your emotions from the rooftop, but we don't. Your feelings should be reserved for kind creatures who deserve your sacred vulnerability. When people are cutting or sly or dickish to you, go cold.

They don't deserve your warmth.

CHAPTER 16

PSA: BOTTOMLESS MIMOSAS ARE TAKING YOU DOWN

Song: "You Know I'm No Good" by Amy Winehouse

This particular weekend warning is going to be short but not-so-sweet. In fact, I'm cutting the sweetness out of your weekend right now, little sister. For you are strictly forbidden to indulge in a sugary, grossly sweet mimosa no matter what. Your lesbian big sister is sick and tired of seeing all of you get dragged down into the ground by the devil that is shitty orange juice mixed with cheap as shit champagne.

Look, I fully understand the temptation. We all love to be super "hangover chic" on a Sunday as we strut into a trendy (but mediocre) West Village restaurant, adorned in expensive distressed clothing with comically large sunglasses strapped to our exhausted little faces. And there is a very specific chill that makes its way down the spine when we FLIP open the menu and see the following words, in gorgeously swirly-whirly colorful font: BOTTOMLESS MIMOSAS ONLY $20!

"Oh my god!" Becky will squeal. "We would be stupid to NOT get the bottomless mimosas." Becky is your best friend, by the way.

"I know!" you'll squeal back at good ol' Becks. I mean, one cocktail is eighteen fucking dollars, and even though you don't care much for mimosas—Becky's got a point, right? You would be an imbecile not to jump on this precious opportunity. You're a young woman just trying to survive in the goddamn city of broken dreams! You need to save your pennies and a deal is a deal, amirite?

You and Becky's eyes will light up like a thousand twinkling Christmas lights the moment that golden-hued pitcher of mixed mimosa liquid is plopped onto your table by your inevitably bitchy twenty-year-old waitress. (It's not our fault she didn't get cast in the shitty, low-budget horror movie she auditioned for last week!)

The sugar-fructose-chemical rush of the artificially enhanced orange juice will make its way down your body as soon as you take that first tiny sip. Your stomach will lurch from the syrupy nastiness you've just ingested. Your eyes will water. You'll want to belch!

"This is good!" you'll lie, because you want to be festive, because no one likes a negative Nancy in the modern-day church that is Sunday brunch. Especially Becky.

In reality, you'll know deep down inside the beautiful crux of your heart that you're drinking toxic, fake orange juice and cheap gas station "champagne." But you'll keep that fact to yourself and chug your mimosa like you're going to the electric chair! After all, we don't order bottomless mimosas because they taste good. We order them with the noble intention of getting buzzed on a budget, baby!

And because the restaurant has promised to give you unlimited mimosas until 6:00 PM, you and Becks will really feel like you need to take advantage of this rare privilege. "We'll take another round!" you'll slur to the apathetic waitress, who will roll her eyes and take twenty-five minutes to grab a pre-made pitcher. She'll set it on your table as if it weighs ten thousand pounds. She will act as if you've barged into her living room and DEMANDED she serves you right then and there.

Her rudeness will only make you want to drink more, to make up for the crappy service you swear you'll Yelp about but never will.

The rest of lunch will be blurry. You'll probably end up on the Lower East Side at a nasty college kid bar tossing back Jägermeister shots with kids in their late teens, popping the cherries of their fake IDs that they bought on St. Marks place a few hours prior.

Whether you end up going home and passing out in your mascara and foundation on the couch in your living room, or turning up all night long—one thing is absolutely certain.

YOU WILL FEEL LIKE SHIT THE NEXT DAY.

In fact, "shit" is the understatement of the year! You'll feel like death, a giant crap on a steaming hot city sidewalk, a piano tossed out the window of a skyscraper, a bug smooshed on the pavement by a careless stiletto-wearing Upper East Side debutante on her way to a Republican fundraiser at the Trump Tower.

Cheap champagne that's teeming with sulfates and additives and fish bladder (I'm not kidding) mixed with that concentrated fructose will kill you. There is nothing more harrowing than a cheap mimosa hangover. Your limbs will be trembling from the surplus of sugar. Your entire body will be inflamed from all the nasty additives. Your stomach will be BURNING LIKE THE INFERNO from all that citric acid. You'll want to vomit everywhere thanks to the gas station-made champagne. Your fingers will be so swollen from the salt and toxins you consumed the night before, you won't be able to squeeze your ring off your poor bloated pinkie. This will send you spiraling into a black anxiety hole. There are few things darker than trying to pry a too-tight ring off your finger—with an apocalyptic hangover, no less.

I don't want you to start the workweek with a mimosa hangover. I want more for you. For us. For womenkind.

If you haven't been living under a radically repressed rock you know that there is a national attack on women's bodies right now. We need to be in our most prime form in order to fight this god-awful patriarchy into the dirt.

Personally, I think mimosas were created by straight men as a way to keep women and gay men down! Mimosas have historically been marketed toward us women and gays. When have you ever seen a Wallstreet dude drink a mimosa? It's the patriarchy, obviously.

So when you're sitting pretty at BRUNCH with BECKY and the GAYZ and you're tempted to get a bottomless pitcher of fructose and fish bladder, I want you to imagine me as your bartender. I'm rocking a low-cut black tee-shirt and you're surprised at how ~ample~ my cleavage looks. I tell you it's because I'm wearing a new ThirdLove bra, and you should really check those bras out because they make your tits look fire. You blush because you're embarrassed that I noticed that you noticed my bulging rack. I wink at you and lovingly pat you on the arm. Right as you're about to go all cheapo on yourself and order the mimosa special, you look deeply into my big sisterly eyes. They're hazel, and are putting you in a trance. A trance that repeats, "Take care of your body. Get a tequila soda and chase it with a large water, OK? You're too old for bottomless mimosas."

A rare, special, powerful but silent energy is exchanged between us. You take a breath. You are grounded in your truth and your posture is perfect. "I'll have a Patrón and soda water with a bunch of fresh lemons, please," you'll purr, your voice sounding as smooth as a Celine Dion song.

I'll smile.

"Bottomless mimosas are offensive because I'm a bottom," I'll say, giving you way too much information about my sex life. You'll be confused and feel shy at my oversharing, but you'll nod your head, because let's be real: You're a bottom too.

CHAPTER 17

Confessions of a Reckless Spender

Song: "Upper West Side" by King Princess

D o you know that famous Oscar Wilde quote, "Anyone who lives within their means suffers from a lack of imagination"? The first time I ever heard that quote I was a spindly little teenager lusting after a Chanel bag more than I lusted after Angelina Jolie and it *instantly* resonated with me. I immediately went to my mother, who also loves big, shiny, glamorous things, and dutifully recited her the quote.

"Damn right, darling," my mother said, her reading glasses sitting at the tip of her very regal British nose. She was tearing through the latest issue of *Vogue*, her favorite pastime. My mother inhaled fashion magazines the way chain smokers inhale nicotine and tar. She read them with a religious fervor, cover to cover, absorbing every wildly expensive trend and grandiose jet-set holiday destination, until they were ingrained right into the crux of her soul. In fact, if you were to peer inside my mother's soul, I'm certain it would be dressed up in a fabulous Jean Paul Gaultier gown, dripping in Chanel costume jewelry with a giant Gucci bamboo handle bag hanging from its Riviera tanned shoulder.

I am my mother's daughter in the very best of ways and in the very worst of ways. I inherited her extreme empathy. She has the ability to feel other people's pain, the ability to emotionally put herself in situations she's never experienced, just like *moi*. I inherited her fluttery-lashed charm, her natural knack for getting whatever the hell she wants effortlessly. I'm unexpectedly tough like her, I'm madly adventurous like her, and the foundation of both of our lives is one-hundred-percent love. I'm proud to be the daughter of the one and only Lynn Barrie.

However, like my darling mummy, I've completely inherited an unhealthy belief that life is just *better* when wrapped in 14-karat gold foil. In fact, I might even be worse than her, if that's even possible. I'll never forget lounging with her one day at a fabulous beach club in the south of France when I was about fifteen. I was sipping on champagne in a rip-off Moschino bikini staring at the European Jet Set dripping in their designer garb the way an art lover would stare at a Picasso painting. "You better make a lot of money, girl," my mother said, her voice a few octaves lower than usual. "I like luxury, but you, my darling, you LOVE luxury."

Throughout my twenties, I was rarely met with big paychecks. I worked my ass off and for the most part, loved my jobs, and always loved my coworkers (even when I had demeaning gigs like pouring shots down throats of businessmen at skeezy, lower east side night-clubs) but I was no young entrepreneur selling my ideas to venture capitalists for millions of dollars. I never worked a day in my life in *finance* or *tech* or whatever other careers young people actually make a substantial amount of money from. I always went for the jobs that gave me the freedom to pursue what I was passionate about, which has always been acting and writing. I've never felt pulled to do anything else with my life except perform and write. (I still don't!) So even though I love expensive things so much I would have sex with them if I could, I'm not motivated by money. (Which is an unfortunate combination.)

When it comes to my career, I'm the most motivated by attaining creative freedom. I worked as a shot girl on the lower east side of Manhattan, where I would pour shots of "Sex on the Beach" down the throats of businessmen for ten dollars a pop. Not a job I loved, but it gave me the gorgeous freedom to audition and write during the day. When I got burned out from the nightly onslaught of sexual harassment, I became a promo girl who handed out free samples of frozen yogurt on the streets of New York during the day. I did that gig merely because it was fun, I could make my own schedule, and it was just enough to pay the bills. I worked the night shift as a receptionist of a film school in North Hollywood, California because once the bosses went home to their wives and kids, I was free to use their printers and staplers to fasten my headshot and résumé together. I worked as a makeup artist behind the cosmetics counter at a famous London department store because I happened to be strangely good at it and I loved the creativity of painting people's faces. I ran a youth outreach theatre group in Florida that paid me under thirty thousand dollars a year because I absolutely loved writing and directing plays with teenagers with every fiber of my being. I wrote for a ton of online and print publications and took on jobs as a staff writer—not because they made me a lot of money (hell no they did *not*) but because writing is the air that I breathe and I was just so ecstatic to be able to do it all day long, even if it meant hardly being able to cover my portion of the rent. I've always chosen my happiness over making money.

It's a very noble thing for one to choose one's happiness over making money—it really is. But in my case, I can't pat myself on the back for putting my passions in front of my finances. Because despite my minimal income, I've always lived (in the words of my mother) "like the Queen of bloody Sheba." Every time I would receive a paycheck, say for two thousand dollars, I would feel the rush of wealth blow over my bones. Literally, the moment the money hit my bank account, I felt like I was suddenly an heiress to a Greek shipping fortune. A rich Manhattan woman who strolls along 5th

Avenue in fur and pearls. I would rush to my laptop and log on to Revolve.com like if I didn't log on right then and there, I would lose the opportunity to buy the perfect dress, the one dress that would drastically improve my wayward life. After all, happiness is always just *one purchase away*, isn't it? My blood pressure would rise to epic proportions, my heart would beat hard and fast as if I'd just done a bump of coke, my pupils would dilate as if I was tripping on acid—all while my eyes scanned a laptop screen bedazzled in beautiful dresses. An ankle-grazing boho maxi dress the color of *sunshine* that seemed to be a key to the chic Mediterranean life I prayed would one day be mine, a black lusty silk slip dress that embodied the feeling of sex itself (perfect for a date), a virgin-white prairie dress with a dramatic Peter Pan collar that promised to erase my sinful past with her village-like innocence (also perfect for a date) all seductively stared at me. I was practically rolling, I was so lit up!

"Ok Zara, you get to choose ONE!" Sharon would coach me, standing behind me, her hot breath hitting my bare neck. But I was under the influence of a spending high, and even Sharon can't get through to me when I'm intoxicated by bags and shoes and clicks and discounts and pretty garments modeled by even prettier models! Sharon would look at me—a girl with her jaw clenched shut, eyes bright red and blinkless, hovered over the computer screen—shoving things into a digital shopping cart in a feverish panic, and she would realize I was a lost cause. She'd light a cigarette, roll her eyes, and get the hell out of there. Leave me to self-destruct in peace.

That's not to say I wouldn't try to "edit" my cart. But the clothing would start talking to me! That sunshine-colored maxi dress would suddenly fly out of the computer screen and tap me on the shoulder. "Zara, you need me in your life! Imagine me cloaked over your pale body, brightening up your sallow skin, as you lounge beneath a palm tree in paradise, sipping on a skinny margarita. I'm your ticket to paradise. If you buy me you'll finally manifest that holiday to the Greek Isles you've been dreaming about forever." *Ok, you're definitely in.* But then the virgin white prairie dress would hand me a basket of the most voluptuous strawberries to ever exist and tell me that I would find love in that dress, that her primness would convince someone really nice that I was girlfriend material, not just some used-up sex columnist in distressed black leather. And then the black dress would purr: "You need me too! When you get that girlfriend you're going to need to wear something sophisticated and sexy on your third date." And then the two dresses would tag team me! "You need ME to score the girl. To fool her into thinking you're as pure as freshly fallen snow. But—" Prairie Dress would say pointing to Sexy Black Slip Dress, "Once you're locked in, you need her to seduce her. To tease her. To yield your sexual power!" Sexy Black Slip Dress would pout and wink at me. The next thing I knew my heart would be pounding out of my chest, literally pounding so loudly I was afraid it would disturb the neighbors, as I filled out my credit card information, sweat pouring down my back. If you've ever done ecstasy you know about "peaking." Peaking is when all the serotonin seems to rush out of your brain at once and suddenly you're in pure high-energy bliss. It's like the moment the orgasm really erupts out of you. That's what would happen right as my fingers hovered over the "confirm this purchase" button. I would confirm, and BAM. It was an orgasm of the body and brain and *heart*.

If you've ever done ecstasy, you also understand that there is a dark comedown that occurs right after the peak. There's a crash. After all, what goes up must come down, my dear. It's a law of gravity. So right after I flew high up in the proverbial sky, and made love to the material gods that live on a giant Versace cloud, I would crash into the ground. Hard. Guilt and shame would slither up next to me like a creepy dude at a bar. "How could you do that? You have to pay your rent in two weeks! FEEL BAD ABOUT YOURSELF, FEEL BAD ABOUT YOURSELF, FEEL BAD ABOUT YOURSELF," Guilt, that useless fuck of a feeling would scream into my ear. "You have no self-control. You're an embarrassment of a human being. You think happiness is just one dress away? How materialistic and vile of a girl *you are*. You say you care about the world? You don't care about the world. You just care about dresses. You're a delusional, materialistic, piece of shit! You have no power over your impulses. Might as well give up trying," Shame, the great demotivator of ever trying to better yourself, would taunt me, in a powerful whisper that reminded me of Meryl Streep's character in *The Devil Wears Prada*. Prada. Prada. Wait, what was I saying?

Guilt and shame are different than anger. When I'm angry with myself, I feel inspired to do better. I feel motivated to make a great change in my life. Guilt and shame make me believe that I'm a hopeless, doomed cause who might as well give up. For so many years I was ashamed and guilty over my excessive drinking and those negative emotions convinced me I was powerless over my partying. I felt too shitty about myself to try and put an end to it all. My lack of control over my shopping was exactly the same as I felt about my substance use.

So what was the result? A constant broke life. Which is fine in your early twenties because all of your friends are broke too (except for those few trust-funders, damn them!). It's expected and slightly cute to blow your paycheck on a night out in your twenties. My whole crew seemed to be under the false impression that they were the next in line to inherit the Walton family fortune on payday—buying rounds of champagne for strangers, purchasing the designer bag that surely would help them move up the social totem pole in the city. But somewhere between the ages of twenty-five to thirty everyone seemed to get their financial shit together. Suddenly my friends had credit cards that they paid off. On time. They had enough money saved up to go on five-day vacation once a year. They didn't seem wracked with fear that their credit card would decline when buying a box of tampons from the bodega on the corner of 92nd and Lexington.

Except for me.

I was still completely stunted when it came to the grown-up art of managing my finances. And despite having a good job as an editor for a popular lesbian magazine, I was broke as a goddamn joke. By no one's fault but my own (purr). I was still stuck in the cycle of excessive payday spending. Of irrationally thinking, "Oh, well I can buy this because a GREAT fortune shall be heading my way soon! Soon as I sell this book. Soon as I sell this screenplay. Soon as I sell this idea. Soon as I sell—".

And then rent would be due. If you live in New York City you understand that rent is usually at *least* an entire paycheck. This city is an outrageously expensive place to live, even if you're well off. (I know people who make a million dollars a year and have no savings—but that's for a different day). One paycheck would go to my rent, leaving me with pennies to survive the next week in New York, and the next paycheck would be blown on clothes and five-star dinners at five-star restaurants that made me feel like I, too, could live a five-star life if I just kept going to the five-star places. It's a vicious cycle that sweeps up lots of girls like me.

I didn't tell my friends, ever, that I was broke. That I was seesawing between a couple of grand and an overdrawn bank account. I didn't tell them because I was deeply embarrassed. Because being broke at thirty is shameful. Especially when your friends see you as someone successful, and because I had a fancy job title and was thus invited to lots of fancy events, my friends saw me as a successful woman. I gripped on to that image, because I didn't feel like one. Plus, my dire money situation was 100 percent *my* fault. I wanted to keep up appearances. I didn't want them to know that I prayed to Lana Del Rey every single time I swiped my credit card, and when the word "approved" would pop up on the little screen I would feel a massive sense of accomplishment. Talk about setting the bar low! My credit card merely being approved was such a rare event that it provided me with a temporary sense of *achievement*. Which would of course later come with a giant sting of humiliation because the pathetic-ness of my situation was not lost on me. That's dark, kids.

I came up with excuse after excuse as to why I couldn't go on trips to The Hamptons with friends. "I have to work!" being the main one, but the truth was usually that I didn't have enough money in my bank account to even cover the gas, let alone room and board and dinners at Nick & Tony's.

The only person who knew the truly dark truth about my financial situation was my darling friend Eduardo. Eduardo is my favorite person on the planet but he's also delusional about money and has a strange sense of luxurious entitlement despite, like me, having no parental help or trust fund or lucrative job. Eduardo is a Mexican immigrant who came to America at thirteen years old. Despite coming from humble beginnings and not having a mother who handed him down copies of *Vogue* magazine, Eduardo is just as bad as me. His mother might not have drugged him with delusions of grandeur, but gay boys are powerful creatures that often transcend their upbringing. He found those damn fashion magazines on his own. He drugged himself with delusions of grandeur! And for years we were each other's reckless spending enablers.

"Pull over," Eduardo would roar to me on a Friday afternoon right before we were about to attend happy hour at the Ritz-Carlton Hotel because we couldn't go where normal twenty-six-year-olds would go, we had to go to the fucking Ritz. "I'm taking out a small business loan."

I would smile in solidarity and tear into the driveway of Wells Fargo. "Me too!" I would cheer.

Let me explain what a small business loan is, in the very specific language of Zara and Eduardo. It means going to the ATM machine and consciously overdrafting your account. It means overdrafting your account to the max it will let you overdraft (for us it was five hundred dollars) and living off cold-cash until your next paycheck. It's not entirely stupid, because if you were to just get overdraft fees by using your credit card, you would get that pesky thirty-two-dollar fee each time. By over drafting the max amount in one delicate swoop, you only get ONE thirty-two-dollar fee, babe. This is the logic of a raging spendaholic. Not very different than the logic of a raging alcoholic.

We were lucky, Eduardo and I, because for a good few years there, we were paid on *opposite* weeks. Both of us were paid bi-monthly, but the Friday I got paid he wouldn't be paid. He would get paid the following Friday. Meaning if he was out of money the Friday I got paid, I would cover him for the entire week. And then when I was inevitably broke by the end of the week, I didn't have to panic. Because Daddy Eduardo was always there to cover me!

Over dinner and drinks, we would lament about how stressed out we were about money. It was a constant source of anxiety, never allowing us to be fully present in our lives. Our money woes were always there in the background, reminding us that rent was due next week and that if we didn't pay it we would be evicted. When you're living on the financial edge you're never really relaxed. You're always worried that you're going to embarrass yourself by not having enough money in your account (even with your small business loan) to cover your half of the bill. But instead of carving out a plan to crawl out of the hole, we took out a shovel and dug ourselves in deeper. We ordered *more* wine. We ordered *another* cheese plate. All you need is one partner in crime in order to prevent yourself from evolving.

It was strange because in almost every other aspect of my life I was evolving. I was taking my health seriously. I was showing up for myself at work. I was giving all of me to the young people I worked with. I was becoming the friend I'd always wanted. In the words of the great Diane Von Furstenberg, I was starting to figure out "the woman I wanted to become." The more I became that woman, the harder and harder it was to ignore the glaring fact that my dysfunctional relationship with money was still stunted.

I think when you've never really made much money—when you haven't had many jobs with 401ks and benefits, you can get into what I like to call the "Last Supper" mentality when it comes to your spending habits. You spend half of the month so completely broke, paying for cigarettes with pennies, that when you do get a lump of money (even if to most people's standards it's a small lump) you *really* want to indulge. Who knows when you'll have money again? And after two weeks of not even being able to afford even the smelly, nasty subway, you just want to party. You want to enjoy life. You know the money will inevitably go away so you rip the Band-Aid off and blow it on a lavish last supper that puts the bible to shame. Whereas normal people get their paychecks and spend a tiny bit each day. They don't diminish it in one sitting. They never have to worry about not having enough money for a box of tampons, because they've never allowed their bank account to get that low. They check their balances daily. Reckless spenders like me, avoid checking our bank accounts as much as I avoid going to the gynecologist. And if you break down the root of my debilitating fear of the gyno, it's because I'm convinced I'll be informed that I have ovarian cancer and that's just too dark of a reality for me to digest. If I look at my bank account and see that it's in the red, it will send me spiraling into the ugly vortex of fear and anxiety, another reality too dark for me to digest.

So I avoid it. Or at least I *used* to avoid it. "People who don't look at their bank accounts are afraid of reality," Alexia, my editor, once told me. She wasn't referring directly to me—it was a general statement that slipped out of her lips during a brainstorming session. I nodded solemnly. I knew that life-truth all too well. If I were to gaze down the barrel of my bank account, it would expose the realest shit about my life. Not just my lack of control when it comes to buying dresses from Revolve. It would expose my blatant cowardice. It would reveal my lack of respect toward my own finances—which translates to a lack of respect for myself. It would show that I am looking for quick fixes to solve my unhappiness—cocktails, dinners, hair appointments. It would show my disgusting laziness. Do you know how much money I spend on sheer convenience? One month I spent eight hundred dollars on *ubers* and could hardly pay my rent. And my deepest fear of all fears is that I am lazy. I was a shitty student at school, you see. I forever think I'm a lazy piece of shit who wants to neglect her homework and hang out and smoke pot with loser boys with lip rings instead of bettering myself or preparing for the future.

I've never loved reality. Just like I was told I was "away with the fairies" as a child, I think as an adult I still tend to get lost in the glitter. The real world has never appealed to me. Adulting has always been a struggle for me. And nothing is more real and more adult than *money*. When I would buy something new and pretty it distracted me from the bleakness of real life. The mundane day-to-day grind of adulthood that depressed me so.

Have you ever dated a healthy person when you're a person still in the process of getting healthy? I know I have! When I was twenty-seven I briefly began to date a woman named Lisa. Lisa really had her shit together. And dating Lisa held up a mirror to how self-destructive my relationship with many things, money included, actually was. Look, you can fool your friends into thinking your credit card "declined" for some mysterious reason. You can fool your coworkers into thinking you've totally got your financial shit together. But you cannot fool the person you're dating. At least not for long. Eventually, they'll catch on to the fact that you are raring toward thirty with no savings account, that you're still living paycheck to paycheck despite the fact that you've been gainfully employed for over a decade. And if they're normal human beings who don't fear the harrowing realities of money, your lackluster approach to planning for your financial future is going to be a great, shiny red flag waving in the distance, telling them to get out of these dangerous waters and steer their boats in the opposite direction.

It's so funny how we always discuss red flags that we see in other people without even noticing that we, ourselves, are holding the biggest red flag the red flag store carries. Being a reckless spender is not cute, no matter how pretty or charismatic you are. It's a red flag. No one who is sane wants to get into a relationship with someone who has shitty credit or is perpetually broke. And if you want to date someone who is sane you have to start engaging in sane habits. Like sane *spending* habits.

Needless to say, Lisa and I didn't work out. I pushed her away because I couldn't handle how together she was; it really drove home how *not* together I was. She pushed me out of my fantasy and into reality, and I wasn't ready for that. Have you ever pushed away a good thing because you didn't feel you were good enough for it? You were too ashamed of your bad behavior and you knew they wouldn't enable your bad behavior so you retreated back into your comfort zone of private self-destruction? It's hard to have relationships when you're self-destructive. You don't want to get too close to anyone stable and sweet because they'll notice how screwed up you are, and try and encourage you to better yourself. And sometimes you just aren't ready to better yourself.

But eventually, I got lonely living in my own pool of money shame. Even Eduardo was getting his shit together. Plus, we lived in different cities now. It was less fun taking out a "small business loan" without my effervescent best friend sitting in the passenger seat of my car, giggling as I consciously removed four hundred dollars from the ATM machine. Plus, no one loves a holiday like yours truly! I was sick of wasting all my money on taxis and dresses, things that were really proving to not fulfill their promises of a better life. I knew I had to get it together. I had kicked everything else.

So, what did I do? I began to look at my bank account. Granted, I still can only look at it on my phone because it's too large and too jarring on my giant laptop screen. Then I went to Wells Fargo, sat shivering like an addict in a methadone clinic in the little plastic chairs until I could speak to a financial advisor.

"I need overdraft protection," I mumbled with a shaky voice. *WHAT ARE YOU DOING?* The dresses from Revolve screamed into my brain. *WE WON'T BE ABLE TO HANG OUT ANYMORE.* I took a deep breath and did my best to ignore those gorgeous garments.

"You're sure?" the financial advisor asked me. Banks love when you overdraw—they make millions of dollars off those thirty-two-dollar overdraft fees.

"I'm sure," I said, totally not sure at all. But if there's anything I've learned it's this: You always know the right thing to do. And the right thing to do isn't always what you *want* to do.

It's been nine months since I've overdrawn my bank account. At thirty-one years old, that's a record for me. Has it been hard? Fuck yes, it's been hard. More than any other demon, money is the one that still haunts me. I still love luxury as much I've ever loved luxury. I still love pretty dresses. And designer bags. And fabulous shoes. And market-priced meals at trendy-wendy eateries. And I don't want to change that about myself. I'm not ashamed of having expensive taste. In fact, I *like* that about myself. I just don't want to those things to steer the ship of my life anymore. I don't want to believe that personal fulfilment is just one maxi dress away. Because it's not. Personal fulfilment lives in gratitude. It never comes from a place of "lack." It comes from a place of appreciating what you already have. And since trying to get my spending shit together that's what I do when I'm fueled with the manic desire to say "FUCK THIS!" and online shop my money away. I take a deep breath. I take out a goddamn journal like I'm some sort lifestyle guru! I write out all of the things I'm grateful for, longhand with a bright pink pen to keep it interesting. I don't put pressure on myself to make this list particularly profound or spiritual. I write what comes to mind: My dog Luka. My cat Wild. My new weighted blanket. The time I got to spend with my oldest friends Owen and Ruba. The two thousand words I wrote this morning. The hot pink sunset last night. My manicure that hasn't chipped. When I take a moment and just point out what it is that I'm grateful for, I am no longer feigning for MORE. Because when I look around, I have a lot. I've always had a lot. Sometimes I just lose sight of it because the pretty shiny things are so shiny, and I have ADHD, so anything shiny distracts me from the beauty of my life.

Spending for me is yet another form of numbing. Because it doesn't crush my spirit and render me sick like booze and drugs, because there is a pretty little package delivered right to my door in lieu of a nasty hangover, it took me a long time to realize that. When you're wearing a new sparkly piece of jewelry, people think you're doing well. When you're stumbling the streets drunk, people do not. So I bought into my own lie when it came to my idea that reckless spending was any different than any other form of self-medicating. You're not thinking of your traumas, your failures, your heartbreak, or your fears when you're purchasing something new. But just like popping a pill, the high you feel is not real. It wears off, like all highs, and leaves you feeling more vulnerable and helpless than ever.

So are things a bit better for me in the ol' money department? Yes. I no longer overdraw my bank account, and that's progress, right? I even had enough money to go to Seattle for my childhood friend Nick's wedding (ironically with Eduardo! The kids are growing up! *Finally.*). Do I have enough savings to do real grown-up things, like buying a house or rearing a child? No, I do not. I'm still a work in progress. I still catch myself being frivolous as hell. I still keep taking the jobs I love over the ones that will give me the extravagant lifestyle I long for as I flip through the latest *Vogue*. Only now I have an end goal with my career. Now I feel motivated to keep doing what I love, and little by little I'm building a brand and a business that I want to be lucrative. I do—for the first time—believe I have the potential to make money. I think the path I've chosen might take a bit longer. Especially with all of the slip-ups I've made along the way. But that's OK. I'm a late bloomer. Big fucking deal.

The reason I share this with you, as I'm still actively struggling, is because I think it's important that women talk openly about their issues while they're still working through them. No one is perfect. Even lifestyle gurus (which I am clearly NOT) have shit swirling through their brains that's still complicated for them. There seems to be this idea that women are only allowed to write about things *after* the fact. They discuss their addictions after they've recovered from their addictions. They discuss their food issues after they've figured out a way to have a healthy relationship with their body. They discuss how they manage their money once they've figured out how to, indeed, manage their money. I think that's great. Most of the stuff I discuss in this book *is* stuff that I've worked through. But I still think it's interesting for all of us to share the train wrecks that are happening in our lives, right as they're crashing. I know I feel less alone in the world when a woman confesses to be thick in the struggle. And if there is anything I want for any of you reading this, it's just that. To feel a little less alone in the struggle. So, there you have it. My name is Zara Barrie and every single day I mess up financially, even though I'm actively trying to get better. Getting better is a long process. And even just writing this chapter, not feeling the need to pretend I know what the fuck I'm talking about, is helping me sort through my money issues. And maybe it will help you too, little sister.

CHAPTER 18

The Great Toxic Relationship Cleanse

Song: "Good as Hell" by Lizzo

I used to be *obsessed* with the idea of "detoxing." Every other week I forced myself to go on a new, trendy (demoralizing and horrible tasting) cleanse. Celery juice sixteen times a day, *no* chewable food! Two gallons of liquid kale followed by a shot of turmeric, raw honey, ginger, and cayenne pepper! An all-vegan cleanse! A plant-based vegan cleanse! A ketogenic cleanse! The *master* cleanse! The latest GOOP-approved cleanse!

"Why on earth are you doing this?!" My best friend Owen would ask me, his eyes filled with disgust at the sight of the charcoal water I'd be gagging down. "That looks miserable." I'd stare longingly at the voluptuous sushi roll he was eating. Oh, how the white rice shimmered beneath the fluorescent lights! How had I not noticed the poetic glitter that exists in a lump of white rice? (Detoxing makes you want to write love songs about food.)

"I need to detox," I would nastily bark back, baring my teeth like a dog protecting a new bone. (Detoxing turns you into a raging bitch.)

"Suit yourself."

"I'm just taking care of my temple, my *body*," I would primly say, smoothing down the flyaway hairs resting at the crown of my frizzy head. (Detoxing makes you insufferable to be around.) Was my obsession with detoxing a pretty way to mask an eating disorder? *Um*. Definitely. I didn't come of age in the body positivity movement, like some of you young kittens probably did. I grew up on my hands and knees worshipping at the altar of hipless, vacant-eyed Kate Moss. I had photographs of her in her underwear taped to the family fridge as a way to discourage all of us from eating. Of course, I had a distorted body image. Of course, I was always on the lookout for weight-loss shortcuts disguised as health kicks. *Of course.*

But there was more to the story. Specifically, with detoxes. Detoxes are a different story than the classic "starve yourself into skinny" or "extreme diet yourself into skinny" tale. They're about cleansing your body of *toxins*, babe. And one only feels compelled to cleanse one's body of toxins if one believes they're consuming so much toxic shit they need to flush their entire bloodstream of it. And don't get me wrong, food can, and often is, toxic shit. All those fillers we can't pronounce that live in the processed foods we consume will wreak havoc on our bodies. But I've never been a processed food kind of girl. I mean, when drunk I might inhale six slices of New York City pizza, or eat an entire pint of ice cream, but I'm not one to eat boxed or canned or fast food. Most girls who obsessively detox have relatively clean diets to begin with. We might drink too much, but if you're drawn to the art of the extreme cleanse you're usually pretty conscious of what you pop into your mouth in your day-to-day life. Look at Gwyneth Paltrow. She loves her annual "elimination diets," and she's so healthy the whites of her eyes are so white they probably voted for Donald Trump.

Based on personal experience, I find that most of us who fixate on the latest and greatest detoxing cleanse out there are subconsciously trying to rid our bodies of toxins—but not *just* the kind that exists in food. The kind that are even harder to kick than sugar, booze, and carbs: toxic people. And until we cleanse ourselves of toxic people, our efforts at cleansing ourselves of anything else are fruitless. For we'll always feel tired, drained, depressed, depleted, sick to our stomachs, and anxiety-ridden when we're shackled to any type of toxic relationship. And I'm not just talking about toxic romantic relationships (though those are particularly nasty). We've already covered that. I'm talking about friends. Family members. Bosses. Coworkers.

I didn't even realize how toxic so many of my relationships were until I did some deep soul-searching with a licensed professional. In therapy you begin to recognize patterns. And I began to notice that my lifelong obsession with health wasn't exactly normal. That I was always expecting these dramatic, life-changing results from my latest dabble in the "plant-based/keto/liquid kale lifestyle" or whatnot and was never satisfied. I was in a constant state of extreme anxiety—but was completely unaware of the source of my anxiety. And anxiety, when ignored, often manifests itself physically. For me, it's all in the gut, babe. I had tremendous stomach aches every day for years. There were incessant knots in my stomach, knots that were so tied up I didn't even know where to start. I was either writhing around, feeling like a war was taking place in my lower abdomen, or bent over the toilet dry-heaving. It was ~extremely~ glamorous.

Not only was the goddamn battle of Hastings happening in my goddamn gut all the time, but I felt so fatigued all of the time I could hardly keep my eyes open at work. I was perplexed as to why I was so goddamn depleted of energy. It's not like I was doing CrossFit sixteen times a day.

"It must be food allergies," I would say to my bored-to-tears coworkers as I frantically googled "WHY AM I SO TIRED?"

"It must be the CRAP that I eat!" I would tell whoever I was dating over dinner. They were always put off—I mean, what's more obnoxious than someone stigmatizing food over dinner at a nice restaurant?

"I'm GOING ON A CLEANSE!" I would shout to my poor mother over the phone. She'd ignore me, she's British, and thus way less mental about food than us American girls.

Finally, I realized my life was starting to mirror *Groundhog Day*. Finally, I realized I was acting like the very definition of insanity: doing the same shit over and over again and somehow expecting different results. I decided it was time to entertain the radical idea that maybe—*perhaps*—I was trying to juice cleanse away a deep-rooted psychological problem. I took a hard, naked look at all aspects of my life. And after journaling and thinking and meditating and speaking with confidants and mentors and shrinks, the blindfold slowly lifted from my eyes and I began to see clearly. And what I saw was a lot of garbage people lounging on my couch, using and abusing my things without so much as offering me one of those hideous fake houseplants from Ikea.

I looked at each person in my life. Like, really, really looked at them without a pretty Instagram filter slapped over their faces. I was amazed as to how many people I had allowed into my life that were toxic. What was even more amazing was that I didn't necessarily want to get rid of these toxic entities. Because I *loved* some of them. That's when Sharon piped up.

"Zara, you can't have this person in your life," Sharon ordered to me, like the no-bullshit coach that she is. "She isn't good for you. In fact, she's causing you emotional harm. She's been doing it for years." Sharon had appeared one afternoon as I was mixing up a strange remedy of cayenne pepper and lemon juice and charcoal. I was wearing a tattered nightgown and hadn't washed my hair in a week. Sharon, on the other hand—her hair was so shiny and bouncy she looked as if she'd just had a blowout in Texas!

"Bu—bu—but…I—" *sob* "*love* her," I cried as snot oozed out of my nostrils.

"You can love someone and still be better off without them," Sharon gently reminded me, running her fingers through her clean hair. *Show off.*

"Are you sure?"

"Absolutely. Just because you feel genuine love for this human being doesn't mean they aren't toxic for your life."

"What does that MEAN?" I eyeballed a jug of tequila sitting on top of my fridge, and fought back the urge to chug it down instead of this nasty detox juice.

"Think of cigarettes. You and I both love a good ciggie, don't we?" Sharon gestured to the cigarette she was puffing on.

I nodded my head. It was true. We did love a good ciggie.

"Ciggies have been there for you when you've been lonely. You've had some good nights that involved cigarettes. But just because you love something doesn't mean they won't kill you in the end."

"You're right," I sighed.

"So you know what you gotta do, don't you kiddo?" Sharon said as she dropped her lit cigarette to the floor and stamped on it with her forest green, strangely chic-looking, Wellington boots.

"I do," I whispered.

Sharon and her clean hair and her wellies bounced away into the night, leaving me, for the millionth time, alone with my thoughts.

I knew it would be hard to cut certain people out of my life. Almost as hard as cutting out cigarettes—which is a real bitch. Real Talk: If you can quit cigarettes you can do anything. And I did quit cigarettes, shortly after Sharon's visit. And after I quit cigarettes, I felt healthy enough to give up the toxic human beings that were causing the same harm to my heart as cigarettes had caused to my lungs.

I didn't cut everyone out all at once. But once I removed a toxic entity from my world, I always felt a giant wave of relief...almost instantaneously. Even if weaning myself from them was uncomfortable, I knew deep down that once I had detoxed myself from their energy, I would feel much better. And after several months, I would feel significantly lighter. No longer dragged down by baggage that wasn't my own. And after about a year, I began to notice that new people and new opportunities were starting to make their way into my life. And pretty soon after that, I started to only have stomach aches when my stomach was actually sick, not just because I was teeming with anxiety over what my unpredictable friend would do next to me. I no longer felt depleted because I was no longer allowing anyone to drink from my cup that wouldn't replenish it after.

And after a couple of years, I realized that this is the greatest cleanse of all: cleansing yourself of the negativity brought into your life by *negative people*. And no amount of organic kale will cleanse away the deadly ickiness of toxic people. I believe that toxic people wreak even more havoc on your system than processed foods. (Do I really have to disclaim, yet again, that I'm not a doctor? Sigh. I'm. Not. A. Doctor. So don't sue me!) In my humble opinion, it's as important to examine your relationship with toxic people as if it is toxic food.

Here are five examples of toxic people I cleansed out of my life, complete with a plan on how to rid your body of them. Let's start with my favorite: the energy vampire.

The Energy Vampire

Energy vampires are a complicated breed and come in many different forms. They can be a best friend, a sibling, a lover. Old. Young. Middle-aged. Teens. But they all have one thing in common: they get their fix by feeding off of your emotional energy. I used to have a close friend who was an energy vampire. She was older than me and far more wealthy and successful, so naturally, I majorly looked up to her (this is common with energy vampires. They tend to live at the top of the social hierarchy and it's common for them to abuse their power/privilege). When we first met she showered me with so many compliments and gifts, that I felt nothing but extreme gratitude for her kindness and generosity. But after a few months of intense friendship, she began to suck my blood out of my body. I began to learn that nothing in this life is free, and sometimes people expect your blood as fair exchange for a nice bottle of wine.

Any time I was celebrating a rare accomplishment, the Energy Vampire would call me frantic, screaming that she needed me NOW. It was like she had an inner alarm system that rang whenever I was having a moment of pure joy. And because I deeply struggled with the word "no" I always extinguished my joy and came rushing her side. And most of the time, her crisis was no crisis, babe. I would rush over to her apartment, heart pounding with fear that she'd been diagnosed with cancer, only to find her slugging back wine with a few other friends.

"What's wrong?" I would ask, skeptically.

"He didn't text me back," she would say, stretching out her legs in her three-hundred-dollar yoga pants.

"But I thought you didn't like him?" I would reply, flummoxed and embarrassed in my twenty-dollar dress from Amazon.

"Well, I feel *rejected*," she would say. "I need you."

Codependent people like *moi*, can get a little aroused by those three seductive words: "I need you." Those words practically made my nipples hard!

I would spend the rest of the afternoon helping my Energy Vampire process the fact that some random dude she met on Tinder dared to not text her back. I would've canceled an afternoon designated for celebration with another friend, just to hold her little hand through her slew of meaningless melodramas. Yet, whenever I needed the Energy Vampire, she never seemed to be able to show up for little ol' me. I'll never forget texting her for support after a close friend of mine passed away. "I'm sorry darling. I'm super busy! I'm working on my book proposal! Which is SO hard. Would love your feedback soon."

I rode this seesaw for years. Actually, I wouldn't say I *rode* the seesaw, I was on the ground the whole time, hoisting her up, as she flew high up in the sky.

And the more I merely accepted this one-way relationship, or justified her selfishness because she *occasionally* picked up the check at dinner or invited me to a glittery celebutante party, the more normal this fucked dynamic became to me. And the more I allowed myself to be drained of life from this blood-thirsty Energy Vampire, the more dead I felt. Being her friend felt like a full-time job with a psycho boss. I was always rushing off to pick up her pieces. I was always giving, giving, giving, and never receiving anything of substance. No wonder I felt so worn out all the time! No wonder my confidence was shot! I was starting to think I wasn't worthy of support or friendship. That my job was to serve, but never be served. I imagined a life spent sitting on the floor, washing the princess's precious feet.

When I decided to embark upon my first toxic relationship cleanse, she was the first person I cleansed out of my life. It was becoming increasingly clear that she wasn't adding anything to my life. It was all monologue and no dialogue. And I'm not a "one-woman show" kind of girl.

So, how did I do it? I began to set firm boundaries with Energy Vampire. When I was in the middle of working on a project or spending time with my family, and she would send me her usual frantic text messages demanding I drop everything and tend to her NOW, I would simply reply "Sorry. I'm unavailable." She was shocked. Pissed. HURT!

I held my ground. And after a few months, she ended up breaking off *our* friendship.

"I don't think I can be friends with you anymore. You're never available," she wrote after I had set normal, healthy boundaries with her. I think I had told her that I couldn't see her for a random drink after work because I had to be up at four AM the following morning.

When an Energy Vampire realizes that you're not going to let them live off your blood supply, they usually are no longer interested in being your friend. These kinds of people seek out friends who are selfless, insecure, and giving. When I became a more confident, strong, person who only gave to people who gave back to me, I was no longer of use to her. Which was fine by me, darling.

My advice with breaking off this kind of dynamic is to set firm boundaries as yours truly did. Maybe they'll evolve to respect the boundaries you set with them! I mean, people can change and I truly believe that most people are redeemable (if no one is redeemable what's the point of living?!). Maybe your resistance to give into their every whim will be the wake-up call they so desperately need.

Maybe *not*. Maybe they'll lash out. Which is OK, babes. You can't control how people react, but you *can* control who you let into your orbit. And the active Energy Vampire does not belong in your orbit. If they don't get the message after you've set boundaries and continue to lash out and hound you, it's perfectly reasonable to explain to any friend why you're unhappy in this dynamic and why you need a break from their company.

The Weight Bitch

The weight bitch is that bitch who always makes a comment on your weight. Whether you've lost, gained or stayed the same, the weight bitch *always* has something to say about the size of your body. And allow me to shout this shit from the rooftop of my Hell's Kitchen high-rise: **There is no need for anyone to comment on anyone's weight. Ever.** We all know that weight is one of the greatest sensitivities a woman possesses. I've never met a woman who isn't self-conscious of her body—even my model friends who get paid ridiculous amounts of money to prance around in lingerie are deeply sensitive and easily triggered about the size of their frame. We've all been reared in a culture that makes money off of shaming us for how we're built. All of us. It's exhausting to be inundated with billboards and magazine ads and Instagram sponsored #ads selling us on how to make our asses bigger and our waists tinier and our legs longer. We don't need to hear that shit from friends and family members, you hear? I used to have a family friend who, before even saying hello to me—after months and months of not seeing her—would comment on my body size.

"Let me see your body! Wow, you've gained a few pounds this semester!" she would say, examining my body as if I were an overripe avocado in the bodega. Each time she commented on my weight I felt as if I had been kicked in the stomach. I felt like I wasn't *worthy* of moving through the world if she declared me "bigger." If she told me I had lost weight, I would feel like I won a *prize*. Knowing that her assessment of me would render me either "confident" or wildly insecure gave her far too much power over me. I would grow increasingly anxious and radically diet before coming home for the holidays. One little comment from her about my body would determine my self-esteem for the following months. Sometimes it would even propel me into a dark bout of disordered eating, binging, and vomiting up my food.

There is something fundamentally toxic about a person who constantly brings up your weight. Deep down they understand that casually mentioning a woman's weight is the most vulnerable thing you can do, yet they still feel compelled to do it. Which means they feel compelled to make you feel like you're nothing *more* than your weight. Which is such a deeply damaging, fucked-up way to feel. I believe that this unyielding obsession with body image and maintaining the "perfect" weight is what brings us women down. It's what makes us feel like no achievement matters if we've been deemed "overweight" or "underweight" by one sicko in our lives. It makes us feel like we're nothing but bodies. But the truth is, we are so much more than our bodies. We are hearts! We are minds! We are souls! We are funny! We are sassy! We have shit to say that matters! People in your life should be bringing up your achievements, or the integrity of your character, or how you're growing mentally, not your goddamn weight. It's also a violation of a firm boundary to bring up someone's body without their consent. Listen to me, ladies: Your relationship with your body is *your own*. You don't need anyone to give you unsolicited advice on what size you should be.

A few years ago, I confronted this family friend. I told her that it made me feel embarrassed when she brought up my size.

"Oh, don't be ridiculous! Stop being so sensitive!" she said.

That was the moment I realized that anyone who tells you to "stop being so sensitive" after you confess to being hurt by their behavior, is *also* someone you don't need in your life. The backbone of all relationships is communication. If a person can't handle you communicating honestly with them about the way their behavior makes you feel, they don't know how to have a relationship. In a loving, safe relationship you should always be able to say how you feel, without your feelings being written off or undermined because it doesn't suit the other person's agenda.

I gracefully walked away from having a close relationship with this family friend after her extreme dismissal of me and my feelings. I gave her the opportunity to have a conversation, I gave the opportunity to change, and she chose not to. Whenever we see each other now, I give her a quick wave and direct my energy on family members and friends who make me feel good about myself. Who ask me questions about my crazy life, not about my boring body.

If you have a weight bitch in your life, I advise doing one of two things. The first can be to confront them. Tell them that their comments sting and that you will not tolerate them commenting on your weight again. Even if it's a "joke." Real friends understand that there are certain things you don't joke about. Real friends will respect you when you tell them they're crossing a line. If you've had this conversation before or are simply burned out from being the target of their body-shaming, you have every right in the world to simply walk away. You don't need to invite someone who makes you feel bad about yourself to social events. You don't have to say yes to going to dinner or drinks with them. You are allowed to pull away from anyone who is making you feel anything less than the smart, nuanced individual that you are.

The Party Enabler

Oh, I swear to Lana Del Rey, I could have an honorary master's degree from Harvard in the party enabler. I've been the party enabler. And I've been *affected* by the party enabler. And holy shit, is this situation as toxic as those cute little vape pens turned out to be.

When you've made the wise decision to cut down on drugs and alcohol, it isn't easy! When you've grown accustomed to connecting with people only when under the influence, when you're so terrified to deal with your emotions sober that you self-medicate with poisonous substances, then the mere idea of raw dogging your feelings and opening up to people without the lubrication of drugs or booze sounds completely unappealing. But when you get sick and tired of being sick and tired and decide that you really want to reach the next step in your life, and begin to realize that all the partying is dragging you into the ground—it's a huge, wild epiphany. Anyone who has ever decided they *need to* make a serious effort to cut down on their substance use doesn't exactly have a casual relationship with partying. If this is you right now, I'm super proud of you, sister. I know that this is daunting and scary but making the decision to be a healthier human being is powerful. In fact, you're about to step into a power you didn't even know you had.

When you tell your friends that you're really trying to stay sober (or at least more sober than you've been) it can feel as emotionally intense as telling them you're pregnant or relocating to Mars. Let me be real with you because your girl has been down this road before (actually I've done about ten laps down this road). Unless you were partying in complete solitude (which is unlikely) you're bound to have at least one friend who is not going to be supportive of your choice to not indulge in the coke or the booze or the pills or whatever else you're using to get blitzed. And I'm here to tell you that you must, *you must*, cut this person out of your life right away.

Anyone who is not in support of a serious life choice you're making, one that involves getting healthier and confronting your demons without a dangerously addictive numbing mechanism, has no place in your life. You want to only surround yourself with people who encourage you to be the best version of yourself! Also, you're putting yourself at high risk by having this person in your orbit. Like I said before, changing your relationship to substance use is one of the hardest things you'll ever goddamn do, girl. It's hard even if you're stranded on an island with only sober people. If you throw a person in the mix who carries drugs and booze on them and then pressures you to take them, you're very likely going to give in. And when you give in, even if it's just once, it's very easy to doubt that you're capable of quitting, which can send you into a spiral bender of using and abusing because feeling incapable of doing anything feels shitty. And for some of us (myself included), feeling shitty can very easily lead to getting shitty off liquor and pills. So for your health and safety, you should stay far away from this person. The people we hang out with, for better or for worse, have major influence over us. When we're spending time with people who are dabbling with drugs and/or making us feel bad or boring or "old" for abstaining, we're eventually going to throw our hands up and mirror their behavior. And that's not the behavior you need to mirror at this critical moment in your life (or ever).

My biggest piece of advice for ridding yourself of this toxic relationship is to cut ties with great empathy. Chances are, this person has a serious substance abuse problem. Only people with substance abuse problems force their friends to engage in drugging and drinking. Healthy people, even if they love to party, aren't freaked out by their friends wanting to abstain from using. I, myself, have felt freaked out to my core when a friend has decided to quit drinking. Not just because I've lost my "partner in crime," but because their choice to change their behavior has held up a mirror to my own behavior, and is forcing me to confront what I'm so desperate to avoid confronting. The fact that I too, need to take a hard look at how I'm living. In hindsight, I completely understand why certain friends in the past pushed me away. I was toxic to them.

I would call this person or meet them for coffee and explain that while you love them, you can't be around them if they're going to push using on you. So how do you confront the party enabler? Explain that this is extremely tough for you, as is, and you need all the support you can get. Tell them that you're ready to hang out whenever they're ready to respect your boundaries, or need help in trying to examine their own relationship with substances. Keep them in your hearts, for they are sick right now. But their sickness is contagious and it is high time you put yourself first.

The beauty of you setting this boundary is that it very well might be the thing that sheds light on their dangerous habit of self-medicating. People who abuse substances rarely get better without consequences. And losing friends because of your hard-partying ways is the ultimate consequence. By not allowing a person who is a bad influence on your health into your orbit, you might even save their lives. I know it's saved mine.

The Toxic Blood Relative

I'm of the controversial belief that it's okay to step away from your family if they're nasty or abusive to you. Just because you are related to a person by blood doesn't mean they get an instant hall pass that allows them to hurt you. If every time you speak with your parents you're in tears and feel deeply unloved and unworthy after hanging up the phone, don't speak to them. Dodge that call like it's a bullet, because it *is*. If your aunt doesn't approve of your sexuality and tells you that you're going to hell every time you come over for family dinner, don't go to family dinner. If your brother has a history of being violent toward you, you don't need to have any relationship with him at all, I don't care if he's your sibling. If your sister insults you every single time you meet up with her for brunch, stop saying yes to brunch. It's that simple.

And that complicated.

I mean, let's take a pause for a moment here, babes. Is anything in the world *more* triggering than family? Does anyone else have the innate ability to get under our skin more than the families we call our own? If there is, please tell me. I have yet to find anything that knows how to twist a knife directly into our hearts better than our own blood relatives.

It's one thing to have spats with your mother occasionally, or get into heated political debates with your dad from time to time—but if you're constantly being torn down by a family member, it's time to protect yourself. An asshole is an asshole is an asshole, regardless of whether they're a friend or a partner or a family member. And when you're trying so intensely to be a positive woman who feels good about yourself (which is HARD in this world), shielding yourself from the family members who make you doubt yourself the most isn't at all a betrayal. It's a wise act of self-preservation. It doesn't mean you don't love them. Like Sharon explained to me that fateful night I attempted to drink charcoal to feel better, *setting a boundary with someone doesn't mean that you don't love them.* Sometimes the people we love the most are toxic for us. Two things can be true at once: You can have giant feelings of affection for someone and be able to see the beauty that lives way back at the bottom of their souls, but also know that it's imperative for you to not allow them into your life because they're knocking you down in a moment when it's direly important for you to stand *tall*.

I can't tell you how to explain to your family member that you aren't interested in speaking with them right now. Every family is so utterly unique. I will say this: It's great to tell them how you feel in person, but it's also okay to write a letter. Or send an email. It's beyond okay, if the situation is extreme, to ghost them or block them (especially if you're afraid of them). You are never obligated to have this "breakup" conversation face to face with anyone, especially if they're manipulative and will twist your words and mind-fuck you until you're limp and defeated. Repeat after me: Put yourself first. Put yourself first. Put yourself first. I know that's a new concept for all of us, because we as women have been raised to put everyone before ourselves, to blindly accept abuse, and always have "empathy"—but this is *your* life. You're in charge, and the only way you'll have control over your destiny is to put yourself first. Tape that on your mirror! Better yet, write it in *lipstick* across your mirror. Bright *red* lipstick.

Anyone who tries to change the core of who you are.

This one is a biggie: Anyone who is trying to change the fundamental core of who you are should not be welcome in your life. When I came out as a lesbian and had my first girlfriend, I had a few friends tell me they didn't "approve" of my "lifestyle" and then tried to set me up on dates with men! At the core of who I am is a woman who happens to love other women. If you want to change that about me, I'll hold the door open for you as you walk out of my life, never to be seen again.

When I stopped running away from my feelings and instead began blogging about them, I had a friend who constantly told me I was acting crazy and needed to stop oversharing. At the core of who I am is a woman who connects to the outer world by sharing her most vulnerable moments through her writing. I ended my relationship with this friend because she was taking up space in my life, and the space she was taking up didn't suit the studio apartment that is my life. Who has room for shame in such a small space? Shame is big. It will bleed its ugliness onto everything else you own.

When I had an editor who constantly told me that I should change my perspective on the world and that my style of writing was too raw, I fired that editor. She wasn't a bad person, but she was trying to change one of the most honest, pure parts about me. I found a new editor who gave me just as many notes, except these were constructive, they made me a better version of myself, not a different version of myself.

The truth is, you can't ever truly change the core of who you are. The parts of you that were alive and thriving when you were a baby. You can *mask* who you are. You can fake your entire personality and live a life performing on a proverbial fucking stage, in order to please the people around you. But you're going to get sick in the end, I promise. Maybe not physically sick, but when you resist who you are at the core, it does something to you. It knocks you out of alignment with your purpose. It gives you extreme anxiety. You won't be able to go to sleep at night or truly look at your reflection in the mirror without feeling like a fraud. You will grow exhausted and ill with fatigue. I think that the root of all the unhappiness in the world is that so many people are living a lie. There is nothing worse than living a lie. I've *done* it. I wanted to die when I was living a lie, because by succumbing to everyone else's vision of what I should be, I lost myself. I slipped through the cracks of my own soul.

On the flip, there is nothing more beautiful than living your truth. Whatever your truth is. Maybe it's pursuing your dream to be an actress. Maybe it's accepting your sexual or gender identity. Or embracing your kooky style or off-beat taste in a romantic partner. There's a reason why people put their lives on the line in oppressive societies, fighting for freedom, fighting for the opportunity to live authentically. When you live your truth, everything else falls into place. The anxiety lifts and dissipates into the sky. You feel comfortable in your skin. Your ego no longer leads you, your heart leads you, and the heart is far more wise than the ego. So don't fux with people who are trying to change the beautiful human being that we both know you are, babe. **There is only one you. There is only right now.** Don't waste another minute of your precious, fleeting, gorgeous life pretending to be someone that you're not. Don't worry about people leaving your life if they want to change you. They don't deserve your light. When you start being yourself, you'll start attracting people that don't dull your sparkle—but instead, add to it.

So simply stop engaging with these toxic people. And start engaging with the real, badass, *you*.

CHAPTER 19

PSA: Beware of Drinking and Bleeding

Song: "Drew Barrymore" by SZA

If you haven't experienced a PMS BLACKOUT you most definitely *know* someone who has, and thus, should keep reading this chapter in order to *look out for* womankind.

OK, let's get down to business. You know when you have raging, soul-sucking PMS? The kind of PMS that gives you body dysmorphia, the kind of PMS that makes you detest humanity, the kind of PMS that makes you weep at McDonald's commercials, the kind of PMS that gives you cystic acne around your chin area, the kind of PMS that gives crippling anxiety not even Xanax can quell, the kind of PMS that makes you feel generally vile in spirit, the kind of PMS that has you incessantly contemplating the meaning of life?

Oh, you do?

Fabulous! Me too!

The trouble with soul-sucking PMS is that it always possesses us with the desire to excessively DRINK. I'll be getting ready to meet up with a friend on a seemingly innocent Friday night, slathering lip gloss on my lips, filled with unnecessary rage. I'll pinch the "fat" on my lower abdomen as I compulsively chow on Flamin' Hot Cheetos (even though I don't care for Flamin' Hot Cheetos).

"NOTHING LOOKS GOOD ON ME!" I'll scream to no one in particular. I'll peel out of my form-fitting black dress, and toss it onto the floor, like a diva in the thick of a mega-bitch meltdown.

I'll proceed to tear through my closet, like a savage, like a woman on a rampage, like a woman on the verge of a *breakdown*, and I'll find some obscure loose-fitted Marc Jacobs dress gifted to me by mother in 2002. I'll toss it over my head and grimace at myself in the mirror. "You're vile!" I'll bellow dramatically into my reflection, pounding my fists against my chest like a gorilla.

By the time I meet up with my friend Dayna, I'll have wept over my "failed career" fourteen times, cursed out the taxi driver, and spontaneously deleted half of my pictures on Instagram whilst in the throes of a hormonally induced episode of mania.

I'll storm into the Cubbyhole where she'll be sitting like a pretty pretty princess, petting her long silky hair extensions with her freshly manicured nails. Mine will be chipped. I'll resent her on the spot. Because she looks happy and peaceful and is sipping a pretty pink cocktail like a lady. And because her nails are perfect, her *life* is clearly perfect. My face will go beet red and I will huff and puff and demand a tequila soda from sweet Lil' Deb the bartender who will make me a strong drink because I'm acting like an asshole, which is wildly out of character for me (I'm an angel).

I'll knock the strong drink back. I'll guzzle it down like it's the answer to my deepest prayers. Because all the FEELINGS I'm FEELING are so intense, because I'm PMSing like a boss, because my body is wracked with so much estrogen I'm like a goddamn milk cow—I'll seek solace in the darkness of booze. But all that extra estrogen and hormonal fuckery and acute stress won't mix well with the booze.

So I'll act out. I'll get nasty. I'll get drunk really quickly. And I'll keep wanting MORE liquor because I'll be that crazy, PMS kind of drunk that leaves you increasingly unsatisfied and mean and bullyish.

And then the next thing I know I'll be waking up in my bed, fully clothed, wrapped in a blanket of shame. My head will be POUNDING and my cramps will have really kicked off, *so hard* it feels like there is a war going on in my uterus!

I'll trudge over to the bathroom, and, as I wrangle out of my underwear, there will be a big flat BLOOD stain tarnishing the gorgeous silk (why do I always wear expensive undergarments right before I bleed?).

And everything will make so much sense. The onset of extreme emotions. The bizarre bouts of anger. The blackout. (Especially if you're like me and suffer from PMDD. Which stands for premenstrual dysphoric disorder and is basically PMS on crack. You experience the symptoms of PMS but in a far more severe fashion. My friend Ruba gets a little testy on her period, I go into a full blast roid rage and wail on public transportation.)

In fact, alone in the bathroom, I'll remember that a gynecologist I interviewed once told me that women are far more likely to over-drink and blackout when PMSing. And even though I'll take a slight comfort in the fact that I'm not the *only* woman who has ever blacked out while PMSing, I'll still be so unbelievably embarrassed in my soul. Humiliation will wrap its arms around my bloated waist. Tears will fall down my bloated face. I'll want to hide my bloated body and deflated ego in my sad apartment all day.

The truth is, nothing sucks more royally than a blackout. Whether it's an Adderall blackout, a heartbreak blackout, a wedding blackout or a PMS blackout—it's all tragic. Life is too short to make memories we'll never remember. Women are too fabulous to put themselves in precarious situations and blacking out always puts you in a precarious situation, one that could subject you to great danger. And the punch in the gut a blackout does to our dignity is *awful*. Losing control and not being sure what words have flown out of our beautiful lips is heart-wrenching!

So if you're PMSing, please stay home.

Or stick to water. Or two glasses of wine, if you're the kind of rare creature that can stick to only *two glasses* of wine. But if you're tempted to chug vodka to make the harrowing PMS symptoms go away, imagine me sitting on your kitchen counter. I'm wearing a dark red dress. A blood red dress. I'm wearing it in honor of periods. Out of respect to the fact that we bleed and can make babies and are so goddamn powerful! My nails are deep red too. As are my lips (which look as if they've been freshly injected with Juvéderm). I flash you a smile. I hand you a cup of tea. I look you deep into your stunning, twinkling eyes and say:

"Babe. Let's stay in. Let's feel our PMS feelings and watch a sad movie like *Blue Is the Warmest Colour* and cry—and enjoy crying! Crying is a great cleanse, babe. Bleeding between our thighs is a great privilege, babe." I'll light up a joint. "You in?" I'll ask, blowing a beautiful ring of smoke out of my suspiciously pouty mouth.

So you decide to stay in and indulge the PMS with me. You decide not to drink the symptoms away, but to rather use them as inspiration for all the great art you'll create during this precious time. Because PMS can make you feel *crazy*. But great art comes from feeling crazy, right? So let's suck all the great content out of ourselves, and waste our sane, boring, un-hormonal nights for the bar, honey.

CHAPTER 20

How to Eat a Piece of Pizza
Without Wanting to Die

Song: "Mess is Mine" by Vance Joy

If I had to define the decade of my 20s in a single word, it would be *unstable*. I was either soaring high up in the sky, reaching my greatest potential, or flailing aimlessly in the air. My heart was shattered to pieces or I was oh-so-passionately in love. I was the brightest shade of blonde or the deepest shade of brunette. I starved myself into a fawn or was in the dark throes of a morbid binge. I was slap-happy wasted or curled up into fetal position reeling from a dire hangover. My life was one giant rollercoaster ride that I rode on for so long, the spinning upside down, the dramatic highs and the terrifying lows felt totally normal. I didn't realize I even deserved to walk on stable ground.

I met Meghan at twenty-nine. I was working for a major millennial media company where I had grown notorious for writing deep personal essays about my haphazard, unhinged life. I wrote about that time I spent eight hundred dollars in a single month on taxis, but not being able to pay my rent. I wrote about waking up in strangers' beds. I wrote about being a psycho ex-girlfriend. I wrote, very candidly, about my tendency to self-medicate and self-destruct. I wrote about shame. I wrote about depression. All of it was real. And I built an audience who related to the rollercoaster of my life. Without even realizing it, I had built a brand entirely wrapped up in my crazy girl identity.

But sometime around twenty-eight, something inside of me started to shift. I can't exactly pinpoint the specific moment I felt myself starting to become stable, it just started to slowly creep up in small moments that carried just enough weight to root me further into the ground. For example, over the past decade I had been scared shit-less of pizza. I know it sounds so goddamn stupid, and I'm ashamed to even admit it, but it's *true*. I loved pizza so feverishly I feared that if I had one tiny bite I wouldn't be able to stop devouring the pizza and the next thing I knew, I would wake up overweight and loveless. And I feared being overweight as much as I feared that I had zero talent and would die a certifiable failure, alone, in Paramus, New Jersey. In fact, the idea of dying alone in Paramus, New Jersey wasn't so bad, so long as I died thin. (Sick and twisted thinking, I KNOW.)

Every Friday at my job, we had "pizza Fridays" where fabulous boxes of juicy New York City pizzas were delivered to the office. The second they landed on the communal table in our kitchen, the entire staff would spring out of their chairs and stampede toward the pizza. I always remained dutifully glued to my chair (along with a few other fucked up girls). It was torture watching my peers shove pizza into their mouths without a care in the world. I would stare at the hot melted cheese and pepperoni like it was a hot woman I wanted nothing more than to sleep with, but couldn't because she was like, *I don't know*, dating *my best friend* or something. Pizza was off limits like a friend's lover.

On one particular Friday, I don't know what came over me, but when the pizza stampede started, I flew off my seat and joined the party. I didn't even think about it. I simply got out of my chair, picked out the sexiest slice I could find, slapped it onto my paper plate, made my way to my desk and ate the fucking pizza. Normally if I were to indulge in pizza, I would manically tear through it, a crazy narrative flying through my head (*you fat bitch you have no control you fat ugly bitch*) and I wouldn't even taste it, let alone enjoy it. You know when you're experiencing trauma and you have an out-of-body experience? Like you ascend into the air and watch the scene from the ceiling fan? That's what would happen to me when eating pizza. But this time was different. I ate the pizza like a normal person. I ate the pizza like my editor Alexia ate her pizza. Casually, pausing occasionally to take a sip of soda, enjoying it, but not enjoying it too much—not enjoying it the point where you aren't eating it, you're making out with it and making everyone around you uncomfortable (which is how I'm told I eat when I'm drunk). After I finished it, I was full. Not painfully full, cozily full. I didn't feel compelled to have sixteen more slices because I'd already "screwed up the day!" I waited patiently for the meltdown, the usual post-pizza breakdown to happen.

It never happened. I wrote an article analyzing a study I read about generation Z and bisexuality and continued my day.

During my walk home from work, I really meditated on the pizza incident. Had I really eaten a slice of pizza and not wanted to slit my wrists? Who was I? *What did this mean?* I had been screwed up about food for so long, it had become ingrained in my identity. Was I a girl *who* engaged in pizza Fridays now?

A few weeks later I went on a Tinder date at The Jane Hotel, a very cool hotel in New York City with a little too much taxidermy for my taste. My date was thirty minutes late. I sipped on my wine and tried not to make eye-contact with the stuffed fox staring at me in the background. My tinder date, Max, came stumbling into the bar completely blitzed, in ripped black jeans and a white tee-shirt so sheer you could see her braless nipples. She was *totally* my type. She exuded a reckless sexual energy peppered in with a hearty helping of narcissism. Girls like that, in the words of my friend Dayna, usually gave me "the pussy flutters."

"Hi, babe," she said plopping down next to me, breathing her boozy breath right in my face.

Babe? I wasn't her *babe.*

Max ordered us a round of shots and proceeded to tell me about her therapist who she happened to be also be having sex with. She put her hand on my leg and asked me if I wanted to go to a leather party with her after the shots. I could smell cocaine permeating out of her nostrils. I know that's strange, but I have a strong sense of smell and no smell turns me off more than the wicked smell of cocaine.

Despite my distaste for the smell of toxic white powder, normally I would be completely wet, drawn to this train wreck of a girl like a moth to a fluorescent bulb. I wouldn't have even noticed that she didn't ask me a single question about my life or my job or my *day* even. I would've taken shots with her, gone to the leather party and had sex with her. I would've woken up feeling empty, like I always did after sleeping with someone on drugs. But tonight, I wasn't even remotely tempted to go home with her. I didn't want to feel empty the next day. I had to work. I had a life to live! Plus, I was uncharacteristically irritated that she was late. I was uncharacteristically annoyed that she was drunk. I was annoyed that she didn't understand the art of conversation and had blabbed to me about her melodramatic life without even pausing to check in with me. I was annoyed that on a date she told me she was *fucking* her shrink. And I certainly didn't want to kiss her booze-addled breath. Since when did I have standards? I left Max to her leather party and went home.

The next morning, I woke up in shock. Why hadn't I at least gone to leather party for the adventure? For the story? For the viral essay I would surely pen afterward? And why did I care that she was a raging narcissist? She was *sexy.* I tried to conjure up feelings of regret inside of me, but they weren't there. That's when the wise woman who lives inside of me, Sharon showed up.

"Girl, you're growing up," Sharon said, sitting on the lounge chair in my bedroom, her legs crossed like a lady. Her signature cigarette was tucked behind her ear and she was wearing a sensible cream-colored button-down shirt and mom jeans. She looked *good*.

"You look really good," I found myself saying.

"Yeah, I'm trying to quit smoking. I haven't had a cigarette for two days. Can you believe it?" She gestured toward her cigarette. "I'm just keeping this here just in case."

"Wow." I was speechless. Who was Sharon without cigarettes?

"Not sure I need these smokes anymore."

"Is it hard?" I asked.

"It's weird, Zara," she said, her voice confident and clear. "I don't really want 'em. I feel like I should want 'em, but I don't."

"Huh," I said, genuinely amazed. It was all a lot to unpack for 6:30 AM.

"Anyway, I'm here to talk about *you*," Sharon said, uncrossing her legs and sitting further back in the chair. "You're evolving. Accept that you're evolving."

"What do you mean, 'evolving'? How?" I really needed Sharon to help me process this sudden growth spurt.

"The things that used to serve you are no longer serving you. You're starting to want real, tangible things in your life. I mean, it's about time. You'll be thirty before you know it. Stop resisting your evolution. You didn't want to have sex with that nut job last night, right?"

I nodded. *Right.*

"And you're beating yourself up about it, wondering what it means, correct?"

I nodded again. *Correct.*

"Stop worrying about it! Let yourself grow. We're supposed to change. Stop holding on to an identity that is no longer you!" Sharon was yelling now, not angry yelling, passion yelling. She opened up my window and threw her cigarette out right on to 92nd street. She grinned at me. And right before I could grin back, she was gone.

A few weeks later I had a date with another woman I'd met on Tinder. We met at a bar on the lower east side during the thick of a Manhattan blizzard. I'd arrived early and was sitting at the bar sipping on a glass of white wine when she sauntered over. She had long legs encased in shiny, wax-coated pants. She was wearing a sheer black shirt that exposed her lacey bra. I looked down at my own outfit. I was wearing a sheer black dress that exposed my own lacey bra. I was doomed. She was hot. She had an air of swag about her that made me weak in the knees. She had to be a narcissist. Hot people are always unpredictable headcases.

Only she wasn't narcissistic or a head case. She was an incredible conversationalist. She asked me questions about my life. She seemed to be extremely interested in my career, my writing process. She had the perfect balance of asking me enough questions, without crossing a boundary or prying. She loved her career—she worked as a creative director in experiential marketing. We were on the same page about everything from music to art to past relationships. I felt like I could open up to her, but I also didn't have an urge to overshare as a way to force a connection. When people overshare it's often less about them wanting to connect, but more about them forcing a connection on you without your consent. It can feel like mind-rape. This didn't feel like mind-rape. This felt like a real, authentic connection. She had her shit together. She had a stable job she was passionate about. She had an apartment and was in close contact with her friends and family. She didn't try to sleep with me, nor did she order shots. We had one glass of wine each. I had never, ever been on a date that wasn't a total booze-fest in my *entire* life. But see, this girl was different. This girl was a grown-up. Not only was she a grown-up, she was interesting. In fact, if I had put my two dates side by side—the one with Max and the one with this sophisticated creature—the one with helter-skelter Max looked dull. That's when it hit me: there is nothing exciting about going on a date with a person who is hammered. In fact, someone who feels as if they have to get hammered before a date must fear that they're not all that interesting. There is nothing more boring than being in the presence of someone who yaps and yaps about themselves and doesn't ask you a single question. Conversations are a give and take. If you don't know how to give to something as simple and as innately human as a conversation, how can I expect you to know how to give in a relationship? (Or in bed for that matter?)

Even the leather party Max had invited me to paled in comparison to having a stimulating conversation with a sexy adult in a cozy little bar downtown. I could've spoken to her for hours. She didn't need the extra bullshit to make herself interesting. She didn't need to be unhinged or a mess to hold my attention.

Her name was Meghan. The girl I met at twenty-nine.

After our date I hopped in a cab to meet up with a smattering of friends uptown. I couldn't stop thinking about how fascinating Meghan was—but how she was fascinating in a way that I wasn't used to. Her mind was interesting. Her grown-up job was interesting. Her unwavering dedication to her family was interesting. If she didn't need to act like a wildcard in order to be stimulating and sexy, neither did I...right?

I wish I could say I came to the conclusion that it was truly time to get it together entirely on my own. But that would be a bold-faced lie. Look, sometimes we're by ourselves on a goddamn solo hiking trip in the mountains when we're hit with massive life epiphanies. Sometimes an epiphany is inspired by wanting to impress a crush. Truthfully, it doesn't matter where an epiphany comes from. So long as you have your own lightbulb moment and understand that *you* have the power to keep that lightbulb on, you're golden. So even though being in the presence of Meghan was inspiring me to take the next step in maturity, I knew in my heart that even if I never ever saw her again, there was no going back from here. If she were to have ghosted me after that first date, I would've stayed on the path of owning my newfound stability. Because my newfound stability was already there, you see. The roots had been planted even before PizzaGate. Meghan had dug deep inside of me and pulled out the roots and tossed 'em in front of my eyes. And once they were in front of my eyes I realized just how damn fucking beautiful they were!

Even a flower isn't as gorgeous as its *roots*. Because roots are deep, and depth is more beautiful than anything.

All the things that used to terrify me were suddenly not scary at all anymore. For the first time I could envision myself as *a mother*. The idea of expanding my family and raising a tiny human being seemed *exciting* to me. The idea of being in a relationship with a person I could actually depend on made me break out into chills, the way a narcissistic fuckgirl would've in the past. The idea of living a real life, that wasn't spent either drunk or hungover sounded blissful. Like Sharon had wisely told me: I wanted something tangible. Something I could hold in my hands. I was suddenly *weary* of the rollercoaster. Rollercoasters are exciting for a while, but eventually they get boring. You don't get to stop and enjoy the epicness of the world when your whole life is spent spinning around and around.

I also knew that if I wanted tangible things I would have to make some serious changes. While I felt a pull toward stability inside of me, old habits die hard, sister. Not only that—but all the hangovers and breakdowns and toxic lovers and reckless spending habits had taken up so much space in my life. There hadn't been room for much else. I was at max capacity. Letting go of these habits meant I would have to find something else to fill the empty spaces in my life. What would I find to fill the giant space in my brain reserved for soul-crushing hangovers? And while it was exciting to think about, it was also scary. Change is always exciting and scary. But at this stage in the game I was astute enough to realize that it's far better to be nervous, to be teetering between fear and giddiness, than it is to be stagnant. It was time to close this chapter and start a new one.

I knew Meghan wasn't going to have stars in her eyes over me if I was unstable. In the past, every person I'd dated had seemed to love how "complicated" (aka drunk and dramatic) I was. They loved it because it took the focus off their own shit. They were able to avoid the lifetime subscription of issues they'd been born harboring, but Meghan wasn't like that. Meghan had done work on herself. She'd been in therapy for years. She had a past, which I loved because, let's get real, a girl like me needs a little grit—but she didn't drag her past into the present like most people I knew did. She was so solid and secure in herself she didn't need a little train wreck to fix in order to make herself feel whole. It was the sexiest characteristic I'd ever experienced. I began to realize the importance of surrounding yourself with positive people if you want to become a positive person.

On our third date we met up with some of her friends at a bar in the West Village. Meghan ordered a drink. Instead of slugging it back and ordering another, she slowly sipped her drink over the course of an hour. I was *shook*. I decided, as an exercise, to attempt to keep pace with her. At first I was nervous; I had relied on alcohol as a social lubricant my entire life. Especially in a bar setting. I took a deep breath. Instead of focusing on getting another drink I decided to focus on her friends. I asked them questions. Anytime I felt the urge to slug down my drink to loosen up, I paused and directed my nervous energy at whomever I was speaking to. Before I knew it, I was in the throes of a lively conversation. I looked at the clock. Over an hour had gone by and I had learned all about her best friend's extremely out-of-the-box childhood. I had debated politics and discussed the nuances of dating in the city with all of her friends.

"Are you sure you're shy?" Meghan asked me, raising her eyebrows. "My friends love you."

I thought about that for a minute. For so long, I had been convinced that I was super shy when it came to conversing with people I hadn't known since birth. That's how I had justified my heavy social drinking. I thought I needed a drink in order to connect with people. But here I was, effortlessly gabbing away whilst completely sober. And the connections I was cultivating were deeper than the connections I made when I was hammered. They were deeper because my senses were sharper—I could really *hear* what people were saying. I could take a minute and, with a clear head, digest what they had said before jumping into a dramatic reaction. Maybe I wasn't shy. Maybe "shy" was yet another lie I had told myself.

I also realized that I was selling myself short with my incessant self-deprecation. I was damn *good* at my job. I drove one million page views to the website a month on my own! Why was I going into meetings acting like I didn't belong there? Why was I saying things like "I'm not a business person," when actually I had a business mind as sharp as any boy in my industry? I began to take my career seriously. Instead of writing emails for potential work opportunities that were desperate and full of exclamation points, I began to own what I had to offer. And I found, to my surprise, I had a *lot* to offer. I'm a great public speaker—why didn't I ever tell anyone that? I never missed a single day of work, so why was I always acting like I prioritized partying over working, when that simply was not true? I was a solid, grounded friend. Why was I making out like I was an unpredictable, narcissistic, headcase of a person, when I was selfless and loyal underneath my leopard print exterior?

I began to realize that I wasn't owning my stability because it gave me an excuse in case I royally screwed something up. When you go out into the world claiming that you're a wildcard, no one expects that much from you. When the first thing you tell people is, "I NEVER FINISHED COLLEGE!" instead of stating your impressive achievements you've earned in spite of having no higher education, no one thinks you're going to amount to anything. And when no one thinks you're going to amount to anything, you don't let anyone down, and not letting anyone down—when your self-worth is completely reliant on validation from others—means not letting *yourself* down. I hung on to my crazy girl identity, because letting go of her meant growing up. It meant stepping up to the plate and understanding my worth. And owning failures, too. And failure scared the shit out of me. But I was starting to see that holding onto a self-destructive identity that stopped me from attaining the life I had always wanted was far scarier than failure.

After peeling back all the onion-like layers of my instability, I found that underneath the hard partying, underneath the chasing of unpredictable partners, underneath the piles of credit card debt and the self-medicating was a giant, spineless ego. And that growing up was about putting him in his fucking place (my ego is totally a dude). I began to realize that my ego had fed me a lie that I couldn't be interesting and *also* stable. That in order to be a creative, sparkly party girl, I had to be a hot mess too. The ego never told me I could be both. I could be more creative than ever and still a healthy, high-functioning human being. I could dive into a beautiful, loving relationship that was as exciting as it was safe. I could embark on wild adventures that didn't result in near death experiences. I could still wear all the silver strapless fit-and-flare dresses I lusted after, and still be a serious business woman. I could be a mom one day, and still be an outspoken badass covered in Lana Del Rey quote tattoos.

I could be stable and still have a memoir-worthy life.

My stability didn't just stay in my relationship with Meghan. Like I said earlier, if you improve in one area of your life, it tends to bleed into every other area of your life, too. I began to show up for myself by taking care of my body, prioritizing sleep, and doing whatever I could do to be the best version of myself.

If you had told me four years ago I was going to be getting married, I would've gagged up the entire bottle of whatever I had likely consumed that evening. The thought of marriage conjured up images of a corset being fastened so tightly over my poor ribcage I couldn't breathe. I have never, ever dreamed of being a wife. While I'm a romantic, I don't have the bridal gene at all. I've craved freedom over security my entire life. I have never wanted to wear one of those virgin sacrifice, hideous wedding dresses, either. In fact, I would rather die than go to Kleinfeilds. I'm that cold.

So you can imagine my surprise when Meghan proposed to me on my Facebook Live talk show a year and a half into dating. I was interviewing her best friend, a fabulous Parisian by way of Cuba, a singer/songwriter named Lisette. We were discussing period stains and unwanted pregnancies and the nuances of sexuality when suddenly Meghan hopped into the frame. Lisette scurried away nervously, like a dog busted for eating the cheese board at the party.

Meghan (who never wants to be on camera, despite me endlessly begging her to be a guest on my show) with the shakiest yet strongest voice I'd ever heard, said: "You know when you find someone who is both wild yet extremely stable, beautiful yet loving, adventurous yet consistent, would you ask them to marry you?" And before I could even take in the words that were tumbling out of her mouth, she got down on one knee, opened up a midnight blue velvet ring box, and asked me to marry her. I was so shocked I didn't even answer, I *squealed*. I cried. I forgot that I was on Facebook Live and that a lot of my readers who have been following me for years and years were watching this go down in real time. Not only that, but my friends and family were watching too (I probably wouldn't have done such a deep dive into the topics of abortion and period sex had I known her Catholic father was watching—but then again, one must always be themselves in this life). Finally, I conjured up the word: yes.

I was so taken by what Meghan had said about me that I didn't even *think* to look at the ring. The old me would've thought I'd be fixated on the ring—after all, I have a reputation for loving shiny things. But who cares about a ring when the person you love most has been able to articulate the woman you've finally become! Meghan had hit the nail right on the head: I was wild yet stable. I could be both. I was both. I could fall in love without losing my identity. I could do this stable, grown-up thing *my way*.

We got married on October 27th at my parent's house in Sarasota, FL. I wore a pink Hayley Paige gown that glittered—because you can take a party girl out of the cocaine-fueled bathroom, but you can't snatch away her taste for glitter, ever. Meghan wore lace pants. Sexy white lace pants that our best friend Courtney designed and made by hand. A mermaid swam in the turquoise pool and a real-life unicorn greeted our guests (Ok, it was a white pony rocking a horn—but he looked like a *real* unicorn). I had ten bride's bitches (my friends are many things, *maids* is not one of them), most of which were gay men who wore bright pink suits. The girls wore floral rompers and mega platforms. The local Sarasota mega superstar drag queen Beneva

Fruitville was our MC. Stacy Lentz, the bar owner of the legendary Stonewall Inn—the place in which the gay rights movement was born—officiated our wedding. There was nothing bleak or mundane or virgin-sacrifice-ish about my wedding. In fact, our wedding represented exactly what my ego had once told me wasn't possible. A fabulous mix of characters, family, fantasy, and real love. And my ego had only told me that because he was so afraid I would get rejected and he would look like a fool. But I've decided many worse things can happen to you than rejection. Like living a life hiding from good things you fear will be snatched away from you, and not experiencing a wedding and a love like I have been blessed to have.

So here's what I've learned on this long journey, kids. You can do the stable adult thing completely on your own terms. You can pick up your kids from school wearing bright red lipstick and you can be a mother who hides handcuffs for your bondage escapades discreetly beneath your very grown-up bed. You don't have to exchange your adventurous spirit for adult milestones. You also don't have to get married to be stable, either. If you *do* fall in love and that person makes you feel like you have to stop wearing your favorite ripped fishnets and Dr. Martens boots because you're getting primed to be a "wife," leave that person. Point fucking blank, *babe*. Find someone who understands that wearing fishnets is not a sign of being immature, it's a sign of being a badass bitch. I will be wearing fishnets until my number is up, that's for damn sure.

You can party with the drag queens until the very end of your life if you want to. I know I'll be partying on Fire Island with drag queens until the day I die, and may my ashes be thrown onto the stage of the most salacious gay club to ever exist. Being stable has nothing to do with being boring. Stability is something that lives inside of you. It's a safe place that no one can snatch away once you have it, because it's something that you build with your own hands. Real stability is not dependent on anyone else. It's what allows you to end the destructive narrative you've written for yourself and rewrite a new story. It's about trading in that death wish you once had for a *life* wish. It's about knowing who you really are and not being too wracked with fear to go after whatever it is that you *truly* want, whether that's marriage, kids, a fabulous career, or a life spent on the road singing songs in bars. In fact, I would say that my life is so much more adventurous now that I've become stable. When I was running around drunk and carousing with toxic entities, that wasn't adventurous at all. Maybe it was for a while—I don't want to dog on my younger self too hard, in fact, I fall more in love with my younger self every single day—but what I'm trying to say is that eventually, my destructive life began to feel a bit like watching the same movie over and over again, you know? Staying up until 5:00 AM having the same drunken conversations with the same people at the same bars no longer felt like an adventure. It began to feel a little empty. A little boring.

In fact, I've come to realize that part of the reason I drank so much was because I was bored. I used alcohol as a medicine to relieve me of my boredom. Writing about the same subjects over and over again, the same mistakes, the same sexual mishaps, that got boring too. Blowing my money on a dress that I thought I needed in order to be happy got *extremely* boring. I wanted to save money to fucking travel the world and have experiences that actually fulfilled me. I wanted to go to places that didn't require extreme drunkenness in order to be interesting! I wanted friends and relationships that were built on the foundation of us having a *true* connection—not just rescuing each other or getting lit together.

I thought I would mourn the death of my instability. I thought maybe I would miss being an eating-disordered sad girl—shit, I built a business around it! But I don't. Plus, she's not totally gone. The crazy girl still lives inside of me and I still catch her standing in line for the rollercoaster every now and then, but she rarely makes it on the ride these days. Because she doesn't run the show anymore. She's not the dominant force ruling my every move. In her place is a strong girl who knows that her life is actually interesting and she doesn't need to be held upside down against her will in order to feel a thrill. The thrill of my life is now all the love I have. Love is my baseline.

Love for myself. Love for my career. Love for my pets. Love for my family. Love for my wife.

These are things I didn't have room to love when that crazy ego dickhead was sprawled out everywhere. I didn't even have room for a pet when he was man-spreading over my brain, let alone a career and a partner. We should name him, shouldn't we? How about Ron? Yes, Ron really got in my way.

Here's the weird thing about stable love. I have found that stable love enables me to take even more exciting risks than I ever have before. Because when stable love is your baseline, you're able to plunge head first into any opportunity. Because you know when you fall, you'll always have this soft-yet-sturdy foundation of love there to catch you.

CHAPTER 21

How to Channel Your Wild Creativity Into Wild Productivity

Song: "Chandelier" by Sia

Before we get started, I *need* you to know something. *This* my sweet little sisters, is the most utterly important chapter in this entire book. Everything we've discussed so far—feeling your feelings, accepting heartbreak, toxic relationships, drug abuse, booze abuse, Adderall abuse, reckless spending, independence, antidepressants, mental illness—all *of it* has been about preparing *you* for this: learning how to take the wild creativity that you have bursting inside of your body and channeling it into wild productivity. Because I solemnly swear to my higher power, Lana Del Rey, no one in this world has the potential to light the world on fire like us former party girls. In fact, part of the reason we've been so drawn to the party to begin with is because we don't know what to do with all this extra energy we have running through us like a puppy high on caffeine.

For years and years, I relentlessly tried to quell the storm brewing inside of me. Since that didn't appear to be possible, I used drinking and drugs as a way to extinguish that burning fire. When I was a teenager, I was ashamed of the fire. I thought the fire was going to be my demise. I didn't know then what I know now: the fire is my greatest gift. While I've always known deep down I had something unique to offer the world, I wasn't sure what that thing was, or how to even begin to access it. When you have this whirlwind of creativity that lives inside of you, a creativity that wasn't nurtured when you were in public school, it often manifests itself as self-destruction, addiction, depression, and anxiety. See, all creative people need outlets in order to survive, they need it as badly as they need oxygen, and if there is one thing I know about you, it's that you're *creative*. All party girls are. All bad girls are. All crazy girls are. All complicated girls are. Almost every girl I've ever met is creative, if I'm being real.

I didn't finish college; it simply wasn't for me. I've always felt like an outsider in a school setting, because there has always been something about the teacher-student dynamic that has felt condescending and demoralizing to me. Not only that, but I don't learn by sitting still and gazing into a blackboard. I learn by *doing*. I learn by experiencing and observing and messing up and falling hard into the pavement and picking myself up again. Plus, the whole notion of "being graded," especially when it comes to anything remotely creative, is completely ridiculous to me. Why can't we discuss the piece, like adults? Art is so subjective, how is one teacher's perspective the "correct" perspective? I gracefully left art school in California after year one and never looked back. I wanted to audition, to be a part of the real world, not sit trapped in a classroom with a bunch of self-important professors who seemed to get off on slashing the spirits of young creatives. Plus, the idea of going into hundreds and thousands of dollars in debt for an experience I knew in the deepest pit of my heart was completely wrong for me wasn't exactly *appealing*.

The trouble with leaving school at nineteen and diving right into the Los Angeles life was that I was lonely and lost and peerless when everyone my age seemed to be seeking higher education. Plus, the message was as clear as day: If you don't go to college, you'll end up a loser. I had heard a father say it once to his seven-year-old daughter while I was working retail. "If you don't go up to college you'll end up doing this for the rest of your life." He pointed at me. I was scrubbing spilled bronzer off a table. The seven-year old looked at me and shuddered in fear.

I didn't know that was a total lie that's been spoon-fed to us by a broken system that makes money off our tuition, and that there are a million and some paths to success. I didn't know that if you don't fit into the neat little college box, you're not completely screwed. (Oh, how *I wish* someone had told me that.) Plus, I had to work so hard to stay afloat in Los Angeles that I could feel myself losing my drive and creativity in the wild survival grind. I would lay awake all night, tossing and turning my scrawny, pimply teenage body, worrying endlessly about what the hell I was going to do with my life. I felt doomed to mediocrity. So many times I considered going back to school to study something "safe" like, I don't know—*nutrition* or something, but I could never make it through the application process without wanting to bite the flesh off my fingers. If the application process was so painfully boring I wanted to ingest my own extremities, how was I to survive a semester? I also wasn't passionate about any of the "safe" career options, and I didn't want to live a life without passion. I mean, passion is the only thing that can pull a depressed body out of bed in the morning, you know? I wanted to have a job that had a purpose. I wanted so badly to make something of my life. I *knew* I had it in me. I just had to figure out a way to pull the magic out and channel it into productivity. With or without school, I was determined to figure it out.

And eventually I did figure out how to unearth my creative power and funnel it into a life that filled me with a beautiful and empowering sense of purpose, a life that I cherish with every fiber of my being. I discovered fabulous outlets for that shameful fire that threatened to burn me alive. It was a hard road with a lot of trial and error to learn how to get over that soul-sucking imposter syndrome that consumes all of us party girls (bad girls, late-bloomer girls, gay girls, slutty girls), and figure out how to parlay my talents into something meaningful.

But I got there. And if I can make the road to wild productivity any easier for you, I will be able to die happy (so long as I die drenched in the most obscure, inaccessible Le Labo fragrance and pointy Lana Del Rey stiletto nails). So let's *do this*.

Here is my official big sister guide to help ~you~ figure out how to channel that glittery prowess into diamond-worthy power.

Remember that teachers are not the keyholders of the truth.

Throughout my whole life, I was told by my teachers that I was distracted, "away with the fairies," crippled at math, cursed with a learning disability, and a terrible student. I'll never forget my guidance counselor telling me my future was in "big trouble" because I failed Algebra 2. Yes, I failed Algebra 2. I have a learning disability when it comes to numbers—I gaze at a page full of numbers and my brain suddenly feels like a bowl of chicken noodle soup (not the soulful kind, the canned, salt-laden kind). Sitting still, strapped to a chair in a public-school classroom with thirty-something kids didn't exactly set me up for success, either. I felt stupid. And when kids feel stupid, they feel worthless, and when they feel worthless, they stop trying, and I'm no exception. I Stopped Trying.™

Oh, how I wish I could scream this right into the ear of my defeated, younger self: YOU WILL NEVER NEED MATH. YOU'LL GET BY JUST FINE WITH A CALCULATOR. STOP WASTING TIME FEELING LIKE A LOSER BECAUSE YOU SUCK AT ALGEBRA! IT. DOESN'T. MATTER.

FYI: Not everyone has to be good at everything. That's the trouble with public school. It judges us based on how well we do in *every single* subject. Rather than pointing out to a kid like me that my writing and reading skills were way above average, and that I should focus my energy on my natural strengths and goddess-given gifts. Instead, it berated me for not being a *numbers* person.

So before you even try and figure out what your purpose is in this cruel, cold world, you must remember that whatever negative garble you were told about yourself in school is *bullshit*. The smartest people I know didn't fit into the stifling little box of public education. Kids who graduated at the top of my class, yeah, some of them are indeed quite successful right now. Some of them are not. Some of us who floundered in school, sucked at every subject even gym class, failed everything, and were endlessly sent to detention, are slaying the real world. School is one tiny (yet very formative) part of our lives. Teachers are not the only keyholders of the truth. So what, they said you had ADHD? What creative person doesn't have ADHD, really? So what, you detested sitting still for eight hours a day when you had the energy of a healthy little puppy? Maybe you were too smart for the system. Maybe you were under-stimulated by your bleak, one-note teacher. Maybe you didn't feel like you fit in with your peers so you retreated inside of yourself. Well if that was the case, congratulations, babe. There is nothing sadder than people who peak in *high school*. Late bloomers *always* win the race in the end.

So get all of the negative opinions about yourself out of that pretty little head of yours. In fact, shake those negative remarks and bad grades off of your body, sweep 'em up with a goddamn broom, and throw them in the trash. Strike a match. Light the trash bag on fire. Watch it burn. It. Burns. *So. Good.* Doesn't it?

Because here's the real tea: Whether you slayed in school or failed school, went to college, dropped out of college, majored in a subject you hated, or majored in a subject you loved—none of it matters now. We're in the real world. And in the real world, we make up our own rules. In the real world, our confidence isn't derived from a grade or a teacher or your parents' approval of you. It's derived from something far more powerful. It's derived from *you*. And owning that is step number one.

Find out what lights you up, what turns you on.

The first step in figuring out what you want to do in your life, what your purpose is, is to figure out what it is that truly lights you up. What do you authentically love doing without mommy's little helpers (otherwise known as Adderall and booze)? I know that when I'm hopped up on Adderall I *love* filing cabinets. When I'm off Adderall, there is nothing I would rather do less than file a cabinet. So clearly filing a cabinet is not what authentically lights me up, because if it did, I would like to do it without the help of prescription speed. Then there is nightlife. I love nightlife. But the idea of being in a nightclub completely sober, with (GASP) no champagne (GASP) sounds like actively choosing to take up residence on the third rung of hell. So clearly, I'm not that passionate about nightlife, because I only enjoy participating in it when loose as a goose on the champers.

In order to find what really lights a flame under your ass, I think it's important to dig deep into your past and pull up some youth! Ask yourself: What did you love doing as a teen? Before money and career and growing up and all that shit made us veer away from speeding toward passions and start driving the legal speed limit down the safe route. Before you started blurring your brain with drugs and booze and boys and girls and sex—what did you like to do for, dare I say, fun?

There were two things I distinctly remember loving as a teen: well, for one, *writing*. In high school I had a LiveJournal—do you remember LiveJournal or are you too young? It was pre-Facebook and pre-Myspace and the primary form of social media at the time (I think). They were essentially these public journals in which young people would detail their lives, diary-style, and share the posts with their friends. None of our parents understood the internet back then, so we didn't have to worry about snooping mothers reading about our acid trips and birth control slip-ups and fake IDs. I couldn't wait to rush home from school every day and share my distressed-denim and side-banged emo angst with the world. I wrote epic, blazingly honest journal entries and ended up developing a loyal following made up of fellow displaced teens all around the country. It ruled.

I also loved being on stage. I loved performing in plays, I loved getting up in front of my class and presenting my *ideas* to them, I loved public speaking and I loved being on camera. Anything that

228

was "front of the house" I loved. When I was referred to as the "talent," I practically started *rolling* it felt so good.

But like most young *artistes*, I was told that none of these talents and passions of mine would ever lead to a sustainable career, so I might as well grow up and give up. So I did. I tucked away my natural born talents into a tiny little box and stuck 'em in the attic of my original childhood home on Long Island. They were lonely in storage and I felt empty without them. But I accepted that eternal emptiness was just part of life.

Until finally, after years of feeling empty and depressed, after years of almost killing myself trying to fill the gaping voids in my life, I finally had enough! I crept back into the attic, pulled out my passion, dusted it off, and gazed into its beauty. I felt whole again, and realized that I didn't give a *shit* if my passion made me money right away. My talents and passions were what I was meant to do, and I would figure out a way to parlay them into a fulfilling career— or at least an awesome passion project—no matter what.

So I ask you: What lights *you* up, babe? What *is it* that brings you joy outside of being around your boyfriend or girlfriend? When do you feel like you're in your zone, in your flow, in alignment? What did you do for fun as a teenager? Did you listen to music? Did you sketch? Play sports? Scrapbook? It's time to crawl into the storage unit of the past and break into that sealed-off box of magic you've abandoned for far too long.

Do it for free. Get used to doing it for the sheer love of it.

When I remembered that I harbored a love for writing, a love that I had neglected for almost a decade, I decided I was going to write my heart out for the hell of it. I wanted to make sure it was something I still loved without even worrying about turning it into a career. Our generation can be a little smug about getting paid for our talents. And I get it! It sucks to work for free. But when you're still in the process of figuring out what you love, it's imperative that you swallow your pride, throw shit out there for free, and see what sticks. You have no business being paid for anything until you've put the time in and honed your craft.

I started a blog called "The Silver Factory Girl." I blogged every single day and experimented with format and topics and style. I paid attention to what resonated with my audience, because part of my passion for writing is rooted in my need to connect with others. After about a year, a local publication asked me to start blogging for them. I didn't ask for payment until I did it for six months. I found time to squeeze in writing (even with an intense, demanding full-time job) and I was ecstatic to have the experience of working for a real publication without the pressure of being a paid employee. I knew writing was an impossibly tough career, so I had to make sure I truly loved doing it for art's sake before I killed myself trying to make ends meet strictly off of writing.

I began acting in plays and short films again, something I hadn't done since I quit acting at age twenty-four. Even though I used to get paid to act, I now gladly did it for free since it had been so long and I was rustier than your redneck uncle's knife collection. And I learned an epic life lesson: I *love* acting, but not as a career. Acting is something I only ever want to do for the naked joy of it. The writing was something I wanted to turn into a career. And I hoped that maybe one day I would be able to perform my own writing to scratch both itches at once. But in the meantime, I was happy just having the emotional outlet of acting.

We all need emotional outlets that have nothing to do with our careers. As soon as something becomes your career there is an added pressure attached to it that sucks the freedom and fun out of it. It's so sad that we feel like the things we love are a waste of time unless it involves tightening our abs or increasing our bank accounts. If I've learned one thing, it's this: Life is so much more than *bodies* and *banks*. And once you explore a hobby that you do just for the love of it, you'll find that the happiness you reap from doing it will make you better in other aspects of your life, ones that have financial benefits.

For example: Acting makes me a much better writer. It reminds me that writing is a performance as well as an intimate look into the brain. It reminds me to play, have fun with words, and improvise. It strengthens my people skills and helps me remember to ground myself when I have anxiety. Something that I do merely for fun has as many (if not more!) benefits to my life as going to the gym three times a week or eating organic food.

Prioritize creativity over partying.

One of my biggest pet peeves is when people tell me they don't have any *free time* to explore their passions. They work *too much*. They are *too tired* at the end of the day. Look—I get it, life is busy and it always will be busy. I used to feel so drained after my soul-sucking job in retail, the last thing in the world I wanted to do was sit down at my desk and write. I wanted to drink wine with my friends and bitch about life! I still want to do that on certain days (and some days I do).

But here's the thing: Drinking wine and bitching with your friends isn't going to get you anywhere. Except for broke and hungover. Plus, negativity is dangerously contagious. If all of your friends are feeling hopeless and downtrodden about life, it's only going to feed your sneaking suspicion that this is all *life* is. So how about you skip the wine and bitch sessions for a month? And commit to channeling that wino energy into a passion project instead? Yes, it seems exhausting after a long, annoying day spent clamoring away doing something you detest. But it only *seems* exhausting. Once you actually do it, you'll find it breathes new life into your body. It energizes you. It lights up the flame inside of you that you thought had been snuffed out for good.

So prioritize doing what you love over partying with your friends. It doesn't mean you don't love your friends. You can love your friends but take some time away to do *you*. I mean, when you think about it, *you* are the only constant in your life. Friends can leave you, but you can never leave you. You're in this relationship with yourself forever, no matter how much you hate yourself. So find what makes *you* happy and hate yourself less and prioritize that. You'll have plenty of time to party and gab and bitch and drink once you've found what makes you tick and what turns you on.

And trust me: If you don't tick at least a few times a week, if you don't want to ravage your passion at least a few times a week, you'll always feel a lingering emptiness inside. And you'll try to fill the gaping holes with other shit, but it won't work. Talent doesn't like to stay dormant. Dormant talent will torture you. Trust me on that one.

Get creative in your thinking.

Okay so let's say your favorite thing in the whole wide world, the way in which you express your best self, is through dance. But, like, let's be honest, the professional dancer ship has long sailed. You might love to dance but you're not delusional. It's no career.

I hear you, but *you*, my friend, are not doomed to a life void of dance! In fact, you can still find a way to channel your love of dance into a career. For example, could you teach dance? If you're rusty as fuck, take a bunch of classes and explore what it takes to teach young kids or teens. Could you start a dance blog? You could call it "Confessions of a Former Bunhead" and write about all of your memories from your dance days and what kind of dance you're into right now. You could even interview professional dancers! Do you know how many former dancers and dance-obsessed people would absolutely *die* for a blog like that? And it's not crazy to think that you could monetize the shit out of, either. Think of all the companies that make jazz shoes and ballet slippers and leotards. What better place for them to advertise their niche items than on a niche dance blog? There are a thousand and some ways to channel your love of dance into a real career. You could do marketing for a dance company. You could choreograph. You could come up with your own method of dance or aerobics for adults who aren't professional dancers but still have the urge to dance their lives away for an hour a day in a non-judgmental environment. I would love to take a class like that. Get creative. If dance calls to you, pick up the phone and call her back, bitch!

Same goes for a love of sports. Or a love of theatre. Or a love of makeup. I had a friend who had a big, important job in hospitality. She hated it. Her true passion was fine art but her parents were old-school and didn't think that painting was a respectable career. She began to paint the faces of her friends for free when they had a wedding or a special event. Each woman felt transformed after my dear friend went to work on their faces. She decided that's what she would do. She would take her talent for fine art and become a makeup artist. Now she travels the world doing what she loves and makes a killing. The possibilities are endless.

Fuck the fear of failure.

Don't worry about going after what you love and failing. Don't worry about it because you will, most definitely, fail. We all fail at new things even when we're naturally talented at them. Do you know how many tone-deaf articles I've written, or how many book proposals I've slaved over that have been rejected by everyone in the industry? Do you know how many times I've been told *no*? Or even worse, the number of times I've been told "yes" and then let the entire team down because my final product missed the mark? Failure is the nature of the beast. The difference between people who make a living doing what they love and the people who don't is simple: People who "make it" don't let failure stop them from persevering. People who give up the first time they get criticized or fired or rejected, don't make it. What kind of person do you want to be? Someone who is a prisoner to the ego (fuck Ron!) and lives in the miserable hellhole of fear of failure?

No, not you. Be the person who understands that failure is part of life, it happens to everyone, and keep trucking along, and eventually, your dreams will fall into place.

Fuck the fear of age.

If I hear one more twenty-eight-year-old proclaim they're too old to start a new career, I'm going to scream. I'm going to rip my eyes out of my skull. I'm going to smash a laptop and relocate to a remote island that houses only people over the age of sixty-five. Your thirties and forties and fifties, even—are an amazing place to start a brand-new chapter of your career. You are far less likely to screw it all up the older you are. I had some amazing opportunities that I completely blew in my twenties because I wasn't ready to for them. I lost out to adults who had thicker skin than I did and more life experience, thus did a better job. Repeat after me: It is never too late to start. Get that tired narrative out of your head. Before you're sitting on your deathbed in your nineties and really *is* too late. Fuck the age stigma and go after what you love. If you're scared of ageism in the workplace, don't tell anyone your age. It's no one's business. So start that career as a stylist, as a poet, as a director, as a writer, as a dance teacher. Everything you've done in your twenties was leading you to this point. Maybe you didn't go for it then because you weren't ready, and deep down you knew that, so you stalled. That's fine. Now you are ready. So get up and go. Wash off your makeup, repaint your face on a clean canvas, and twirl out into the world. Because nothing is more youthful than twirling out into the world. And that youthful energy will be infectious to everyone, regardless of your age. Age is an energy just like everything else in this life.

Be real, be vulnerable, be tough.

Whatever it is that you decide you love doing, you need to be unafraid to be vulnerable in order for it to be powerful. Create from the heart. Ask for help. Admit to yourself that you're new to this or that you haven't done this particular thing in a really long time and seek out a mentor. Don't suck your mentor dry, but find *someone*, a teacher of sorts, that maybe you offer to help with their social media (or something else our generation is naturally good at) for free in exchange for advice or the opportunity to shadow them. Read every book in existence about your passion. Watch every YouTube video. Immerse yourself in your passion just like you immersed yourself into partying and sex and toxic love. And keep going. Keep going no matter what. Even if you're not sure if it's going to work out, just keep *going*. It will work itself out so long as you don't give up. You might not end up on the exact path you imagined you would, and that's OK. Usually, it ends up turning into something better than you'd even imagined. When all I wanted to do was act on stage, I was heartbroken when it didn't work out. But I kept writing and I kept doing theatre for free and eventually I began to perform my own words on stage to packed houses in New York City, collaborating with big brands like Samsung 837. Am I on Broadway performing famous plays written in the 1800s like I had suspected I would? No. But what I'm doing now is so much cooler and suits my natural rhythms so much more than being in a Shakespearean play ever would. I'm performing my own damn words. And I love it far more than I've ever loved being in a play, reciting lines I didn't write. You just have to stay open. You just have to keep going. Don't think, do. And while the rest of your friends are thinking about their next move, you'll wake up one morning having already *done it*.

CHAPTER 22

You Are Your Own Ride or Die

Song: "We Might Be Dead by Tomorrow" by Soko

I will never be a girl who undermines the earth-shattering force that is a romantic relationship. Sometimes I feel embarrassed to admit it, but if I'm being real as fuck with myself (and with you), I'll confess that I'm a very uncool romantic. A *wild* romantic. I'm a hop-a-train-in-the-middle-of-the-night-to-another-state-just-to-see-the-person-I-love-in-the-morning kind of romantic. I'm a fuck-this-party-let's-leave-and-have-sex-under-the-stars kind of romantic. I'm a *Lana Del Rey lyric* romantic: "When someone else's happiness is your happiness, that is *love*."

While I never dreamt about finding my person, I always dreamt of a tragic, inconvenient, against-all-odds kind of love. I watched a lot of movies growing up, Baz Luhrmann's adaptation of *Romeo + Juliet* being my favorite. I think I was in fourth grade when that movie came out, and like most of the kids in my generation, that movie is fully responsible for my notion that love is hard. Love is painful. Love is death. I wanted to be Claire Danes dressed as an angel staring at my forsaken lover through a fish tank at a bougie costume party. I mean, what is love without life-or-death stakes?

Boring, I thought. Boring like the love I witnessed from watching my friend's parents in the flat suburbs: bleak TV dinners on the couch. Sweatpants and kids. The occasional night out at a mediocre restaurant in one of those depressing, stale towns forty-five minutes outside of New York City.

So it should come as zero surprise that I actively sought out volatile relationships because I thought love was supposed to be "passionate." I was one of those girls who confused chaos and emotional abuse for passion. I was addicted to the chaos and the fighting and the endless crying because it made me *feel.* It conjured up a powerful feeling inside of me that nothing else could: A feeling of "we are ride or die." Like no matter how horrible we are to each other, no matter how deeply we stick the knife into each other's hearts, we'll always be there. I'll always hop on the back of your motorcycle and venture into the dark and dangerous neighborhood for you, even if it means I get shot in the chest in the process. Lovers put their lives on the line for each other, right? What a passionate, scary, yet exciting feeling *that* was.

But then I got older and I began to realize that even those sex-laden volatile relationships were leaving me pretty unfulfilled. Something was always missing. Sometimes I would start horrible fights just to try and provoke those feelings of fear and rage—those feelings I foolishly mistook for passion—back into my body. Sometimes I would act in ways that I consciously knew would trigger my partner just so we could get down and dirty in a massive screaming match that left me crying in a heap on the floor. Because at least when I was crying in a heap on the floor I was *feeling.* I didn't have the dreaded deadness. Nothing is worse than the dreaded deadness.

When my relationship would inevitably end, I would crumble. I would crumble into nothing because without this person I *was* nothing. All of the feelings that my heart harbored had been poured into another human being, and when that human being was gone, I was an empty vessel with no emotions. No identity. I was blank. Beige. Nothing.

Sometimes I didn't seek out the volatile. Sometimes I sought out the kinds of people who were inclined to rescue *me*. And holy shit, there were there a lot of women who seemed to want to rescue me. I was a helpless fawn who didn't love herself and it was blazingly transparent. Helpless fawns who don't love themselves attract a very *specific* type of person. They attract people who are controlling and lonely—an utterly dangerous combination. People that want to nurse you back to health, but don't want you to get *too* healthy, because if you get *too* healthy you'll leave them. And because only super codependent people are drawn to helpless fawns who can't fend for themselves, their deepest fear is that you'll learn how to fend for yourself and when you do, you won't need them anymore and you'll get the fuck out of dodge, fast. So they snatch the reigns out of your shaky hands and take control of your life. Make it so you're only functioning and healthy around *them*. They keep you down by enabling your drug-use. They tell you your friends are ill-intentioned. They put a wedge between you and your family. They make you feel like you will die without them there, that they're the only ones in the world who care about you, and everyone else is scum who is taking advantage of your helplessness. And the sickest part about it is you *let them* make you feel that way.

These are the people you attract when you don't love yourself. There is a certain energy that radiates out of the pores who girls who don't love themselves yet. And that energy magnetically attracts toxic, sick people into your toxic, sick orbit. Sick likes to be with sick, and two sick people stay sick because they keep each other infected.

Sometimes I would get to the point where I simply had enough of all this toxic bullshit. I would begin the process of working on myself. Maybe I'd start seeing a new shrink. Maybe I'd start journaling or listening to inspiring podcasts and reading self-help books and going to yoga regularly. The very moment I would start to feel like *"holy shit*, I can ACTUALLY do this," another sexy human would come skipping into my life. At first I would be a healthy person with firm boundaries and such, but because I hadn't really done the work on myself—only *sort of* done the work on myself—I would quickly get lost in whomever I was dating. I would allow them to interrupt my journey of bettering myself because I was still vulnerable and had not yet really healed. If an addict leaves rehab early, even if she has been doing AMAZING in the program, she's likely going to relapse. I would relapse on my own personal recovery because I wasn't ready to be out in the dating world again. Before I knew it, I would be neglecting therapy and yoga and all the shit that makes me feel whole, and instead I would fill those spaces with fighting and fucking and a neediness that can never be quelled no matter how much sex you have.

What I'm really trying to say here is that, as important and as amazing and as earth-shatteringly orgasmic as love is, it's an extremely powerful, dangerous force of nature that will knock you down with its destructive hurricane prowess if you haven't yet built a strong foundation inside of yourself first. After getting blown to bits time and time again by the wild shitstorm of "love," I finally reached a breaking point. I had no house to live in. I had to build my own four walls from *scratch*. But when I built myself a home with my own bare hands I was able to slowly build the foundation of my house, and I made sure that shit was strong as fuck. I laid down my own floorboards. It took time, but it was hurricane-proof. I knew it. Because *I* made it. I made myself strong enough to withstand love by taking time away from channeling it toward another person, and instead, channeled it back into myself. This time, it was a deeper process than simply going to therapy and reading books. It was about looking in the mirror and learning to accept the way I looked without a filter. It was about finally refusing to bend my body in order to fit into a box that I didn't fit into. It was about stretching out my limbs and being comfortable living outside of the box. It was about loving that I was too big for the box. It was about not making myself small anymore.

It was about getting up every single day, and instead of fighting the way I felt, thanking myself for having such deep feelings because those deep feelings were sacred, not shameful; they were my inner guidance system letting me know that I was where I was supposed to be. It was about not running from the truth about my past, but clasping its hand and finding the beauty in it, even if it wasn't classically beautiful. It was about learning to accept that I'm not classically beautiful, I'm exotic and not everyone's taste and that's OK. Mainly: It was about forgiving myself. Forgiving myself for all the stupid shit I've done. Forgiving myself for all the time I'd wasted in life by being distracted, drinking, and doing drugs. Forgiving myself for living in the shadows. Forgiveness was the hardest part. If you're holding onto resentments you have for yourself, your relationship with yourself is poisonous. The only way to have a healthy relationship with yourself is to really, truly forgive yourself. To say to yourself: "You did what you thought you had to do at the time. You know better now. It's OK. *I love you.*"

Learning to fully forgive leads to the deepest love—with other people, but especially with yourself. Holding onto your mistakes and feeling constantly angry and disappointed in yourself will lead to feelings of worthlessness. And when you feel like you have no worth, you self-destruct. So if you do anything, I beg you, just let it all go. I don't care how bad the thing you did was. Let it go. Let it go. Let it go. Breathe. You're a good girl. I *promise.* There is no such thing as "bad girl." There *is* such a thing as a badass boss bitch (which you are) but no girl is "bad." Be gentle with yourself. If life dealt you a screwed-up hand of cards, you're fully capable of snatching that deck back and re-shuffling them. But you must forgive yourself first. Nothing can change with tension and meanness; things can only be changed with gentleness and kindness.

Once I forgave myself, really, truly forgave myself, I learned the most valuable lesson I've ever learned, one that I will carry with me forever and ever and ever. There is no such thing as the one. You are the one. You are your own ride or die. Even if you fall in love with the greatest person ever, they could still leave you, babe. I've seen people who I never in a million years would've thought would've ever gotten a divorce, get a divorce. I've seen people die completely unexpectedly, leaving their lovers behind overnight. I've seen people who once were so in love they were attached at the soul, fall out of love. It *can* happen. There is no guarantee in life. I am newly married and I love my wife deeply. I am grateful to have this beautiful love. But I still cherish the fact that she didn't come into my life until I was whole without her. Until after I'd learned how to truly love myself without the validation she gives me. Because while I hope we're together forever, I know that this could fall apart one day. I know that something could happen that could tear us apart. I know that it would be brutal and painful and heartbreaking if she were to ever leave me. But I know I would be OK. Because she isn't my ride or die. I am my own ride or die. I am the love of my life. And because I have fully owned that my relationship with myself is my number one, I don't have to worry about me leaving me. Because I *can't* leave me. I'm *stuck* with me. I am the only relationship I'll ever be in for life. So thank Lana Del Rey that I have cultivated a fabulous relationship with myself.

So little sisters, fall in love. Please. Falling in love is such a beautiful, humbling, vulnerable experience. But fall in love with yourself before you even think about falling in love with another human being. You don't have to be perfect to love yourself. Fuck—you don't even have to like yourself every single day in order to love yourself. You can still be in the process of figuring out your relationship with booze, you can still be in the process of getting your shit together, you can be in the process of figuring out how to be a better friend or employee or daughter—and you can still love the shit out of yourself. That's one thing you don't need to wait to do. You can do it today. Right now. Because the love you have for yourself isn't conditional at all. It's not "OK, I will love myself once I start meditating and writing gratitude lists." No. You must love yourself when you're hungover. You must love yourself when you're lazy. You must love yourself when you're feeling jealous. You must love yourself when you're simply a flawed, fucked up human. Forgive yourself. Breathe. Breathe. Let it go. And let in love. Your *own* fucking love.

Acknowledgments

Song: "Maps" by Yeah Yeah Yeahs

First and foremost, I have to thank my goddamn, fabulous, impossibly chic, wild contradiction of a mother, the one, the only, the legend of a woman: LYNN BARRIE. Thank you from the bottom of my oh-so-distracted heart for telling my teachers to "fuck off" when they suggested I go on Ritalin because I was "away with the fairies" all the time. Thank you for understanding that being "away with the fairies" is a beautiful, magical, wonderful place to be, for fairies live in the land of wild creativity, and there is nothing in this world I love more than wild creativity. Thank you for teaching me that the arts are just as important (if not more important) than academia and for never shaming me for my deplorable math and science grades. You rolled your eyes at "the system" and instead, struck the perfect match that lit up my burning creative desires. Thank you so much for picking me up from my stuffy Connecticut school in your cool as fuck Dr. Martens boots with your waist-length blonde hair and your long black dress with the bright red AIDS ribbon fastened to it. You didn't care that the other mothers wore khaki pants and polo shirts and hideous Lilly Pulitzer dresses. You *never* conformed. You did *you*. And because of that, I do *me*. And going through life as yourself is the only way to live. What a gift you've given me! Thank you to my amazing, quick-witted, golden-hearted, ever-generous, business-genius of a DAD. Thank you for never pressuring me to play tennis like my brother or to score high on the SATs like you did. Thank you for driving me every single Saturday throughout the entirety of my adolescence into the thick of Manhattan so I could go to acting class in "the city." Thank you for dropping everything whenever I call you because I desperately need my social security card or birth certificate or tax return RIGHT THEN. Thank you for always picking me up from the airport at horrible, traffic-laden times. You have taught me that love is not passive. Love is active. Love means sacrificing your precious Saturday when you work all week, just so your misfit teenage daughter can sit in a theatre class in the East Village with a bunch of chain smoking twenty-five-year-old "actors." I know now that love means traffic and keeping receipts and making photocopies of annoying shit like driver's licenses and contracts. No one loves more actively than you do, which means no one loves as authentically, as deeply, as real-ly as you do. You're a north star in a sports car, Frame. Thank you to my opinionated, magnetic, hilarious brother Blake for introducing me to cool music at a young age, music that inspired this book! Also, thank you for offering to beat up that horrible boy who incessantly bullied me in middle school twenty-something years ago. No boy ever fucked with me again after you and your cool skater friends scared everyone off that year, and I'm grateful to you for that because middle school is hard *enough*, you know? I might not have made it if wasn't for you. (Also thank you to *that boy* because you've made me SO GLAD TO BE GAY.) Thank you to my creative partner-in-mega-platform-boots, the ultimate dyke princess and writer extraordinaire, Dayna Troisi. I could not have written this book without you. Thank you for hysterically sobbing at the Andrea Gibson show with me, thank you for dissecting poetry with me whilst drunk at the Dinah Shore, thank you for your brilliant edits, your seemingly endless well of talent + creativity, and your kickass, badass, Daddy Dayna support throughout this whole process. I would rather be bionic than a goddess if it means I can be exactly like *you*, sister. Thank you to Amy Lesser, Corinne Kai, Alexia LaFata, Kaitlyn Cawley, Faye Brennan, Kevin Schlittenhardt, Emily

Mccombs, Sheena Sharma, Gigi Engle, and Candice Jalili for helping me find my voice as a writer, for teaching me how to ward off internet trolls, for being my first editorial collaborators in this crazy writing world! Thank you to my best friends & absolute *muses*: Owen Gould (my soul), Ruba Audeh (my muse), Eduardo Anaya (my sister), Courtney Adams (my Sharon), HL Ray (my moment), Matt Craft (my husband), Joshua Beadle (my fellow party girl in pain), Harriet Sokmunseur (my star), Tatyana Sharoubim-Stewart and baby P! (my positive energy), Petra Rueangaram (my baddest boss bitch), Molly Klauber (my step-sister and biggest supporter), Bailey McAvenia (my downass bitch forever) and Nick Diamond (my brother and the only person from Westport, CT invited to my lesbian wedding). I have no story without you in it. I have no love in my life without you in it. You are all over this book. Your presence and energy and your beautiful craziness color every blank, bleak page. Thank you to my agent at CAA, Anthony Mattero, for not giving up on me and for believing I do, indeed, have a powerful story to tell and for being able to see through the glitter party girl exterior and recognize that beneath the sparkle and the chamPAIN is an important story that deserves to be told. Thank you to anyone who has ever rejected me, both professionally and personally. They say rejection is protection and I believe that. Because I am surrounded by the people I was MEANT to work with and be around, people sent to me by my higher power Lana Del Rey and I know she protected me from all of *you* who rejected me. Thank you to Lana Del Rey, for teaching me all about the bad girls, honey and for singing the most beautiful poetry to ever exist. Thank you to my thoughtful, brilliant, kind, editor Allie Woodlee. Thank you for *getting* it. Thank you for elevating my work without changing my voice. I adore you so. You are a rare gem. You have amazing goddamn taste, too. Thank you to Post Hill Press for believing in me and the rest of the undermined, underestimated party girls in the world who deserve to be heard and seen and need a safe place to deal with their traumas. Speaking of *party girls*: Thank you to all of my followers throughout the years. You are my best friends. You give my life purpose. You keep me going when I want to throw the towel in. You inspire everything I do. Being your lesbian big sister has been the greatest honor of my life. Thank you to my original kittens (you know who you are). Thank you, KT Curran, for being the first adult who ever saw the light behind my eyes and thank you for teaching me how to channel the angst, the energy and the relentless feelings into *art*. I really owe *everything* to you. Thank you to Jaymie Klauber and Audra Barrie and Amanda Brooks for being my iconic older sisters who never took shit from boys and always spoke your badass minds and dressed unapologetically hot and have never been afraid to take up space in the world. Thank you to Auntie Frances and Auntie Marie for all the tea and all the love. Thank you to Samsung 837 for supporting all of the wild creatives, I love you *so* much. Thank you to my fur babies: Luka, Wild, and Bowie. Thank you for getting all Grey Gardens weird with me when I isolate myself in the house and walk around in robes and write and chant and be an unhinged weirdo. Thank you for being the gayest, fiercest, most unique pets on the planet. Thank you to girls who live in the tri-state area and smack their gum and write poetry and blast sad songs on their headphones (I love you). Thank you Zach Overton. Thank you Prozac. Thank you Nick, I will never stop trying to energetically release you from this hell of a situation. Thank you to all the little boys who can't help but wear blue nail polish to school even if they know they will get beat up, but they just can't NOT express themselves (I love you). Oh! And thank you to that asshole theatre director I had in high school who never cast me in the school plays which made me turn to writing as an emotional outlet instead of acting and I am much happier as a writer than as an actor! And MOST OF ALL thank you to my wife, my life, my wolf-eyed, gazelle-legged, bombshell of a partner: Meghan Dziuma. They say love is like falling, and it is, only our love never hit the ground. I want to stay suspended in the air for lifetimes upon lifetimes with you in this bliss. Lana sent you to me, and me to you. We are the lucky ones. *This time*. It's all part of the great design, right?

Love is safe and exciting at once and I felt that first in your arms on your murphy bed in Lower Manhattan and it was the biggest burst of transformational emotion I've ever experienced, ever.

Girl, Stop Passing Out in Your Makeup—Playlist

"I Am Not A Robot" by Marina and the Diamonds
"This Is What Makes Us Girls" by Lana Del Rey
"Pills" by St. Vincent
"bad idea!" by girl in red
"Nineteen" by Tegan and Sara
"Lover I Don't Have to Love" by Bright Eyes
"A Better Son/Daughter" by Rilo Kiley
"Seventeen" by Troye Sivan
"Hunger" By Florence + the Machine
"Nighttiming" by Coconut Records
"Coachella" by Lana Del Rey
"8 Ball" by Waxahatchee
"Wet Blanket" by Metric
"Mariners Apartment Complex" by Lana Del Rey
"Everybody But Me" by Lykke Li
"all the good girls go to hell" by Billie Eilish
"You Know I'm No Good" by Amy Winehouse
"Upper West Side" by King Princess
"Good As Hell" by Lizzo
"Drew Barrymore" by SZA
"Mess is Mine" by Vance Joy
"Chandelier" by Sia
"We Might Be Dead By Tomorrow" by Soko
"Maps" by Yeah Yeah Yeahs